Kabbalah's Secret Circles

Time Line & Insights into Jewish Mysticism,
the Ancient *Kabbalah*,
& The *Kabbalah* Wheel

By Robert E. Zucker
QBL

Namaste

Robert E. Zucker
4-25-17

KABBALAH'S SECRET CIRCLES: TIMELINE TO JEWISH MYSTICISM,
THE ANCIENT KABBALAH & THE BOOK OF FORMATION (SEPHER YETZIRAH)
By Robert E. Zucker

Published by BZB Publishing
P.O. Box 91317
Tucson, Arizona 85752

Web: http://emol.org/kabbalah
Web: http://Robert-Zucker.com/qabalah
Email: publisher@emol.org
Phone: 520-623-3733

ISBN: 978-1-939050-14-4

Cover art ("Spirits," 1975) by Robert E. Zucker. Abulafia's Circles from CHAYE HA-OLAM HABA. Credited illustrations from Zedcor, Inc. copyright-free graphics collection.

This book contains Divine Names, please handle with care.

"In order for science to study Force,
It must be manifested into some objective Form." [1]

---

[1] Quote by Robert E. Zucker from the introduction to HERMETICS: CONSCIOUSNESS & HYPER-PERCEPTIVITY (1976), a college research manuscript written for multi-course credit. In science and Jewish mysticism, once a force is able to be measured, its "form" is usually depicted in a symbolic or numerical value.

𝒦abbalah's 𝒮ecret 𝒞ircles 𝒞ontents

Note: All Hebrew and non-English words are in *italics* and book titles are in CAPITAL LETTERS. Foreign language titles are in *ITALIC CAPITAL LETTERS*.

The *SEPHER YETZIRAH,* known as the BOOK OF FORMATION, or THE BOOK OF CREATION, is one of the oldest preserved manuscripts on Judaic mysticism– possibly more than two thousand years old. This image is the cover of the Mantua edition of *SEPHER YETZIRAH,* printed in 1562.

Opening the Kabbalah Circle

Jewish mysticism often sparks the imagination with scenes of nefarious rituals and Medieval incantations. What once was a spiritual and deeply religious experience become distorted through generations of wives-tales, books, movies, television, and history.

There are many legends about biblical figures and famous rabbis with superhuman talents who could explore the hidden realms of the Heavens, conjure angels, and enliven artificial creatures. They claimed to possess a secret and sacred knowledge to manipulate nature and human consciousness.

For centuries, this knowledge was verbally shared among small circles of followers who studied the metaphysical [2] aspects of the *TORAH* and related religious literature. Over time, many of these ancient Jewish oral teachings (*mishna*) and traditions (*aggadah*) were put into writing and became known collectively as the *Kabbalah*.

Rather than rehash the fundamentals of *Kabbalah*, this volume explores the development and practices of Jewish mysticism from history's most prominent religious leaders, including a comprehensive historical survey of the infamous BOOK OF FORMATION (*SEPHER YETZIRAH).*

For someone who is unfamiliar with the *Kabbalah*, this volume presents an insight into a hidden side of Jewish culture. A person with knowledge of those practices will be able to optimize this

---

[2] Metaphysics is a branch of philosophy that explores the basic nature of 'being' and the world that encompasses it.

information and further their path to enlightenment.

This book is actually three books in one. The first part covers more than 5,000 years of Jewish mysticism. Discover how these age-old traditions began and how to utilize some of the techniques once kept hidden from the public for millennium. Many of these principles are divulged in the words of famous Jewish authorities who shared their understanding of the cryptic, esoteric messages in Judaic literature. Based on their discussions, an ancient device has been uncovered– the *Kabbalah* Wheel.

The second section presents the first two chapters from *SEPHER YETZIRAH* (also known as the BOOK OF CREATION)– the book that greatly influenced Jewish mystical thought over the centuries.

The highlight of this volume are the instructions to assemble an ingenious, homemade, device I call the *Kabbalah* Wheel. This unique gadget is revealed for the first time in eight centuries to decode the mysteries of the 231 Gates described in the first two chapters of the *SEPHER YETZIRAH* and the historical survey provided here.

Included in this volume are copies of my some of my personal notes, art work and charts used over the past four decades to map this path across time. For further study, there are more than 700 footnotes that reference books and articles used in this research.

While these pages cannot cover the entire spectrum of Jewish mysticism, enough information is presented to unravel some of the mysteries surrounding the *Kabbalah*.

Robert Zucker
January 1, 2017

Graphic depiction of *Chockmah* (Wisdom), representing the 2nd *Sephiroth* (sphere) of the Tree of Life, drawn by Robert Zucker in 1976. The archangel *Raziel* is the personification of *Chockmah* (Divine Wisdom). [3] Rabbi Moses Maimonides called *Raziel* the Chief of the Order of the *Erelim*, (*Aralim*) a rank of angels mentioned in *Kabbalah*. [4]

---

[3] Davidson, Gustave, A DICTIONARY OF ANGELS, page 242-243.

[4] Ibid. Also, from Moshe Maimonides, MISHNA THORA.

Jewish Mysticism and The Kabbalah

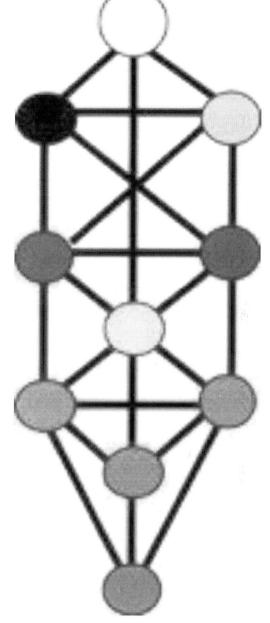

J ewish mysticism bridges the connection between the material and the spiritual worlds in order to become closer to God. This practice, secretly shrouded with legends and traditions, is called the *Kabbalah.*

The word '*Kabbalah*' (*Q-B-L-H* ק ב ל ה) is derived from the Hebrew "to receive, reception" or "tradition." The *Kabbalah* [5] is the collection of traditions received from our ancestors.

These traditions may have originated with the first man– Adam, who supposedly acquired a magical book from the angels that contained the secrets of the Universe.

Part of these "traditions" may have also been received by Moses on Mt. Sinai along with the written Ten Commandments. Legend says that Moses communicated these secret teachings to Joshua, his successor. This sacred knowledge was passed on through generations until it was written down about 2,000 years ago.

Graphic representation of the Tree of Life.

---

[5] The Modern English spelling of *Kabbalah* is used in this volume instead of the more traditional *Qabalah.*

For centuries, only a few select rabbis and their followers kept this hidden from the general public, although the fundamental concepts of *Kabbalah* permeate all Jewish religious services and thought.

The Medieval term "cabal" is used described a clandestine circle of people who share similar interests at the exclusion of outsiders. *Kabbalists* were members of their own secret society. It was so secret that only those "in the know" were aware of its existence. However, the advent of the printing press over 500 years ago, and some prolific writers, made it possible for the masses to eventually have access to this occult knowledge.

There is no one authoritative book on the *Kabbalah*. Since these teachings were transmitted verbally over hundreds of generations there are numerous interpretations. By the time they were written down, much of the original intent was lost in time.

The ancient manuscripts of the *SEPHER YETZIRAH*, the *BAHIR*, the *ZOHAR*, the *TANYA* and *SEPHER RAZIEL* are some of the most popular handbooks on *Kabbalah* that still exist today to carry on these teachings. These works, including the *TORAH*, provide the cornerstones to understand this secretive, mystical practice.

There is an underlying theme common among all of these important texts. This is embodied in the concept of the Tree of Life– a symbolic representation of humans and their interaction with the Universe.

Some practitioners only focused on the religious aspects of the Tree of Life and its ten spheres (called *Sephirot* in Hebrew). Other groups employed practical applications such as meditation exercises, elaborate ceremonies, and cryptic letter permutations techniques. Either way, they depended on the basic principles of the *Kabbalah* to achieve their goals.

While the true knowledge is buried deep in the early Hebrew culture, these concepts were introduced into the general populous during the Middle Ages. Jewish *Kabbalists* followed the original traditions and Christian Cabalists interpreted the Semitic teachings through the veil of their own religious views.

But, *Kabbalah* is not a religion. The *Kabbalah* is based on elementary ideas and their interrelationships. It is used as a meditative gaze into one's soul. Understanding the deeper, symbolic meaning and relationships between each of the 22 Hebrew letters is the Key to understanding oneself and the universe around us.

Judaic Mysticism in Biblical Times

A lthough the *Kabbalah* is not specifically mentioned in the OLD TESTAMENT, there are many passages that allude to this secret knowledge. These teachings are attributed to biblical ancestors like Adam, Moses, and Abraham.

This privileged knowledge was passed on by word of mouth for generations between learned men. It probably first written down about the turn of the 1st century C.E. [6] when a manuscript called *SEPHER YETZIRAH* (in English, it is titled the BOOK OF FORMATION or BOOK OF CREATION) began to circulate among select circles of adherents.

One group associated with early Jewish mystical practices might have been the Essenes who lived throughout the land of Judah from about the 2nd century B.C.E. [7] through the 1st century C.E. [8] The original Dead Sea Scrolls may have been a part of the Essene's uncovered library along with many other esoteric writings.

The inherent dangers, and the rewards, of studying these mysteries are emphasized in numerous legends that have spawned from several biblical, *TALMUDIC* passages, and rabbinical discussions. As one example, early traditions reveal Adam's role in obtaining these secrets and his risk handling this sacred knowledge.

---

[6] C.E: Common Era, after the birth of Christ. 1 C.E. is the same as the year 1 A.D. (Anno Domini).

[7] B.C.E.: Before the Common Era, before the birth of Christ. 1 B.C. is the same as 1 B.C.

[8] Kaplan, Aryeh, *SEPHER YETZIRAH*: THEORY AND PRACTICE, page xvii, Samuel Weiser, 1990. This is one of the foremost books on the subject and has been studied by this author for decades to interpret the mysteries of the *SEPHER YETZIRAH*. See Appendix for additional suggested authors.

The *Angel Raziel's* Secrets

"Each day the angel Raziel makes proclamations
on Mount Horeb, from heaven,
of the secrets of men to all that dwell upon the earth,
and his voice resounds throughout the world." [9] [10]

---

[9] From the *Targum* on Ecclesiastes 10:20. A *Targum* is a version or "a translation."

[10] Image from Zedcor Graphics collection.

The archangel *Raziel* [11] played a major role in early Jewish mystical tradition. His name is first mentioned in the BOOK OF ENOCH, composed sometime before the Common Era (C.E.). [12]

Raziel sits among the highest class of archangels with *Michael, Raphael,* and *Gabriel.* The archangel *Raziel* was the transmitter of secrets and author of the legendary BOOK OF THE ANGEL *RAZIEL.*

In a rabbinical explanation (called a *Targum*) about the above passage, *Raziel* stands on the peak of Mount *Horeb* and shouts out the secrets of mankind for all to hear. To preserve this wisdom, *Raziel* collected all of the knowledge of the Universe into a book– the BOOK OF *RAZIEL* (*SEPHER RAZIEL*) or the BOOK OF SECRETS. According to some legends, this "book" was originally inscribed on a sapphire stone. [13]

The Hebrew word *raziel* (רזיאל) means "Secret of God."

- *RAZ–* (רז) is Hebrew for "secret."
- *–AL* (אל) is the suffix used for the word "God."

The BOOK OF *RAZIEL* disclosed everything from the astrology of the planets to the creative life energy– birth, death, reincarnation of the soul, and other occult subjects. [14]

The archangel explained that the contents of the book contained "all things worth knowing (that) can be learnt, and all mysteries, and it teaches also how to call upon the angels and make them appear before men, and answer all their questions."

This "book" contained the sacred 72 branches of wisdom and 670 sacred inscriptions. In the middle was a "secret writing explaining the thousand and five hundred (1,500) Keys which were not revealed even to the holy angels," according to the *ZOHAR.* [15] [16]

The *ZOHAR* is the compendium of Jewish mystical tradition compiled in the 13th century from

---

[11] *Raziel* is also spelled as *Razeel, Reziel, Ratziel* and *Galizur.*

[12] *Raziel*, by Crawford Howell, Ludwig Blau, from JEWISH ENCYCLOPEDIA. The unedited full-text of the 1906 Jewish Encyclopedia.

[13] "*BOOK OF RAZIEL*," from JEWISHENCYCLOPEDIA.com.

[14] Davidson, Gustav, A DICTIONARY OF ANGELS, pages 242-243.

[15] *ZOHAR* 1, 55a-b.

[16] Gaster, Moses, Ph.D., THE SWORD OF MOSES, AN ANCIENT BOOK OF MAGIC, Samuel Weiser, Inc. 1973, page 15.

more ancient sources. It described how God handed this "book" of Secret Knowledge to the Archangel *Raziel*, the "angel in charge of the holy mysteries."

Raziel stood near the Throne of God and recorded everything spoken, hence, this title of keeper and communicator of secrets. [17] But, he wasn't known as one to keep secrets. *Raziel's* role in flagrantly revealing hidden mysteries is described in this passage from Ecclesiastes:

> *"Curse not the king, no not in thy thought;*
> *and do not curse the rich in thy bedchamber,*
> *for a bird of the heavens will carry the sound and the*
> *winged creatures will make the matter known.* [18]

Adam and the Book of *Raziel*

The BOOK OF *RAZIEL* is called the first book ever written since Adam was the first human to possess its contents, according to Judaic legends. [19] *Raziel* shared this knowledge with Adam who read the book aloud to the angels. But, he was warned.

The holy angel *Hadraniel* [20] implored Adam not to reveal these secrets to the other angels. It was only Adam's privilege to possess this knowledge.

---

[17] JEWISH ENCYCLOPEDIA, p 335.

[18] OLD TESTAMENT, Ecclesiastes 10:20.

[19] See "The BOOK OF *RAZIEL*" in THE LEGENDS OF THE JEWS, by Louis Ginsberg, pages 90-93 for a narrative of events between *Raziel* and Adam.

[20] *Hadraniel's* name means "majesty [or greatness] of God," the gatekeeper at the second gate in Heaven, from Davidson, Gustave, A DICTIONARY OF ANGELS, INCLUDING THE FALLEN ANGELS (1967), page 132.

"Adam, keep the glory of your Master concealed.
For permission has not been given to celestial beings
to know about the glory of your Master,
it has only been given to you."

Spoken by the Angel Hadraniel, from the ZOHAR. [21]

Adam obliged. According to one legend, however, the angels were so envious of Adam they took the book away from him and threw it in the sea. The angel *Rahab* [22] was ordered by God to return it Adam, and he did. [23]

Another legend related that Adam continued to practice these secrets until he had "transgressed the command of his Master." Because of his infraction, the book "flew away from him" and it was cast into the ocean.

One version claimed that after Adam and Eve were expelled from the Garden of Eden, [24] Adam took with him the "knowledge of the leaves of the tree," [25] a subtle reference to the allegorical Tree of Life described in *Kabbalah*. To prevent Adam and Eve from reentering the Garden, *Cherubim* (holy winged-creatures) were placed at the entrance.

Adam eventually passed this sacred knowledge on to his son Seth and it was transmitted through the generations until it came into the possession of Abraham, and later Enoch, [26] [27] a Biblical figure mentioned in Genesis and the great-grandfather of Noah. [28] This may be why this collection of Wisdom was called "the book of the generations of Adam" in the OLD TESTAMENT

---

[21] *ZOHAR* 1:55a-b.

[22] The angel *Rahab*, angel of the sea, is named by Davidson, Gustave, A DICTIONARY OF ANGELS, page 243 and in Louis Ginsberg, THE LEGENDS OF THE JEWS, I, pages 155-157.

[23] Ginsberg, Louis, THE LEGENDS OF THE JEWS, I, pages 156-157.

[24] Gaster, Moses, THE SWORD OF MOSES, AN ANCIENT BOOK OF MAGIC, Samuel Weiser, Inc. 1973, page 15.

[25] *ZOHAR* 1, 56b.

[26] *ZOHAR* 1, 55a.

[27] See "Enoch," Wikipedia.com.

[28] OLD TESTAMENT, Genesis 25-30. Enoch begat Methuselah who begat Lamech, who begat Noah.

(Genesis 5:1), where the future generations of Adam were revealed. [29] [30]

Adam and Eve being banished from the Garden of Eden by *Jophiel,* [31] an angel of the order of *Cherubim*. Graphic courtesy of Zedcor Graphics.

---

[29] Genesis 5:1 lists the generations from Adam to Noah. "This is the book of the generations of Adam. In the day that God created man, in the likeness of God made He him."

[30] Also, mentioned in ZOHAR 1, 55b.

[31] Mentioned in Genesis 3:4, *Jophiel, Yofiel, Iophiel,* etc. ("Beauty of God") guards the Tree of Life. As one of the seven archangels, he is the archangel of Wisdom, Understanding and Judgement (according to Pseudo-Dionysius's *DE COELESTI HIERARCHIA* (CELESTIAL HIERARCHY), a 5th-century work on angelology). *Jophiel* directs 53 legions of angels, according to the ZOHAR.

Enoch's Book of Secrets

Enoch is the prophet who "walked with God" (Genesis 5:21-24). Although no human can be together with God and live, [32] Enoch did survive. He gazed upon the secrets of Heaven and Earth and returned from his journey through Heaven.

According to tradition, Enoch acquired this "book of *Raziel*," and it became incorporated into his own BOOK OF ENOCH. [33] Enoch's book may not have contained all of the mysteries of *Raziel*, but the collection of writings was a major contributor to early Judaic mysticism. THE BOOK OF ENOCH, however, was not included among the stories in the OLD TESTAMENT, because it was not considered scripture.

These mystical secrets of the universe eventually came into the possession of Enoch's great-grandson, Noah, [34] who used its instructions to build the ark. When Noah studied the book, the Holy Spirit came to him and he gained the sacred knowledge he needed. That book, "made of sapphire stones," was enclosed in a golden casket and placed in the ark.

The magical text was eventually passed on to King Solomon who used it to practice his magical skills. [35] Many medieval *grimoires* (magic textbooks written in the Middle Ages) revealed the secrets of King Solomon's magic with talismans, amulets, corrupted Hebrew inscriptions and prayers to communicate with the angels in order to perform supernatural feats.

---

[32] Genesis 5:21-24. "And Enoch lived sixty and five years, and begot Methuselah. And Enoch walked with God after he begot Methuselah three hundred years, and begot sons and daughters. And all the days of Enoch were three hundred sixty and five years. And Enoch walked with God, and he was not; for God took him."

[33] Richard Laurence, The BOOK OF ENOCH, translated from Ethiopic. London, 1883.

[34] See the story of Noah and the book of *Raziel* in A DICTIONARY OF ANGELS, by Gustave Davidson, page 154-157.

[35] Ginsberg, Louis, THE LEGENDS OF THE JEWS, I, pages 156-157.

The Fate of the Book of *Raziel*

S o, what happened to the secrets of *Raziel?*

Although the original manuscript is now lost, the contents were supposedly acquired by Rabbi Eleazar of Worms in the 12th century and were included in his SEPHER RAZYA HA-SHEM (BOOK OF SECRETS OF THE HOLY NAME) along with his commentary on the SEPHER YETZIRAH, the BOOK OF FORMATION. After his death, multiple versions circulated.

The English translations, however, stray far from the original Hebrew. The surviving content also contains numerous errors. Jewish scholar Mordecai Margalioth, [36] discovered fragments of earlier texts in the Cairo Genizah in 1963. [37] He published it as *SEPHER HA-RAZIM*. It was translated into English in 1983 by Michael Morgan [38] and in 2007. The book is split into seven sections, and contains a list of angel names and instructions to perform certain rites. [39]

Early folklore advises the owner of the BOOK OF *RAZIEL* to keep a copy in one's home to bring a special Divine blessing and to protect the home from fire. People also kept miniature copies in their wallet or purse, or slept with it under their pillow. It was also recommended for pregnant women to assist an easy birth. Today, the medieval version of the BOOK OF *RAZIEL* can be found on the shelves of almost any bookstore or occultists' library. [40]

---

[36] Margalioth, Mordecai, *SEPHER HA-RAZIM*. Jerusalem: *Yediot Achronot,* 1966.

[37] The Cairo Genizah is a collection of more than 300,000 Jewish manuscripts and fragments found in the storeroom (Genizah) of the Ben Ezra Synagogue in Old Cairo, Egypt. Source: Wikipedia.com.

[38] Morgan, Michael A. *SEPHER HA-RAZIM*: THE BOOK OF MYSTERIES. Chico, CA: Scholars Press, 1983.

[39] *SEPHER HA-RAZIM,* Wikipedia.com.

[40] See Steve Savedow's English translation of *SEPHER REZIAL HEMELACH*: THE BOOK OF THE ANGEL *REZIAL*. This rough translation is the only English version available. There is a 1701(Amsterdam) full Hebrew version in public domain circulation called *SEPHER RAZIEL HAMELECH.*

Noah is being instructed by the Lord to build an ark and assemble animals. Zedcor Graphics (BIBLE 13).

Angelic Beings

A *Cherub*, a winged-angel, guiding a meditative rabbi to a brighter vision. Zedcor Graphics.

The imagery of supernatural beings permeated early Hebrew literature during the late 7th century B.C.E., prior to the Jew's captivity in Babylonia. Angels– *malach* (מלאך) in Hebrew– were the messengers of God's word. They interceded between the Holy One and humans [41] and often sung the praises of the Lord. The concept of angels may have originated in the Mesopotamian culture of the Babylonians, Assyrians and Sumerians. In one Babylonian

---

[41] Example, 1 Kings 19:2: "Then Jezebel sent a messenger (*Malach*) unto Elijah…"

myth, *Annunaki* ("princely offspring of the sky god *Anu*"), sank below the horizon and became underworld deities and the judges of the dead. [42] The Hebrew archangels *Michael* and *Gabriel* were Babylonian in origin. [43] Angels are also cited in the Ethiopian ENOCH I, [44] where the seven archangels are listed as *Michael, Gabriel, Raphael, Uriel, Raguel, Zerachiel* and *Remiel.* [45]

Although there are hundreds of references to angels throughout the OLD TESTAMENT, on the whole, biblical writers did not speculate much about them. The first mention of an angelic being by name in the OLD TESTAMENT was in THE BOOK OF DANIEL. [46] One of the most well-known archangels, *Michael* [47] (Hebrew for "Who is like God?"), appeared to the prophet Daniel and provided him with dire prophecies about the future of Greece and Persia.

Around the time the *TALMUD* was put to writing (4th-6th century C.E.), the works of Dionysius the Areopagite [48] ranked the various classes of angels and explained their heavenly powers. There are three triads of celestial hierarchies between God and man, according to these texts. The first triad, and the closest to God, were composed of the *Cherubim, Seraphim* and *Ophanim*; the 2nd triad, which was a reflection of the first, comprised the Dominions, Virtues and Powers; and the 3rd triad, ministering directly to man, are the Principalities, Archangels and Angels.

Enoch's BOOK OF DREAM VISIONS vividly describes the hierarchy of the Archangels, the Fallen Angels, spiritual entities known as the "sons of God" or "messengers of God (*beni Elohim* בני אלוהם), and the history of Israel up until his lifetime. [49] [50]

---

[42] Leemings, David, OXFORD COMPANION TO WORLD MYTHOLOGY, Oxford University Press (2009). p. 21.

[43] Archangels, NEW WORLD ENCYCLOPEDIA and A DICTIONARY OF ANGELS, Including the Fallen Angels, by Gustav Davidson, 1980, Free Press Publishing.

[44] Estimated to have been written about 163–142 B.C.E.

[45] In the late 5th to early 6th century, Pseudo-Dionysius lists them *as Michael, Gabriel, Raphael, Uriel, Chamuel, Jophiel,* and *Zadkiel.* Pope Gregory I lists them as *Michael, Gabriel, Raphael, Uriel, Simiel, Orifiel,* and *Zachariel.* From A DICTIONARY OF ANGELS, Including the Fallen Angels, by Gustav Davidson, 1980, Free Press Publishing.

[46] Daniel 10:13: "But the prince of the kingdom of Persia stood against me for 21 days, and behold Michael, one of the first princes, came to help, and I remained there with the kings of Persia." See also Daniel 10:21 and Daniel 12:1.

[47] See STRONG'S CONCORDANCE #4317 for the OLD TESTAMENT and Strong's #3413 for the New Testament.

[48] Dionysius the Areopagite on the Heavenly Hierarchy.

[49] *Beni Elohim* are mentioned in Genesis 6:2, Job 1:6, Job 38.7 and Psalms 29:1.

[50] Example of the *Beni Elohim* in Job 38:7: "When the morning stars sang and the Sons of *Elohim* shouted for joy."

Graphic of Archangel *Raphael*, drawn by Robert Zucker in 1976. *Rapha-el* means "God has healed." The original art is an illustration in William Hayley's THE POETIC WORKS OF JOHN MILTON (1796).

Cherubim– Guardians of the Tree of Life

"And He placed the Cherubim to the east of the Garden of Eden and the flame of sword revolving to guard the way of the Tree of Life." [51]

Cherubim graphic. Zedcor Graphics

C herubim (*cherub,* also *kerubim*), the first heavenly beings named in the OLD TESTAMENT, belong to the Order of Celestial Beings. They are not actually classified as angels and their role in Judaic literature has never been fully revealed. But, they are repeatedly mentioned in the OLD TESTAMENT and play a part in early Judaic mysticism.

The word *karubu* [52] ("interceding deities") is Assyrian or Akkadian in origin. In Assyrian art, *karubu* were depicted as huge winged creatures with human faces and bodies of bulls or sphinxes.

---

[51] Passage from Genesis 3:24. *Cherubim* are named 91 times in the OLD TESTAMENT, including Exodus 25:18, the *cherubim* of gold; Hebrews 9:5, the *cherubim* of glory shadowing mercy seat; Ezekiel 10:14, each of the *cherubim* had four faces; Kings 6:23, in Solomon's Temple, there are carved out of olive wood, etc.

[52] In Akkadian the word *Karibu* means "one who prays," or "one who intercedes."

They were often placed at the entrance to palaces, temples as guardian spirits. [53] Phoenician art of the 8th century B.C.E. depicted winged-like creatures carrying godlike figures across the sky. They are usually displayed as a human adult or child features with huge wings.

Just before God banished Adam and Eve from the Garden of Eden, He remarked that man has "become as one of us, to know good and evil." So, He placed two *cherubim* at the east of the Garden with their "flame of whirling swords" [54] to protect the "Tree of Life" and keep Adam and Eve out of the Garden after they were expelled.

In God's instructions to build the Ark of the Covenant, He explained how to make two *Cherub* of gold, one for each end of the Ark, and have them face each other. [55] God is also described as riding a *Cherub* in Psalms 18:11 and 2 Samuel 22:11.

During the Exodus in the 13th century B.C.E., the *Cherubim* were the only supernatural beings represented on the desert Tabernacle [56] and in the Jerusalem Temple [57] they were portrayed in a more decorative, architectural fashion than religious. They were prominently displayed in the Temple until the end of the 2nd Jewish Commonwealth in 70 C.E. when Jerusalem was seized and looted. In the Babylonian *TALMUD*, the *K'rub* are called *rabia* and described as being "childlike" and appeared youthful. They surrounded the Ark of the Covenant as winged guardians. [58] The most famous description is given by two major figures in Biblical times– Ezekiel and Enoch.

When the Ezekiel preached to the Jewish captives of Babylonia in 6 B.C.E, [59] he gave an eye-witness account of the *cherubim*-like being he called Holy Living Creatures. In Ezekiel's vision,

---

[53] Davidson, Gustave, A DICTIONARY OF ANGELS, page 86. Also, see Frederic Nye Lindsay, KERUBIM IN SEMITIC RELIGION AND ART. NEW YORK, 1912, THESIS, COLUMBIA UNIVERSITY.

[54] Genesis 3:24: "He drove the man out and placed on the east side of the Garden of Eden *cherubim* and a flaming sword flashing back and forth to guard the way to the Tree of Life."

[55] Read Exodus 25:18-22. See Exodus 25:22: "Above the cover between the two *cherubim* over the Ark of the Covenant, I will meet with you and give you all my commands for the Israelites."

[56] Exodus 25:19: "Make one *cherub* on one end and the second *cherub* on the other; make the *cherubim* of one piece with the cover, at the two ends." And Exodus 26:10 the Tabernacle with ten curtains of finely twisted linen and with blue, purple and scarlet yarn, with *cherubim* woven into them by a skilled worker."

[57] 1 Kings 6:21: "For the inner sanctuary, he (King Solomon) made a pair of *cherubim* out of olive wood, each ten cubits high." Their wings stretched out so that one wing would touch the other.

[58] Exodus 25:18-22. "And make two *cherubim* out of hammered gold at the ends of the cover... above the cover between the two *cherubim* that are over the Ark of the Covenant law and I will give all of my commands to the Israelites."

[59] The generally accepted date corresponds to July 28, 593 B.C.E.

he saw four *Cherubim* with the form of winged men each with a four-fold head. [60] Ezekiel described the living creatures as "angels of fire" [61] who support the Throne of God." These "Holy Living Creatures" (*Hayyoth ha-Kadosh*), mentioned by Ezekiel and *Merkabah* literature, are another class of celestial beings, sometimes equated with *Cherubim*.

Enoch gave an eyewitness account of his vision of the *Cherubim* in 1 B.C.E. He wrote that after awakening, he saw the appearance of two men, or angels, who guided him through the various levels of Heaven. "Behold," Enoch wrote, [62] "I saw a very great light, and all of the fiery hosts of archangels, and the incorporeal powers and the lordship, and the principalities, and of the dominions: *Cherubim* and *Seraphim*, thrones and the watchfulness of the *Ophanim* ("many wheels, or many eyes")." [63] Rabbi Pinhas ben Yahir, a 2nd century C.E. Palestinian teacher, remarked that the two *Cherubim* over the Ark of the Covenant corresponded to the two Holy Names of *Yahweh* ("Lord") and *Elohim* ("God"). [64] When they are displayed as a pair, *Cherubim* symbolize the realms of Heaven and Earth. When shown as four, they represent the four directions or winds. [65] After the 5th century, *Cherubim* earned angelic status when ranked among the First Order of Angels by the Greeks. [66] John Milton often drew on the images in Ezekiel's vision of the *Cherubim.* They also played a role in sleep as the body transitions through several stages, according to an ancient *midrash.* Angels never sleep but always watch the Throne of God. [67]

---

[60] Ezekiel 1:5: "The four living creatures…in the appearance of a man." Ezekiel 1.6: "Each had four faces and four wings."

[61] Ezekiel 1:5: "Within the fire was the appearance of four living creatures with a human form."

[62] BOOK OF ENOCH, chapter 20:1 describes Enoch's vision when he was escorted into the 7th Heaven.

[63] Ophanim are referred as "Angels of the wheels of the moon" and are among the Order of Thrones. Ginsburg Louis, ESSENCES AND THE KABALAH, page 90.

[64] *Midrash Tadshe*, ed. Jellinek, *BET HAMIDRASH III*, page 164, from Patai, Raphael, THE HEBREW GODDESS, page 83.

[65] Ezekiel 10:11: "As the *Cherubim* moved, they would go in any one of the four directions that they faced, but the wheels did not turn about as the *cherubim* went."

[66] *DE COELESTI HIERARCHIA (THE CELESTIAL HIERARCHY)* is a 5th century Greek work on angelology. *Cherubim* were ranked alongside *Seraphim* and *Chayyot* (Living Creatures), among the three Orders of the Angels recognized by Pope St. Gregory I (see Wikipedia.com. THE CELESTIAL HIERARCHY was translated into English in 1899 (Dionysius the Areopagite on the Heavy Hierarchy).

[67] BOOK OF ENOCH 70: 9: "Then the *Seraphim*, the *Cherubim*, and *Ophanim* surrounded it. These are those who never sleep, but watch the Throne of His Glory."

Abraham's Book of Holy Letters

The secrets contained in the Oral Tradition continued to be transmitted by select scholars from generation to generation until it was written down by Abraham, [68] the Father of the Jewish people.

Abraham is considered to be the original author of the ancient book of Jewish magic called *SEFER YETZIRAH*– the BOOK OF FORMATION. Although no copy of Abraham's original "book" has been found, some parts of it may have been inscribed centuries later. [69] Some editions of the *SEPHER YETZIRAH* were also called *OTIYYOT DE-AVRAHAM AVINU* – Letters of Abraham Our Father. It doesn't necessarily mean he composed the book. Instead, it alludes to the principles that were taught by Abraham. [70]

According to a statement in *ROKEAH* (*Hasidut Zakuyyut 'Arum*), at age 48, Abraham was moved by the deeds of the generation of the Tower of Babel to reflect on God and the Universe. Abraham meditated on the Laws of Creation before he received his first revelation from God. [71]

Abraham contemplated on these holy concepts for three years by himself, until he became so wise he wrote down the words to what would be known as the *SEPHER YETZIRAH*– the BOOK OF FORMATION. Then, God appeared to Abraham. He "took him unto Himself, kissed him, called him His friend, and made a covenant with him and his descendants forever," according to the *SEPHER YETZIRAH*. [72] [73] [74] Abraham practiced those principles upon his conversion from idol worshipper to the religion of the One God.

---

[68] "Abraham," Jewish Virtual Library. Abraham was born about 1946 B.C.E. and died in about 1771 B.CE. He was born in the Jewish year of 1948 after Creation.

[69] Ginsburg, Louis, LEGEND OF JEWS, page 210.

[70] Kaplan, Aryeh, *SEPHER YETZIRAH:* THEORY, page xii.

[71] Genesis 12:1-31: "The Lord said to Abram: "Leave your country, your family, and your relatives and go to the land that I will show you. 2: I will bless you and make your descendants into a great nation. You will become famous and be a blessing to others. 3: I will bless anyone who blesses you, but I will put a curse on anyone who puts a curse on you. Everyone on earth will be blessed because of you."

[72] *SEPHER YETZIRAH* 6:7.

[73] Ginsberg, Louis LEGEND OF JEWS, page 210, from *Sepher Yetzirah*.

[74] Kaplan, Aryeh, *SEPHER YETZIRAH*: THEORY, page xiii.

Abraham's Souls in Haran

One odd passage in Genesis tells where Abraham and his wife, Sarah, were instructed by God to gather "the souls they made in Haran." [75] [76] This phrase has been interpreted mystically to mean that Abraham "created" these souls, or *golem,* with the knowledge he learned from the concepts of the *SEPHER YETZIRAH.*

Did Abraham actually create artificial beings or did he only convert those souls to his following? The intended meaning of this passage has been debated for centuries. *Kabbalists* insist that these "souls" were not human beings, but actually man-made creatures called *golem.*

How could Abraham accomplish such a feat? Jewish legends contend that humans who possess a certain Wisdom have the capability to mimic the actions of the Creator.

---

[75] Genesis 12:5: "Abraham also Sarah, his wife, and Lot, his brother's son, and all of their possessions, and the souls (people) they had gotten in Haran."

[76] Haran, Charan or Charron is identified with an ancient city in Upper Mesopotamia. Harran is now a village in Turkey. Haran was a temporary home for Abraham. See "Haran (biblical place)," Wikipedia.com.

Moses Receives the Oral Tradition

When Moses received the Ten Commandments– the "Written Law"– on Mt. Sinai, during the Exodus from Egypt about 1440 B.C.E., legend claims he also received another, more sacred, Wisdom that was not written in stone. This is the *"Torah Shebe'al Peh,"* the unwritten Oral Tradition.

Jewish legend claims that Moses verbally transmitted this sacred knowledge to Joshua, who passed it on to the Elders.

The Elders shared these "traditions" with the Judges. From the Judges it was passed to the Prophets.

The Prophets then entrusted this knowledge with the most learned men in the synagogues, and they passed it on to other wise men. [77] [78] This collective knowledge eventually became part of today's *Kabbalah.*

Moses with the Ten Commandments graphics. Zedcor Graphics.

---

[77] Kaplan, Aryeh, *SEPHER YETZIRAH*: THEORY, by page 343. Moses studied the letters on Mt. Sinai, from *PIRKEY* RABBI ELEAZER OF WORMS, 48 (Warsaw, 1852), 116a.

[78] Nissan, Dovid Dubov. THE ORAL TRADITION, Chabad.org.

The Ancient 72 Triplet Names

19

ויסע מלאך האלהם ההלך לפני מחנה ישראל וילך מאחריהם ויסע עמוד

20

הענן מפניהם ויעמד מאחריהם:

21

ויבא בין מחנה מצרים ובין מחנה ישראל ויהי הענן והחשך ויאר את הלילה

ולא קרב זה אל זה כל הלילה:

ויט משה את ידו על הים ויולך יהוה את הים ברוח קדים עזה כל הלילה

וישם את הים לחרבה ויבקעו המים:

Exodus
14:19-21

19: And the angel of God, who went before the camp of Israel, removed and went behind them; and the pillar of cloud removed from before them, and stood behind them;

20: and it came between the camp of Egypt and the camp of Israel; and there was the cloud, and darkness here, yet gave it light by the night there; and the one came not near the other all the night.

21: And Moses stretched out his hand over the sea; and the Lord caused the sea to go back by a strong east wind all the night, and made the sea dry land, and the waters were divided.

The above three passages from Exodus (14:19-21) describes Moses' miracle when he departed the Red Sea. In early Jewish mysticism, these passages also hold a very mystical, and secret, meaning. A special arrangement of the 216 consecutive letters in the three passages reveals the hidden 72-triplet Names of God. Moses was said to have used this formula in order to spread the waters. Medieval magicians would use permutations of the three verses to construct angels' names. According to the *BAHIR*, [79] the 72 Holy Names are comprised from each one of those three verses in Exodus.

---

[79] *BAHIR* III, page 43. "This was the explicit name (*Shem Ha-MeForesh*) which permission is given that it be permutated and spoken (according to Numbers 6:27).

33

Jewish rabbi in Egypt graphic from Zedcor Graphics (Jewish27).

The knowledge of the 72 Triplets is one Key to unlock the secrets of the *SEPHER RAZIEL.* One of the most important *Kabbalists* of the 13th century, Rabbi Abraham Abulafia [80] was among the first to discuss its purpose and provide the exact formula to construct the Sacred Names. [81]

According to Abulafia, one of the methods to accomplish this is through letter permutation

(*tzeruf* צרף), the activity of forming letter combinations, and contemplating on the meaning of

---

[80] Abraham Abulafia was born in 1240 C.E.

[81] Abulafia, Abraham, *CHAYE HAOLAM HABA* (LIFE IN THE FUTURE WORLD— THE AFTERLIFE).

each permutation to produce new knowledge and a spiritual experience. [82]

To start the process, Abulafia instructs the student to inscribe the three verses of Exodus 14:19-21 in the following order to create one Triplet (3-letter Name). [83] There is a total of 24 Triplets that contain the 72 letters, according to Abulafia.

- Write the letters of the 19th verse in <u>forward</u> order
- <u>Reverse</u> the order of the 20th verse
- Write the 21st row in its original, <u>forward</u> order

To construct the first Triplet:

- Take the <u>first</u> letter of the 19th verse, which is a *Vav* (ו).

- Take the <u>last</u> letter of the 20th verse, which is a *Heh* (ה),

- Add the <u>first</u> letter of the 21st verse, which is a *Vav* (ו).

- Combine these three letters to produce the first Triplet, *V-H-V* (והו)

Follow these same steps to create the 2nd Triplet: *Y-L-Y* (ילי):

- (י) *Yod*– 2nd letter of row 19

- (ל) *Lamed*– 2nd from the end of row 20

- (י) *Yod*– 2nd letter of row 21

The following chart, from Rabbi Abulafia's book, depicts the Triplets of Names when all three verses are placed in a grid layout.

---

[82] Kaplan, Aryeh, MEDITATION AND *KABBALAH*, page 92.

[83] Excerpts and quotations are from Abraham Abulafia's *CHAYE HAOLAM HABA*. Most of Abulafia's book is translated in MEDITATION AND *KABBALAH* by Aryeh Kaplan, pages 93-106. The English translations are provided by Kaplan.

Start

This chart displays the 72 Names of God, derived from the three verses in Exodus, provided by Abraham Abulafia, *CHAYE HAOLAM HABA* (LIFE IN THE FUTURE WORLD).

"Start" marks the beginning of the first Triplet *VHV* (והו). Read from right to left.

The results provide the three-letter consonants to form each of the 72 Holy Names. The final output should look like the chart above. Using that example, read the first three Triplets (top row, from right to left):

- The 1st Triplet is *V-H-V* (והו) and pronounced as *Va-He-Va.*

- 2nd Triplet is *Y-L-Y* (ילי) and is pronounced as *Yo-La-Yo.*

- 3rd Triplet is *S-Y-T*, (סיט) and is pronounced as *Sa-Yo-Te,* etc.

When all of the 72 Names are written out, one must meditate on the meaning of each Triplet (3 letter set).

The rabbi further instructs, "After you have depicted all this, prepare your mind and heart so you should understand the many things that come to your thoughts through the letters that your heart imagines." Each Triplet has a relation to a specific passage in the OLD TESTAMENT. For example, *VaHeVa* would be invoked through Psalms 3:3. [84] The 2nd Triplet, *YoLaYo,* is connected to Psalms 22:19. [85] There are numerous attributes, however, so no one list can be truly accurate.

Each letter is also paired with a specific vowel sound, Abulafia explained. [86] Pronounce the "Name [of Seventy-Two] using the natural vowel sound of each letter." There are five Hebrew vowels (O, A, E, I, U). Breath in when speaking the letters and exhale with the vowels. Each Triplet involves twelve breaths.

"Clear your mind completely," Abulafia instructed, "then, with complete concentration, and a proper, pleasant, sweet melody, pronounce the Name of the 72." With the pronunciation of each Triplet, one soon experiences an uplifting feeling and is prepared to receive the 'Divine Influx,' called the *shefa* (שפא). "We have a tradition that the Divine Influx will come to a perfected individual after he completes (pronounces) the 24 Triplets," Abulafia wrote.

The divine influx will carry the meditator to a point where "your soul is separating itself from your body" as you obtain this overwhelming spiritual feeling. When you achieve that level, stop and take a break. Each pronunciation has a specific head movement as well as correct pronunciation to achieve the full spiritual effect.

When the power of the Influx begins to manifest and reveal itself to the one gazing in the "mirror," the letters and the *Sefiroth* begin to appear like lightning flashes, as the visions of the *Chayyot* ("living creatures") as in the biblical passage: "The *Chayyot* ran and returned, like a vision, or appearance, of lightning," [87] Abulafia revealed in his writings.

In the *SEPHER YEZIRAH*, the phrase "Their vision (*tzafiyah*), is like a flash of lightning," refers to prophecy and the mystical vision, such as "one who gazes (*tzefiyat*) at the Chariot *(Merkabah)*." The prophet Ezekiel had such a vision when he described the "living creatures that ran and returned like lightning flashes." [88]

---

[84] Palms 3:3: "Many there are that say of my soul: 'There is no salvation for him in God.' *Selah*"

[85] Psalms 22:19: "They part my garments among them, and for my vesture do they cast lots."

[86] The vowels have specific names, *Cholem* (o), *Kametz* (a), *Tzere* (e), *Chirek* (i), and *Shurek* (u).

[87] Ezekiel 1:14 and *SEPHER YETZIRAH* 1:6.

[88] Ezekiel 1:14.

The 72 Names of the Angels

Sometime during the Middle Ages, however, the use of the Holy Names became corrupted by secular "magicians" who used the 72 Names to conjure angels and conduct nefarious biddings. Medieval *grimoires* that circulated among the masses only encouraged the unskilled to attempt dangerous acts that many people believed could influence others and nature.

The 72 angel names were composed out of the Triplets extracted from the verse in Exodus 14:19-21. Each three-letter set forms the prefix of an angels' name. The suffix of the angel name is comprised from one of the two Holy Names. These were also known as the 72 angels of Jacob's Ladder.

Since only the Temple High Priests were allowed to speak the Holy Name, and only on High Holy Days, substitutions for the suffix of the angel's name were made by using "nicknames" to avoid using the actual Name of God. Today, the Name is still uttered during the High Holy Days, but the true pronunciation is only known to a few. Instructions to form the Divine Name are mentioned in the *BAHIR*, the *ZOHAR*, and written about among several prominent rabbis, especially during the Middle Ages. [89]

To form an angels' name, either the suffix -*AL* (אל), for an angel of mercy, was added at the end of the three-letter Triplet. *YH* (יה), representing an angel of judgement, was added at the end of the angel's name. The word *AL* is found in other Semitic languages as Phoenician and Aramaic.

For example, start with the first Triplet *V-H-V* (והו) and add the suffix of *YH* (יה). The first angle's name is והויה – *Vehuiah*. This is demonstrated on the following chart in the upper right column (indicated next to the four descending X's– read from top down). The second angel name would be *Ieliel YLVAL* (ילואל). The 72 Angel Names were published in medieval magic *grimoires* such as the *LEMEGETON* [90] and were used invoke miracles, healings and other superhuman powers, especially among Christian Cabalists. [91] Each angel had his own power, sigil, influence, correspondence in nature.

---

[89] See also Agrippa, Heinrich Cornelius: *DE OCCULTA PHILOSOPHIA*, book III, chapter 25 for a discussion from a secular view.

[90] De Laurence L.W., The LESSER KEY OF SOLOMON, *GOETIA*, THE BOOK OF EVIL SPIRITS (1916), Is also known as the *CLAVICULA SALOMONIS REGIS or LEMEGETON*. See pages 22-45 for names, attributes, followed by observations, times, etc. This book also includes the sigils assigned to each angel. The book was republished in English in 1916

[91] Burton, Dan and Grandy, David, MAGIC, MYSTERY, AND SCIENCE: THE OCCULT IN WESTERN CIVILIZATION, Indiana University Press, 2004, page 69.

This is the chart of the 72 3-letter triplets in Hebrew and the angel names when either *EL* or *YH* is added at the end of each triplet to form what is also called 72 angels of Jacob's Ladder. This chart was produced in THE MAGUS, in 1801. [92] The First three squares (read downwards) in the upper right contain the first name. The fourth square is the 2-letter suffix (*YH*- יה or *EL*- אל) to create the angel's full name. The second column to the left contains the second name, etc. [93]

[92] Francis Barrett, THE MAGUS, 1801. Page 243.

[93] The 72 Names are also known the 72 angels of Jacob's Ladder.

Teraphim– the "Nourishers"

"The teraphim are built according to the forms of men and this form is made [in such a way as] to receive the power of the superior [beings]." [94]

Teraphim are ancient human-shaped miniature household figurines used for worship in the home and mentioned numerous times in the OLD TESTAMENT. [95] The Hebrews acquired their use of *Teraphim* from inhabitants of lower Mesopotamia.

It was believed that these handmade figures would bring fortune and good luck to its owners. *Teraphim* were called the "givers of prosperity," "guardians of comforts," and "nourishers" by the Roman Lares and Penates of the early Hebrews, although the practice was generally considered heathen among religious leaders. [96]

Teraphim could be hidden away in the pack saddle of a camel, similar to the ones described in Genesis. Rachel stole them because she was afraid they would tell Laban her direction when she fled to elope. [97] Others were life size. Some may have represented family members.

According to another passage, found in Samuel, [98] Michal took a *teraphim* and laid it on the bed on a pillow of goat's hair at its head and covered it with David's clothes in an attempt to conceal

---

[94] From SEPHER HA-HAYYIM attributed to Rabbi Abraham ibn Ezra (Idel, Moshe, GOLEM: JEWISH MAGICAL, page 86), from a 12th century discussion of biblical *teraphim* of Lavan.

[95] In addition to those passages mentioned here, see other examples in Judges 18:14, 17, 18 & 20; Hosiah 3:4.

[96] *Teraphim,* JEWISH ENCYCLOPEDIA.

[97] Genesis 31:34: "Rachel took the household *teraphim* and put them insider her camel's saddle and was sitting on them. Laban searched through everything in the tent but could not find them."

[98] Samuel 19:11-13: "Saul sent messengers to David's house to watch him, because he might kill Saul in the morning. But Michal, David's wife, told him, 'If you do not escape with your life tonight, tomorrow you will be killed.' So, Michal let David down through the window and he fled away and escaped. Michal took *teraphim* and she laid it on the bed and put a pillow of goats' hair at its head and covered it with her clothes."

his absence. But, in a passage from Zechariah, [99] *teraphim* "speak falsely" and would lead believers on a misguided path.

The great philosopher Moshe (Moses) Maimonides (1135-1204) said that "the worshippers of the *teraphim* claim that as the light of the stars filled the carved statue, it was put in rapport with the intelligence of those distant stars and planets who used the statue as an instrument. It is in this manner that the *teraphim* taught people many useful arts and sciences."

---

[99] Zechariah 10:2: "For the *teraphim* have spoken in vanity, and the diviners have seen false visions, and they dream falsely, they comfort in vain; therefore, people follow them like sheep, they are afflicted, because there is no shepherd."

Egyptian *Ushabti*- The Answerers

The rite of enchantment used by the Egyptians may be similar to the Jewish *teraphim* and the vivification of the *golem*, believed historian Ibn Khaldun (1332-78 C.E.) when he saw a ceremony performed with an *Ushabti* in Moslem Egypt.

Ushabti (also called *shabti*, or *Shawabti*) are magical, clay figure statuettes produced in the early dynasty of the ancient Egyptian empire. *Shabti* is the Egyptian word for "answerer."

Shabti were used from the Middle Kingdom (around 1900 B.C.E.) until the end of the Ptolemaic Period (about 2,000 years later). The term applies to these figures prior to the 21st dynasty (21st) of Egypt. After the 21st Dynasty, the term *ushabti* was used.

Originally, slaves or captives were sacrificed and buried in the tombs of their masters with the belief that they would continue to serve them in the afterlife. Their bodies were eventually replaced by statuettes called "answerers." These small, handheld statuettes held various tools of labor in their crossed hands. Below the chest, a special charm and title of the deceased was inscribed.

These Egyptian funerary figurines were placed in the tomb with the deceased to complete the work of its owner in the netherworld. A prayer was made to the statue to do its earthly biddings.

Most *shabti* were made of clay, some were made of hardstone, sandstone, limestone and some were wood carved. The power of dirt, or clay, was believed to have life-giving properties.

Like the *Teraphim* and the *golem*, the *shabti* are supposed to obey the orders of the owner. But these statuettes are animated to specifically serve the soul of the deceased whose name is carved into its chest along with a prayer to "carry the water" from the canals and to "do the work" in the netherworld. The writings engraved on the object often contain a portion of the 6th chapter of the EGYPTIAN BOOK OF THE DEAD.

The earlier *shabti* may have planted the cultural seed for the later *golem* and *teraphim* legends. When the spell was uttered, the figure would become alive and do whatever was necessary. This is a typical prayer to the *shabti*, often inscribed on the figurine body in hieroglyphs:

"Hail, Shabti, this, if be decreed,
that I am to be adjudged to do labors
which are to be done in the underworld,
to fill with water the canals,
to carry sand from the East to the West,
such work shall be performed for me by thee
and no obstacle to doing so shall be put in thy way."

The shabti then replies:
"I will work, verily I am here [when thou] callest thee." [100]

---

[100] Budge, W., EGYPTIAN BOOK OF THE DEAD, page, 233-4

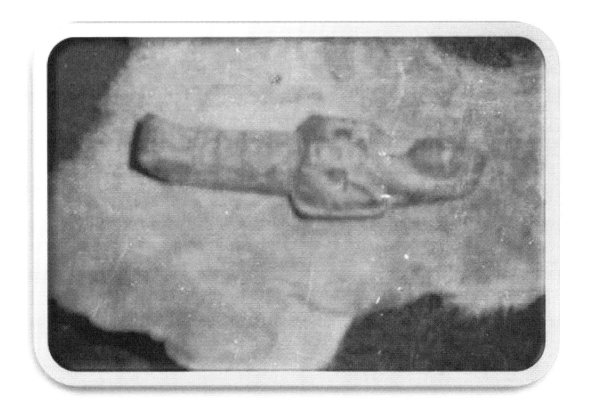

A *shabti* from a private collection.

Clay Figurines in the Middle East

Mystical funerary objects are found in several early cultures. The Sumerians buried idols under floors of houses and chambers where men lay sick. They were also used to protect property and guard against the devil.

In the homes or bedrooms of ancient Babylonians protective figures either stood at the doorway or were buried under the threshold. At Ur, for example, clay figures were found in boxes of burnt brick placed under the floor against the walls. These boxes, provided with lids, had one end open, facing the center of the room, which the figures watched and guarded.

There were human figures clad in a garment composed of a pointed hat and a long robe painted with scales– these were fish-men, creatures mentioned in mythology. Some had figures of human bodies and the heads and wings of birds, some were long-bearded, long-robed, and some had closed hands folded across the breast as though grasping some object. [101]

The Assyrians kept images of gods in their homes that were believed to have power to ward off spirits. Chinese witches fashioned statuettes in clay, paper, wood or jade to "give them life." The witch placed inside of the figure not only the reproductions of vital organs– heart, liver, lungs– but also a small living animal like a bird, insect or reptile.

They believed that when the soul leaves the animal after its death, it will inhabit the talisman. Amulets and talismans were common part of everyday life during Paleolithic [102] and Neolithic periods. [103] They evolved into small carved figurines of lime, wood, ivory, sandstone, clay and metal of the early magicians.

---

[101] Saggs, H.W.F., THE GREATNESS THAT WAS BABYLON page 301.

[102] The Paleolithic period was the early phase of the Stone Age when human started using stone tools.

[103] The Neolithic period, the New Stone Age, began about 10,000 B.C.E. in the Middle East and ended between 4,500 and 2,000 B.C.E.

The 'Life from Clay' Theory

*"And the Lord, God, formed
man of dust and of the ground."*
Genesis 2:7

id life actually evolve from earth (clay) rather than water? A developing concept known as the Life from Clay Theory is based on the idea that clay, as a substance with it transference properties, provides the necessary factor to spark life from organic matter.

In *golem* folklore, life can be embedded into a solid substance, i.e. dirt or dust, just as the body is formed from the Earth. This primordial dust is clay.

Several scientists from California support the emerging theory that life on earth began in clay rather than the sea, according to an article in the NEW YORK TIMES. [104] The discovery, announced at a symposium in 1985, showed that ordinary clay contains two basic properties essential to life: to store and transfer energy.

When the scientists analyzed common ceramic clay, they discovered evidence that the formation of clay crystals may have created the condition to trap and retain energy. Clay can act like a catalyst during chemical reactions.

The "primordial soup" theory, proposed by A.I. Oparin in the 1930's, suggested that "compounds that contained carbon and hydrogen and some other chemicals accumulated particularly in the earth's early waters. Energy from lightning and solar radiation then caused the compounds to evolve spontaneously into living matter."

The experiments demonstrated how to evoke the spark of life, or energy, into an inanimate object.

Scientists were later able to re-create what may have been similar to the original spark of life on

---

[104] NEW YORK TIMES, April 3, 1985. Armin Weiss of University of Munich and Research conducted experiments with a team of scientists at the National Aeronautics and Space Administration's Ames Research Center in Mountain View, California. The leader was Dr. Lelia Coyne, research associate at Ames and San Jose State University.

Earth, according to researchers. During lab tests, a laser zapped clay and a chemical mixture that simulated the energy of an asteroid as it sped to Earth.

The laser-zapping experiment produced all four chemicals needed to create "what can be considered crucial pieces of the building block of life." There are additional steps necessary for life to emerge, but this was the starting point. [105]

According to ancient Judaic mysticism, [106] God conferred life by the "vapor of the pronunciation of the letters." Those sound vibrations induced vitality into the dust [107] and infused a soul (in Hebrew, *Nephesh)* into an inanimate object, the *golem*.

---

[105] "Scientists re-create possible origin of life," by Seth Borenstein, The Associated Press, December 10, 2014. The experiment was conducted by lead author Svatopluk Civis of the Heyrovsky Institute of Physical Chemistry in Prague.

[106] *AMIRAT HA-'OTIYYOT*," fol 43a.

[107] Idel, Moshe, *GOLEM*, JEWISH MAGICAL, page 91-92.

Judaic Mysticism in the 1st Millennium C.E.

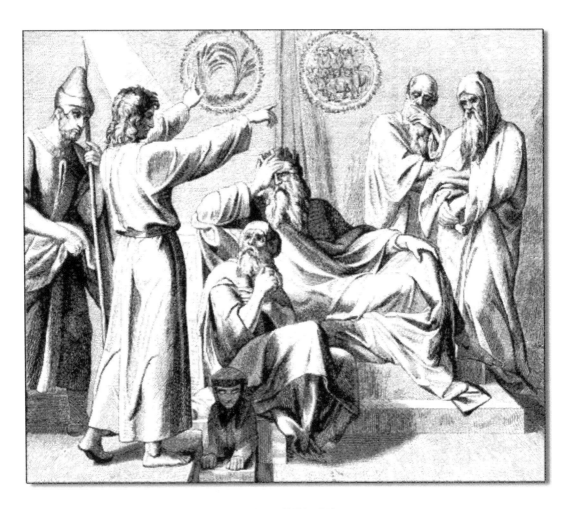

Scholarly discussions, from Zedcor Graphics (Bible 35).

D uring the first century after the birth of Christ, the Jewish residents in Jerusalem greatly suffered. In 66 C.E., the Jewish people rebelled against the oppressive Roman Empire.

On a fateful day of the 9 of Av in 70 C.E., Roman legions under Titus destroyed the Second Temple [108] in Jerusalem. The Temple's treasures were plundered and the Romans occupied the city.

In this tumultuous time of Jewish history, many sacred and mystical texts were put into writing and secretly circulated among followers. In the shadows, rabbi's and learned men carried on the traditions hidden from the rest of the world over the next centuries.

This early *TALMUDIC* period in Palestine was also the beginning of a movement where meditative techniques were used to obtain spiritual enlightenment. Many formulas consisted of the repetitive use of the Divine Name in conjunction with letters of the Hebrew alphabet.

In the last decade of the Second Temple and after Jerusalem was destroyed, Johanan ben Zakkai, an important Jewish sage, and his pupils were among the first to receive these sacred teachings and circulated a written manuscript outlining the secret teachings of the Oral Tradition. [109]

Mishnaic sage Rabbi Shimon bar Yochai [110] and his son lived during the time when the *TALMUD* and other Jewish teachings were forbidden. Before Yochai died, he revealed deep secrets of the *Kabbalah*.

Rabbi Yochai's memory is honored every *Lag BaOmar* (18th of Iyar) when he died 19 centuries ago. He was attributed as the original author of the great *Kabbalistic* work, the *ZOHAR* (BRILLIANCE), widely circulated 700 years later. [111]

---

[108] The Second Temple period was 349 B.C.E. (Before the Common Era)-70 C.E.

[109] Johanan ben Zakkai, by Solomon Schechter and William Bacher, JEWISHENCYCLOPEDI*a.com.*

[110] R. Yochai known by the acronym *Rashbi*, born in 100 C.E. and died in 160 C.E.

[111] Published by Rabbi Moses ben Shem Tov de Leon near the end of the 13th century.

Merkabah– Riding the Chariot

The *Merkabah* [112] literature is collection of ancient Jewish mystical texts including esoteric observations of the Babylonian *TALMUD*. It contained descriptions of the heavenly palaces (*Hekhalot*), personal accounts of ascents into Heaven, [113] and the secret names the initiate needed to guarantee safe journey to each level of Heaven. The goal was to receive the Vision of the Divine Chariot (*Ma'aseh Merkabah*). [114] The *Merkabah* was a popular topic in early Jewish *Hekhalot* [115] literature. [116]

Many of the concepts found in the *Kabbalah* are based on these ancient *Hekhalot* texts. Most of the material was composed between 100-1000 C.E. and was later studied by the *Chasidic Ashkenazi* during the Middle Ages (12th-13th century). [117] It covered various theories and visions connected with the Throne of Glory and the chariot.

The earliest Biblical reference is found in 1Chronicles 28:18, where it described the "altar of incense refined gold by weight; and gold for the pattern of the chariot, even the *Cherubim*, that spread out their wings, and covered the Ark of the Covenant of the Lord."

A reference in a *MISHNA HAGIGAH* passage stated that, "One may not expound the Laws of Creation before two, nor the Divine Chariot before one, unless he is wise and understanding from his own knowledge." [118] Ezekiel's vision of the *cherubim* included a description of the "chariot" (*Merkabah*). [119]

---

[112] *Ma'aseh Merkabah*; Merkabah mysticism; the name given in *MISHNAH HAGIGAH* 2.1, to the first chapter of Ezekiel.

[113] The *HEKHALOT ZUTARTEY* is the account of Rabbi Akiba and *HEKHALOT RABBATI* is the account of Rabbi Ishmael

[114] *Ma'aseh Merkabah* is also translated as "The Labor of the Vision" and "The Mechanics of the Vision."

[115] *Hekhalot* is from the Hebrew word for "Palaces," the visions of ascents into heavenly palaces.

[116] The *HEKHALOT* literature from this time included: *PERKEI HEKHALOT*, or Chapters on Ascent, describes the kingdom of the heavenly hosts, and instructs the mystic on the correct approach to the King. *GREATER HEKHALOT* describes the journey through the 7 palaces, as described by R. Ismael, and *LESSER HEKHALOT*, speaker R. Akiba (earlier origin than Greater).

[117] *Merkabah* Mysticism, See Wikipedia.com.

[118] *MISHNA HAGIGAH* 2:1.

[119] 1 Chronicles 28:18.

Ezekiel's Vision is a c. 1518 painting by Raphael. This plate is from the first Protestant Bible published in Spanish. Zedcor Graphics.

Ezekiel's Vision of the Chariot

Those fantastic visions witnessed by the prophet Ezekiel during his 22-year exile in 593 BCE [120] spawned an entire mystical tradition–

the "Vision of the Chariot" (מרכבה *Merkabah*). [121]

Followers of the *Merkabah* indulged in recreating the supernatural visions such as those suggested in the first chapter of the BOOK OF EZEKIEL in the OLD TESTAMENT and the Temple vision of Isaiah. [122]

In Ezekiel's vision of the Heavenly Throne, or the Chariot, he described the sight of the four living creatures (*Chayyot*, הייﬨ) who have a general human form, but with four faces, each one looking in a different direction.

One had the face of a man, a lion, ox and an eagle. They each had four wings, joined one to another. Their feet were similar to the hooves of a calf. Within the midst of these four was an "appearance like burning coals of fire like the appearance of torches." [123] "And the living creatures ran and returned as the appearance of a flash of lightning," Ezekiel accounted. [124]

The comparison of lightning to the "running and returning" of the living creatures is a major theme in development of the *Kabbalah* [125] and a centerpiece of the *Merkabah* movement during the first centuries C.E.

---

[120] According to Ezekiel in the OLD TESTAMENT, it was on the "fifth day of the fourth month in the thirteenth year." This is approximately July 28, 593 B.C.E.

[121] Scholem, Gershom, JEWISH GNOSTICISM, MERKABAH MYSTICISM, AND THE TALMUDIC TRADITION, 1965. The term *Ma'aseh Merkabah* was coined by Gershom Scholem, in the 20th century to refer to the collection of manuscripts written during this period,

[122] Isaiah 6: 1-13 describes Isaiah's vision of the Lord on a throne surrounded by *Seraphim*.

[123] Ezekiel 1:13.

[124] Ezekiel 1.

[125] *SEPHER YETZIRAH* 1:8, "The *Chayyot* running and returning." From Ezekiel 1:24.

Four Rabbis in the Garden of Eden

There is a famous Jewish tale mentioned in several early *Hekhalot* texts and the Babylonian *Talmud* [126] about four rabbis who enter the Garden of Eden– the Orchard.

The Orchard ("*Pardes*") is a symbolic reference to the knowledge of the mystical Works of Creation, *ma'aseh bereshit* (ברשת).

In this Garden stands the Tree of Life, the proverbial symbol of the Universe and all of its knowledge.

The story alludes to the rewards and perils of studying the mysteries of Creation.

The fate of the some of these four rabbis, however, was not so bright. Rashi (1040-1105) said that they attempted to ascend to Heaven by permutating the Divine Name through letter combinations and meditating on the permutations of the letters. This act would induce spiritual enlightenment.

When Simeon ben Azzai, Simeon ben Zoma, Rabbi Elisha ben Abuyah (known as *Acher*), and Rabbi Akiba ben Joseph "entered" the Garden they each had a life-changing experience. Zoma and Azzai were not actually certified rabbis, as they died young, but they did earn the honorary title. They were religious teachers, or *tannas,* [127] and possibly a part of the inner mystical circle

---

[126] *Chagiga* 14b, *Zohar* I, 26b and *Tikunei Zohar, Tikun* 40. The story is also accounted in the *Merkabah* text of *Hekhalot Zutarti*.

[127] A *tanna* is a "teacher" or "repeater" whose views are recorded in the *Mishnah*.

among Rabbi Joshua ben Hananiah's followers. [128]

Three of the rabbis did not return from the viewing the "Garden of Esoteric Knowledge" without some kind of harm.

When Ben Azzai "gazed" into the Garden and saw the Divine Glory of God (Divine Presence, the *Shekhinah*) he died; Ben Zoma "looked" and went insane, and *Acher* destroyed the Garden. But, Rabbi Akiba had the wisdom to enter and leave without succumbing to the Garden's temptations.

The Scriptures are quoted in regards to Azzai's fate: "Precious in the sight of the Lord is the death of His saints." [129] Azzai was so zealous in his studies that he lost sight of the world around him. An explanation of his early death may have occurred because of the belief that man cannot cast his human eyes upon the face of God and live." [130]

Ben Zoma, also a *tanna* who lived in the first third of the 2nd century, gazed into the Garden's delights and he went insane. The quote from Proverbs in the Scriptures is used regarding Zoma's fate: "Hast thou found honey? Eat so much as is sufficient for thee." [131] Zoma apparently indulged too much into the studies of the mysteries and suffered for his excessiveness.

According to one story, Rabbi Joshua ben Hananiah were out walking and passed by his disciple, Ben Zoma, who did not notice Hananiah. Zoma later replied he was "lost in the thoughts concerning the account of Creation." Hananiah later declared that Zoma was "outside" the allowable realm of contemplation on the subject– hence, he became mentally unstable.

Rabbi Abuyah, a rabbi born in Jerusalem sometime before 70 C.E., was said to have mutilated the plants in the Garden. His fate is summarized in Ecclesiastes: "Suffer not thy mouth to bring thy flesh into guilt." [132] He was accused of betraying his people and taking a heretical worldview, hence the nickname *Acher* (the "Other One"). The Babylonian *TALMUD* said that Rabbi Abuyah kept forbidden books hidden in his clothes. [133]

Rabbi Akiba is the only one who entered the Garden and departed in peace. [134] One clue to

---

[128] See more on the life of these *rabbis* and *tannim* on Wikipedia.com.

[129] Psalms 116:5.

[130] From *SHMOT* 33:20, and quoted by *Rashi*, *Hagigah* 14b.

[131] The Scripture quote is from Proverbs 25:16. The statement is from *HAGIGAH* 14b.

[132] Ecclesiastes 5:5.

[133] *HAGIGAH* 15B.

[134] from the *TOSEFTA* (*HAGIGAH* 2:3-4), also in the Babylonian *TALMUD* (*HAGIGAH* 14b), and Jerusalem *TALMUD* (*HAGIGAH* 2:1).

Akiba's survival was something he said to the others who entered into the Garden with him: "When you arrive at the "pure shaking" stones, do not say 'water, water.' For it is said: 'He who speaketh falsehood shall not be established before mine eyes.'" [135]

The overall lesson is that the study of the mystical teachings of the *Kabbalah,* found writings such as the SEPHER YETZIRAH, must be studied with caution and humility.

Image of a Rabbi having an ecstatic experience while meditating on the rising sun. Zedcor Graphics.

---

[135] Psalms 101:7.

The Book of Formation– SEPHER YETZIRAH

ספר

יצירה

The manuscript chiefly associated with the *Kabbalah* is the *SEPHER YETZIRAH* [136] (translated as the BOOK OF FORMATION, also called the BOOK OF CREATION). [137]

Out of all of the Hebrew texts that have survived over the centuries, the *SEPHER YETZIRAH* continues to amaze and confound those who study its contents.

The *SEPHER YETZIRAH* is considered to be the first systematic treatise of Jewish mysticism and one of the oldest and most studied and commented works of Jewish esoteric lore.

Almost all of the prominent Jewish leaders throughout history were well versed in the study of

[136] *Sepher Yetzirah* is also spelled as *Sepher Yetzira*, *Sepher Yetsirah*, etc. In Hebrew, the word *Sepher* (שפר S Ph R) means "book." Many Hebrew books had the word *Sepher* in the title. The words Formation and Creation have been both used in translating the title, although the more accurate translation is Formation.

[137] Photo of the cover of a Medieval copy of the *SEPHER YETZIRAH*.

the *SEPHER YETZIRAH* according to legends, commentaries and historical records.

The book is filled with mystery, shrouded with myths and illusions. Through proper study, one can eventually discern the confusion and understand the laws of the letters and the forces behind them. Then, all riddles can be solved.

Rabbis and *Kabbalists* have pondered, and argued, for centuries about its obscure meanings and the variety of conflicting interpretations, speculations and delusions found in its pages. Although each 'school' of *Kabbalah* differed in emphasis, they all relied on some common principles of the *SEPHER YETZIRAH*.

All of the versions of this small, mysteriously written "book" contained instructions to re-enact Abraham's meditations on the laws of creation immediately before his first revelation from God and revealed the methods to obtain spiritual experience.

Legends also attribute great magical feats that can be accomplished with its knowledge. It explained the entire process of the Universe in 22 basic concepts where each of the 22 letters and numbers of the Hebrew alphabet are endowed with special creative powers.

This ancient and cryptic manuscript made its appearance in the late *Talmudic* period (300-600 C.E.). Since the multitude of handwritten copies that have survived over the centuries are riddled with errors, there is no known authoritative text to study.

The oldest reference to one of the major concepts of the *SEPHER YETZIRAH* is found in the *TALMUD* (70 C.E.), [138] "Ten agencies through which God created the world, vis, wisdom, insight, cognition, strength, power, inexorableness, justice, right, lore, mercy." These agencies are also the characteristics of each of the ten *Sephiroth* of the Tree of Life.

---

[138] *HAGGIGAH* 12A.

The Path of the SEPHER YETZIRAH

The story of the *SEPHER YETZIRAH* coincides with the development of the *Kabbalah* and the history of the Jewish people. There are numerous speculations how the BOOK OF FORMATION was actually created.

According to the tradition, the Jewish patriarch Abraham originally wrote down the keys to the *SEPHER YETZIRAH*. Abraham gave it to Jeremiah the Prophet and then to his son, Ben Sira (Zira), who passed it to his son, Joseph ben Uziel. Other legends claim it was also acquired by Moses and then given to Joshua, passed on to the Elders, the Judges, and then to the Prophets. Its teachings continued to be transmitted by word of mouth until the famous Rabbi Akiba, one of the sages of Jerusalem, put it to writing at a time when the Jewish culture was under attack.

Rabbi Joshua ben Hananiah, [139] who lived in the 1st century C.E., is credited with the earliest known reference to the *SEPHER YETZIRAH* when he stated, "I can take squashes and pumpkins, and with the *SEPHER YETZIRAH*, make them into beautiful trees." This rabbi was a disciple to the famous Rabbi Johanan ben Zakkai (47 B.C.E.-72 C.E.), who led the Jews after the destruction of the Temple. [140] A *Talmudic* story was told about Rabbi Sira, Rabbi Hananiah, and Rabbi Oshaya's magical creations when they employed the instructions found in the *SEPHER YETZIRAH*. [141]

The *SEPHER YETZIRAH* was originally a very short handwritten manuscript, perhaps a few hundred words long. But, with all of its simplicity, this cryptic manuscript has evoked speculation and controversy for centuries. While hundreds of copies of the *SEPHER YETZIRAH* have been discovered and preserved over the centuries, there are probably hundreds or thousands more that have been lost or destroyed. As different versions were rewritten over the centuries and distributed among small groups of *Kabbalists*, anonymous authors and scribes added and changed the original content. This created many errors in the texts. Even though they were very similar in wording, the letter correspondences provided in various versions conflicted. Yet, these errors were copied over and over and the true arrangements have become lost. Even centuries later, no one seems to agree on the correct order of the combinations to achieve these miraculous results. This confusion has led to misconceptions and errors that have altered the understanding of the *SEPHER YETZIRAH*. But, the basic principles remain the same.

---

[139] Rabbi Joshua ben Hananiah, who died in 151 C.E., was a leading *tanna,* or Rabbinic sage, who practiced Judaic mysticism after the destruction of the Temple.

[140] Kaplan, Aryeh, *SEPHER YETZIRAH*: THEORY, page xvi. Kaplan discusses the chain of succession among the rabbis who obtained this knowledge during this period of time.

[141] *SANHEDRIN* 65b, 66b and 67b.

Unraveling the SEPHER YETZIRAH

One of the big mysteries about the *SEPHER YEZIRAH* is its purpose. On first glance, the *SEPHER YETZIRAH* does not explain what to do with this knowledge about the Universe and its mechanisms or how to produce supernormal events. But, throughout history numerous commentaries and legends have revealed bits and pieces of the mystery to fill that gap of knowledge.

The *SEPHER YETZIRAH* reads like a grammar and instruction manual. It utilizes sounds, shapes, concepts and numerical values of the Hebrew alphabet to achieve wisdom, spirituality and understanding. It details the origin of the universe in the combinations, reversals, and augmentations of the letters of the Hebrew alphabet and symbols which underline all human speech.

Some commentators claim that the *SEPHER YETZIRAH* contains the knowledge of how to manipulate the foundations of the Universe, Time and the Body (the soul). It was composed in a series of riddles. To unravel the mysteries of the book is to understand the origins of creation and know how to 'create something out of nothing.'

As described in the *SEPHER YETZIRAH*, creation out of nothing (creation *ex-nihilo*) begins with several human acts: <u>Writing</u> (as in writing symbols or letters), <u>Number</u> (as in order or placement of these symbols), and <u>Speech</u> (using the voice to speak).

All three processes are based on the Hebrew root *SPhR* (שׁפּר) because they are from a common spirit (L. *spirare*, to breathe) as an emanation between God and man. When a symbol or letter is spoken, it is as if it were spoken by God Himself.

Creation of the world is achieved by sound, numbers, and the 22 letters of the Hebrew alphabet, as stated in the *SEPHER YETZIRAH*. The 22 letters are combined according to an ancient formula to produce a series of 231 letter combinations or "Gates." The teachings then demonstrate how to use these Holy Gates. Humans can then take part in this creation process, a feat reserved for God Himself.

While the *SEPHER YETZIRAH* presents these concepts in an organized order, it can be confusing to the average reader. There is also a massive cultural and language divide since the original material was probably first written down sometime after the birth of Christ.

Because of that, many of the mystical secrets of the *SEPHER YETZIRAH* have yet to be uncovered and many interpretations have been corrupted or mistranslated.

Rabbi instructing student in the ways of the teachings, Zedcor Graphics.

HILKHOT YEZIRAH VS. SEPHER YETZIRAH

Rashi said of R. Abraham Yagel...
"he was wrong since he did not distinguish between the "HILKHOT
YEZIRAH" and "SEPHER YEZIRAH," thinking as he did that they are
identical and explaining that they [the Talmudic masters] were
practicing combinations of the letters of the [divine] name by which
the Heaven and Earth were created, etc. since SEPHER YEZIRAH,
attributed [ha-mekkuneh] to Abraham our ancestor is, in principle
following the way of combination of letters in 231 gates, known to the
Kabbalists, by which they may create a man and a spirit and a soul
in his nostrils, and other creatures...as the sages say there"
"Rava said, If the righteous desired
they could create the world." [142]

---

[142] R. Abraham Yagel, *AVODAT HA-QODESH*, Ms. Oxford, 1301, fol 47a, from Moshe Idel, *GOLEM*: JEWISH MAGICAL AND MYSTICAL, pages 181-2, 191. There is a difference between *"Hilkhot Yezirah"* and the *"Sepher Yezirah"* according to Rashi. *Hilkhot* refers to the Rules (or Laws) of Creation while *Sepher Yezirah* is described as a separate teaching, see Aryeh Kaplan, *SEPHER YETZIRAH*: BOOK OF CREATION, page xix.

Creative Acts by Humans

Creation of a Calf–

"ha-Bore'm Agalim"

"...by means of (the SEPHER YETZIRAH) they created a third-grown calf and ate it."

Babylonian *TALMUD* [143]

One of the most enduring legends (*aggadah*), found in the ancient Babylonian *TALMUD,* is how two famous rabbis used the Laws of Creation to create a real-life calf (*"ha-Bore'm Agalim"*). [144] Both of the rabbis were *Talmudist* members of the prestigious *Amoraim* of Israel.

About the same time the *SEPHER YETZIRAH* appeared between 300-600 C.E., stories about Rabbi Hananiah [145] and his brother Rabbi Oshaya's [146] ability to create a calf by means of *HILKHOT*

---

[143] Babylonian *TALMUD* Tractate *SANHEDRIN* 67b. Cow graphic, Zedcor Graphics.

[144] The Babylonian *TALMUD* was written between the 1st century CE through the 7th centuries A.D. and is one of the major works of the Jewish people.

[145] R. Hanina was the second and third generation *Amora* Sage of Israel and brother of the famous *Amora* sage, R. Oshaia, reference by Wikipedia.com.

[146] Oshaya is also spelled as Hoshaiah, Hoshiah, and Oshaia. He died about 350 CE.

YEZIRAH [147] ("Rules of Creation") widely circulated among the Jewish communities. The rabbis spent their Sabbath Eve's studying this book on creation until they were able to create a "third-grown calf," [148] which they ate." This was considered an acceptable act of magic according to the *TALMUD*. [149] [150]

Another acceptable practice among the disciples of Judah the Prince (135 C.E.-217 C.E.) was the act of creating a man, or a *golem*.

The *TALMUD* indicated that Bezalel, the chief artisan of the Tabernacle, [151] "knew how to permutate the letters" to cause wondrous deeds. [152] Rabbi Nathan Yehudah (220-299 C.E.), the founder of the Babylonia Academy in Pumbedita, was one of the "Elders of Pumbedita" who was knowledgeable in the sacred arts of letter permutation.

French priest William of Auvargne (1190-1249), who served as Bishop of Paris, wrote that "Men have tried to produce, and thought that they succeeded in producing human life in other ways than by the usual generative process." [153]

The renowned Jewish mystic and Rabbi Eleazar ben Judah of Worms (Germiza) [154] wrote in the early 12th century that "in the case of the creators of the calves, they have shortened." [155] He referred to the secret technique to combine the letters of the Hebrew alphabet to create a *golem*. He used the phrase "*ha-Bore'm Agalim*" ("The Creation of the Calves") in connection with the specific set of combinations used to create a calf. Rabbi Eleazar reportedly used a similar technique to create his own *golem*.

---

[147] THE *SEPHER YETZIRAH* has been equated with the *HILKHOTH YETZIRAH,* but they may actually be two separate manuscripts, according the preceding quote from Rashi about Rabbi Yagel.

[148] This may refer to either a three-year-old calf or a calf that is one-third the normal size.

[149] Babylonian *TALMUD, SANHEDRIN* 65b.

[150] The same story is repeated in a second passage in *SANHEDRIN* 67b.

[151] Bezalel was in charge of building the Ark of the Covenant, according to Exodus 31:1-6 and chapters 36-39.

[152] Kaplan, Aryeh, *SEPHER YETZIRAH*: THE BOOK OF CREATION, page xxii-xix.

[153] Trachtenberg, Joshua, JEWISH MAGIC AND SUPERSTITION: A STUDY IN FOLK RELIGION, page 286.

[154] R. Eleazar of Worms was also known as Eleazar ben Judah ben Kalonymous and sometimes called Eleazar Rokeach (Eleazar the Perfumer). He was born in 1176 and died in 1238.

[155] Ms. Oxford 1566, fol. 44b. From GOLEM: JEWISH MAGICAL by Idel, Moshe, page 274; 280.

At end of 13th Century, Rabbi Abraham of Esquira wrote that there were some who were acquainted with this practice. They would engrave an image of a cow on a wall and change it into a living cow, which they would slaughter and eat.

According to Rabbi Yehudah, this appearance was actually a vision that takes place in the imaginative power of man ["*ela 'shehyah mar'ehu ha-Bore' be-dimyon'*]. The creature is endowed with motive and sensitive qualities. [156]

Several other statements written in the 13th century claim that the creation of an artificial man followed the same pattern as that of a calf, or a cow, with the latter being consumed as food.

One 13th century writer castigated those who say they can duplicate the feat of Rabbis Hananiah and Oshaya and proclaimed that "they themselves are dumb calves." [157]

An untitled 15th century work by Rabbi Yhanan Alemanno compiled a list of animals that can be created by the combinations of the letters using the instructions from the *SEPHER YETZIRAH*. [158]

In some *Ashkenazi* manuscripts, certain combinations of the letters of the Divine Name, along with the letters of the alphabet, were vocalized according to the pattern of the *Notariqon* (a technique of letter substitution) to create a calf. One text stated that "there are '*Alephim* (letters) for creation of the calf." [159]

---

[156] Idel, Moshe, *GOLEM: JEWISH MAGICAL*, by page 50.

[157] Trachtenberg, Joshua, JEWISH MAGIC AND SUPERSTITION: A STUDY IN FOLK RELIGION, page 86.

[158] Ms. Paris (BN) 849, fol. 6b: "ox, sheep, and a calf." From *GOLEM*: JEWISH MAGICAL, b y Idel, Moshe, page 281.

[159] Ms. Firenze-Laurentiana, 44, 16, fol. 4b. From STUDIES IN *KABBALAH*, by Moshe Idel, page 274 and 281.

The Enlivened Broom *Schtick*

In a related account about enlivening an object, Lucian, the 2nd century satirist, [160] wrote a short story in Greek called PHILOPSEUDES (LOVER OF LIES) in 150 C.E. [161]

In this tale, also called the Egyptian Miracle Worker, Eucrates is an apprentice of a magician priest of Isis called Pancrates. When the magician leaves, Eucrates enlivens a wooden pestle with a three-syllable spell that he overheard. He ordered it to carry water.

When the jar was filled up, he told it to stop. But, it would not obey him and kept fetching more water as the house flooded. The animated pestle became uncontrollable. The apprentice took an axe to chop the pestle in two, but each part picked up a jar, filled it with water, then emptied it in the house. Finally, Pancrates, the Magician, returned, saw what was going on, broke the spell, and turned the pestle back into wood. [162]

This tale of the Egyptian Miracle Worker became part of the story of the Rabbi's *golem* in the late 1580s. The theme later became the foundation for several later legends, including the basis for Goethe's "The Sorcerer's Apprentice" in 1797, and the inspiration of the famous 1940 Walt Disney animation of the magician's wayward magical broom.

---

[160] Lucian of Samasota was an Assyrian born in Turkey in 125AD and died in Greece in 180AD.

[161] THE WORKS OF LUCIAN: From the Greek, Volume 2, by Lucian (of Samosata), page 329-331.

[162] Source: A. M. Harmon, translator, LUCIAN, vol.3 (London: William Heinemann; New York: G. P. Putnam's Sons, 1921), pp. 371-77.

Creation of the *Golem*

> *"Thine eyes did see my unformed substance (גלמי),*
> *and in Thy book they were all written even the days that were*
> *fashioned, when as yet there was none of them."*
> *Psalm 139:16*

Out of all of the persistent Jewish traditions, the ability of humans to create a *golem* (גלמ) has permeated literature and religious discussions for centuries.

A *golem* is an apparent semi-living creature, brought to life by secret techniques described in the ancient magical and mysterious manuscript of the *SEPHER YETZIRAH*. The *golem* is activated by meditating on specific formulas that are revealed after studying and fully understanding the contents of the *SEPHER YETZIRAH*.

The word *golemi* (גלמי) appears once in the OLD TESTAMENT to mean an "unformed substance," although the word is probably a derivative of *gelem,* meaning "raw material."

Adam was initially created as a *golem* when his dust was "kneaded into a shapeless husk," according to a passage in the Babylonian *TALMUD*. [163] Adam was originally a "body without a soul." The topic of Adam as a *golem* was often discussed among the Gnostic rabbis. [164]

Tannatic sage R. Hananiah, who reportedly created a *golem* with Rabbi Oshaya, explained the 12 steps to form Adam: (1) his dust was gathered; (2) it was kneaded into a shapeless mass (*golem*); (3) his limbs were shaped, (4) a soul was infused into him, (5) he arose and stood on his feet, (6) he gave the animals their names, (7) Eve becomes his mate, etc. [165]

The creation of a *golem* was often discussed among the rabbis as being merely an image, similar to

---

[163] Babylonian *TALMUD TRACTATE SANHEDRIN* 38b.

[164] "God created Adam as a *golem*; he lay supine, reaching from one end of the world to the other, from the earth to the firmament (Ḥag. 12a; comp. Gen. R. viii., xiv., and xxiv.; JEWISH ENCYCLOPEDIA i. 175," from "*Golem*," Jewish Encyclopedia.

[165] *SANHEDRIN* 67b.

an apparition, which is an outline of a physical aura. Rabbi Hananel ben Hushiel, in the mid-11th century, commented on the *SANHEDRIN* passage about the creation of a *golem*. He believed it was actually a production of a phantasma, a mass hallucination– a "[technique of] illusion; [*ahizat 'enayim*]. The term *ahizat 'enayim* ("seizing the eyes" or creating an illusion) occurs in the *TALMUD* in the context of the creation of a man. [166]

In the late 13th century, a *Kabbalistic* passage used a similar meaning for the term *golem* and *tzelem*. The figures drawn of a man on a wall are called "*tzelamim*" [167] which are, at the same time, known as "*gelamim*" being without form. Both words stand for the static, soul-less form. Some commentators claimed that the *SEPHER YETZIRAH* also holds the key to the creation of a *golem*, an artificial creature. Many say that it is both– a manual about how to manipulate nature and secretly gives the recipe to create a *golem* as proof.

Most of the major rabbis throughout history seemed familiar with the creation of a *golem* by use of the letter combination techniques. The *golem* was often a topic along-side of discussions about the *SEPHER YETZIRAH*. Preserved writings extensively discussed and argued about these details over the centuries.

The *golem* has its appearances in non-Jewish mysticism as well as Egyptian, Greek, and our own Americanized version of Frankenstein.

---

[166] Idel, Moshe, *GOLEM*: JEWISH MAGICAL, page 48.

[167] *Tzelem* (צלם), as in *"B'tzelem Elohim,"* "In God's Image."

Rabbi Ben Sira & Jeremiah's *golem*

"Rava (the Rabbi) said: If the righteous desired it,
they could [by living a pure life] be creators.
It is written, [168]
'But your iniquities have distinguished
you between you and your God.'
Rava created a man (by means of "Sepher Yetzirah")
and sent him to Rav Sira who spoke to him.
But, Rabbi Sira received no answer,
the man was unable to speak.

The Rabbi then said to him,
'Thou art a creature of the "magicians."
Return to thy dust.'" [169]

---

[168] Isaiah 59:2, "But your iniquities have separated you from your God; your sins have hidden his face from you, so that he will not hear."

[169] This quote is from the Babylonian *TALMUD,* Tractate *SANHEDRIN* 65b.

That passage from the Babylonian *TALMUD* about 500 C.E. explained that the practice to create "a man" was considered acceptable Jewish magic and not sorcery. There are two versions of the same story that are used to validate this exercise in human-induced creation.

Accordingly, a rabbi (*Rava*) had "created a man" and sent it to another rabbi, named Ben Sira,[170] who was an actual prominent Jewish *Talmudist*. Rabbi Sira questioned the creature but it would not speak. So, he commanded the *golem* to return to its source– dust.[171]

In this particular legend ("*aggadah*"), Rabbi Ben Sira was studying the *SEPHER YETZIRAH* on his own. A heavenly voice told Ben Sira to "find a companion" in order to study the mysteries of creation. After three years of study, Rabbi Sira created a *golem* with the help of his relative, Jeremiah the Prophet.[172]

Using the secret knowledge found in the *SEPHER YETZIRAH*,[173][174] they were able to create a "new man"[175] after they combined and permutated the letters of the Hebrew alphabet. The, they engraved the Holy Name (*Tetragrammaton*) *YHVH Elohim AMT* (אמת אלהום ילהי)– "The Lord is Truth"– on the forehead of a figure that they molded from dirt. The creature came alive.

In another twist to the legend, the *golem* had a knife in its hand and erased the first letter, *Aleph*

---

[170] Rav Joseph ben Sira is also spelled as Sira, Zeira, Zira or Ze'era). He was born in Babylonia and was a 3rd generation Talmudist who lived in Israel about 300 C.E.

[171] Babylonian *TALMUD*, *SANHEDRIN* 65b.

[172] Jeremiah the Prophet was born about 650 BCE and died about 570 BCE. He is the author of the biblical book that bears his name. From "Jeremiah," by J. Philip Hyatt, ENCYCLOPAEDIA BRITANNICA.

[173] Kaplan, Aryeh , *SEPHER YETZIRAH*: CREATION IN THEORY AND PRACTICE, page xv. See footnotes on page 343 for more references. Also, see "ORIGINS OF LETTERS AND NUMERALS ACCORDING TO *SEPHER YESIRAH*," by Phineas Mordell, Philadelphia, page 531-535, from "The Jewish Quarterly Review," Dropsie College for Hebrew and Cognate Learning, 1913. And see, *KABBALAH* IN ITALY, 1280-1510: A SURVEY, by Moshe Idel, page 248. According to A.E. Waite (in the "HOLY *KABBALAH*, 111), there is a manuscript called *MISHNAT*, written by Uziel, in the Bodleian Library in Oxford, from A GARDEN OF POMEGRANATES: SKRYING ON THE TREE OF LIFE, by Israel Regardie, Chic Cicero, Sandra Tabatha Cicero, page 15.

[174] Mordell, Phineas, ORIGIN OF THE LETTERS AND NUMERALS IN THE *SEPHER YETZIRAH*, from The Jewish Quarterly Review, Volume 3, edited by Cyrus Adler, Solomon Schechter, Abraham Aaron Neuman, Solomon Zeitlin. Page 533.

[175] Idel, Moshe, *GOLEM*: JEWISH MAGICAL, page 65, from *SEPHER HA-GEMATRIOT*, from the collection of works from the disciples of R. Yehudah he-Chasid during the late 13th century.

(א)– of the word *AMT* (אמת "truth")– leaving the word *MT* (מת) ("dead").

The *golem* feared Jeremiah the Prophet would be considered a god by the people for creating life. He instructed Jeremiah how to circle around the figure and pronounce the letters backwards to destroy the *golem* so it could return to its dust. [176]

This technique to use the combinations of Hebrew letters while moving in a circle around molded dust is common in all legends. The *golem* is destroyed by reciting the original combinations backwards and circling in the opposite direction. [177] [178]

Rabbi Meir ha-Levi Abulafia, [179] in the late 12th and early 13th century, rejected the idea that the *golem* was merely an illusion. He pointed out that Rabbi Sira was in a different location when *golem* was sent to the second rabbi. Therefore, it couldn't have been a hallucination, because both people saw the creature from different places.

In the 14th century, R. Shem Tov ibn Shapprut wrote in his *PARDES RIMONIM* that the production of an illusion for this purpose is not prohibited by Jewish lore. But, the idea of an object infused with some type of magical property is not unique in the Jewish culture or the OLD TESTAMENT.

---

[176] *PERUSH SHEM SHEL ARBA OTIYYOT* Ms. Florence 2:41, from TREE OF SOULS: THE MYTHOLOGY OF JUDAISM by Howard Schwartz, page 280. Also, cited in THE EARLY KABBALAH by Joseph Dan, pages 54-56; and Idel, Moshe, *GOLEM*: JEWISH MAGICAL.

[177] Idel, Moshe, *GOLEM*: JEWISH MAGICAL, page 92-93.

[178] Marla Segol, WORD AND IMAGE IN MEDIEVAL *KABBALAH*: THE TEXTS, COMMENTARIES, AND DIAGRAMS, page 177-178.

[179] Rabbi Abulafia is often known as *Ramah* short for Rabbi Meir ha-Levi. He was born in 1170 and died in 1224.

The *golem* of Jacob's sons

*"Joseph brought an evil report of them
unto his father, Jacob."*

Genesis 37.2

The mystical interpretation surrounding this biblical passage about Jacob's sons still stirs controversy– why were the sons of Jacob denounced by their brother Joseph when "Joseph brought to his father an evil report of them?" [180]

R. Isaiah Horowitz [181] suggested that the brothers were accused of using the teachings of the *SEPHER YETZIRAH* to create and slaughter animals. [182] Since those techniques weren't classified as a sin they did not need to perform a *Kosher* slaughter, according to Judaic laws.

Horowitz believed that the animal may have been a *golem* calf– not a real creature, but one that was created through the use of mystical letter combinations of the Hebrew alphabet which was an acceptable practice.

There is also a story that the brothers had some type of relations with Canaanite maidens. Rashi, [183] the medieval Jewish mystic and famed rabbi, indicated that Joseph accused his brothers of having relations with twin sisters, or 'unspecified' females. [184]

The women may have been female *golem* and the brothers "walked" [*"hayyu metayyilim"*] (had carnal relations) with the women, suggested R. Zevi Hirsh of Munkacs in the 19th century. The female *golem* cannot be considered a human being from a *Halakhic* point of view, he believed.

---

[180] This story is also told by *RASHI*, in connection to a passage in Genesis 37:2, "Joseph brought an evil report of them unto his father."

[181] Horowitz, Isaiah, *SHENEI LUHOT HA-BERIT*. Horowitz, a 17th century mystic and rabbi was also known as *Shelah ha-Kados*– the Holy *Shela*– named after one of his popular books.

[182] Kaplan, Aryeh, *SEPHER YETZIRAH*: THEORY, page xiv.

[183] *Rashi* is an acronym for Rabbi Shlomo Yitzchaki, born in France in 10140 C.E. and died in 1105. Rashi wrote many important commentaries on the *TALMUD, TANAKH*, and the *SEPHER YETZIRAH*.

[184] Rashi on *Bereshit* 37:2. "Et Dibatam Ra'ah."

Based on this, the female *golem* was denied any human quality. [185]

In the 18th century, R. Hayyim Joseph David Azulai [186] wrote in his *MIDBAR QEDEMOT* that the secrets of the *SEPHER YETZIRAH* were given to the "sons of Leah, and they created maidens [*ne'arot*] and they walked with them." [187]

---

[185] Idel, Moshe, *GOLEM*: JEWISH MAGICAL page 236.

[186] Hayyim Yosef David Azulai was a rabbinical scholar born in 1724 in Israel and died in 1806 in Italy.

[187] Idel, Moshe, *GOLEM*: JEWISH MAGICAL, page 236. "Walking" is a euphemism for intercourse.

Rabbi Akiba's Secret Alphabet

The prominent Rabbi Akiba (Akiva) ben Joseph, [188] a student of R. Joshua ben Hananiah, is often attributed as the author of the first written copy of the *SEPHER YETZIRAH*. Other sources suggest that the concepts of the *SEPHER YETZIRAH* were first written down after Akiba's death in 137 C.E. Rabbi Akiba, called the father of rabbinical Judaism, lived in time of Emperor Hadrian and lost his life in support of claims of Barchocheba, a false *Messiah*. [189]

R. Akiba is attributed to be the author of a *midrash* [190] about the names of the letters of the Hebrew alphabet called The ALPHABET OF AKIBA BEN JOSEPH (*OTIOT DE-RABBI AKIBA*).

The *Midrash* says that the 22 Hebrew letters have a dual, or mystical, meaning only known to initiates. The letters were presented in allegorical form for children to memorize in order to preserve the ancient wisdom. During the beginning of the 3rd century, in the time of Joshua ben Levi, school children were taught mnemonic exercises derived from R. Akiba's alphabet lessons. [191]

At least five different systems were outlined by R. Akiba in his book. [192] These different letter combination techniques (called *Tzeruf*, in Hebrew) were subsequently used over the next millennium as a way to achieve spiritual and mystical attainment.

---

[188] Rabbi Akiba was born about 50 C.E.

[189] "Akiba ben Joseph," JEWISH ENCYCLOPEDIA.

[190] A *Midrash* is a portion of the *TORAH* reading along with stories taught by the Sages of the Post-Temple era. Wikipedia.com

[191] Shab. 104. "Alphabet of Akiba ben Joseph," Wikipedia.com.

[192] Gaster, Moses, THE SWORD OF MOSES, page 11.

The Mystical 22 Hebrew Letters

א
ב
ג
ד
ה
ו
ז
ח
ט
י
כ
ל
מ
נ
ס
ע
פ
צ
ק
ר
ש
ת

Today's English alphabet developed from the ancient Hebrew letters. But, the early Hebrew letters were more than mere symbols. They were vessels that contained an inherent power embedded within each letter– a concealed life-force– the soul of the letter. [193] [194]

The written and spoken Hebrew alphabet uses one set of symbols to represent letters and one to represent numbers. For example, the first letter *Aleph* (א) also assumes the role for the number one (1). The first 10 numbers are represented by the first 10 of the 22 letters of the Hebrew alphabet.

The *SEPHER YETZIRAH* explained how all of the words that ever existed, or will ever exist, are formed from those 22 letters.

These 22 "foundation letters" are expressed in three ways– written, enumerated, and spoken (written within a Space, enumerated by Time and spoken through the Soul).

In *Kabbalah,* these three sets, (called *Sepharim* or "books"), [195] depict the boundaries between the mental and physical worlds– the mind and the body. The letters are written within a designated space to convey thoughts via words and numbers.

By giving these letters a form, linking them to a numerical value, and an audible sound, the "soul of all that is formed and all that will be formed" can be created. [196] This is the inherent power contained in every letter– something is created out of nothing. [197]

The assumption is that if one combines the letters properly, the creative process used by God in the formation of the world can be re-enacted. This is accomplished by forming,

---

[193] Idel, Moshe, LANGUAGE, *TORAH*, AND HERMENEUTICS IN ABRAHAM ABULAFIA, page 7; notes page 140.

[194] right) Column chart of the 22 Hebrew letters.

[195] *SEPHER YETZIRAH 1:1*: "He created His universe with three books (*Sepharim*), with text (*Sepher*), with number (*Sephar*) and with communication (*Sippur*)." From Kaplan, Aryeh, *SEPHER YETZIRAH*, THEORY, page 5.

[196] *SEPHER YETZIRAH 2: 2*: "The 22 letters…He depicted all that was formed and all that will be formed." From Kaplan, Aryeh, *SEPHER YETZIRAH*, page 100.

[197] A Latin phrase meaning "out of nothing." *Creatio ex-nihilo* is often used to indicate "creation out of nothing."

weighing, combining and transforming the letters in a precise manner.

According to the *SEPHER YETZIRAH*, the world was created by a certain combination of the letters with the Divine Name (called the *Shem Ha-Meforesh* or the *Tetragrammaton*). Each permutation of the letters condensed the divine light into a life force degree by degree until it becomes a material object.

This concept is one of the foundations of Judaic mysticism and the premise of the *SEPHER YETZIRAH*– THE BOOK OF FORMATION.

A chart in the Appendix shows the 22 letters, the equivalent numbers and their meanings.

"The names in the Holy Tongue are the very
"letters of speech" which descend degree by degree from the 10
utterances by means of substitutions and transposition of the letters
through the 231 gates
until they reach and become invested in that particular created
thing to give it life.

"Everything is clothed in some Emotional Attribute
which brings [soul] to think that thought.

This attribute is the vivifying force of that thought.
From the letters of thought produce
letters of speech, speech brings to action wisdom
is beginning and source of life force." [198]

_____

[198] From the *TANYA, SHAAR HAYICHUD VEHAEMUNAH* (THE GATE TO UNDERSTANDING GODS UNITY AND FAITH), chapter 1, by Rabbi Shimon Bar Yochai (died 18 C.E.) in the *Mishnaic* period.

The Sound of the Letters

The vibration of the sound produced when each letter of the alphabet is pronounced is associated within specific dimensions of space (outline form) and occurs at a defined time (tempo).

Sound is made from tiny vibrations in air pressure. Through the voice, vibrating vocal chords break up the stream of lung air so that pulses of high pressure alternate with pulses of low pressure. [199]

This produces sound, similar to the screeching noise made when holding the opening of a filled balloon to release air. Various pitches are produced by loosening or tightening the opening (its mouth). The consonants depend on vowel sounds to properly pronounce a word. The diverse combinations of the 22 letters, with the proper sounds, can reveal many mystical secrets.

Rabbi Saadia Gaon, a prominent 1st century C.E. Jewish philosopher, was probably the first to divide the 22 letters of the Hebrew alphabet into five groups, based on their phonetic pronunciation.

Rabbi Isaac Luria, a 16th century Jewish mystic, organized them as five levels, or parts, of the soul. According to the *SEPHER YETZIRAH* the letters are "engraved with the voice, carved with the breath and set in the mouth in five places." [200]

---

[199] Ladefoged and Johnson, ARTICULATION AND ACOUSTICS, Chapter 1, page 7. Contains studies on Speech Production. Sound Waves. Places of Articulatory Gestures, the Waveforms of Consonants, and the Articulation of Vowel Sounds..

[200] *SEPHER YETZIRAH* 2: 3.

The five places in the mouth and associated Hebrew letters include:

Name	Part of Mouth	Corresponding Letters
Gutterals	throat	*Aleph, Chet, Hey*, and *Ayin*
Palatals	palate	*Gimel, Yod, Kaf*, and *Qof*
Linguals	tongue	*Dalet, Tet, Lamed, Nun, Tav*
Dentals	teeth	*Zayin, Samech, Shin, Resh, Taz*ik
Labial	lips	*Bayt, Vav, Mem*, and *Pe*

The Living Soul

"And when a man sleeps, his body tells his spirit (Neshamah), the spirit tells the soul (Nephesh), the soul tells the angel, the angel tells the Cherub, and the Cherub tells him that 'hath wings' and he that 'hath wings' tells the matter- to whom? To Him at whose word the world came into existence."

MISHNA, LEVITICUS RABBAH 32.2 by Rabbi Abin
[Lev. R. xxii.; Eccl. R. x. 20] [201]

---

[201] Illustration from "Une semaine de bonté" ("A Week of Kindness"), a comic and artist's book by Max Ernst, first published in 1934. Wikipedia.com.

Even the most primitive people in the world believed in the existence of the soul. Its nature has been a topic of discussion and argument among our ancestors and still continues among philosophers and laymen of today.

There still is no definite conclusion about what the soul actually is or if it even exists. Most people agree that there *is* something that makes a living being a truly *living* creature and a *spiritual* being. In Judaic tradition, the physical evidence of the soul is speech, believed to be possessed only by humans.

The soul is a concept often discussed in Judaism and *Kabbalah*. Jews believe that all souls are originally one soul, without separation of the sexes (male and female). The separation occurs when the soul journeys below to earth, according to tradition.

Only God knows where the two halves of the original soul reside. Sometimes, the two separate parts of the soul do meet in the physical world. This is the meeting between "soulmates."

The soul contains a certain amount of vitality (*hayyot, Chayyot* חיית), which is the source of its acts.

There are five descending layers of the human soul, according to the *ZOHAR*. These levels of consciousness include the: [202]

- animal soul (*Nephesh*)
- the spiritual or vital soul (*Ruach*)
- breath (*Neshamah*)
- the life-force (*Chayya*)
- and "oneness" (*Yechida*).

---

[202] As given by R. Isaac Luria (1537-1572), recorded by his disciple R. Chayim Vital in *SHA'AR HA-GILGULIM* (GATES OF REINCARNATION).

The Animal Soul: *Nephesh*

"And God said, bring forth
the earth's living creatures (Nephesh Chayyot)..."
Genesis 1:24

The *Nephesh* [203] (נֶפֶשׁ) is most basic component of the soul. This is the "animal soul" that contains the spark of life, *"pikuach Nephesh."* The *Nephesh* keeps a body alive and provides the raw vital energy necessary for its maintenance. When a person is born, his *Nephesh* enters him, according to Rabbi Luria. [204]

The Hebrew words, *Nephesh Chayyot* is often translated as a "living soul" or "vitality" – the "spark of life."

The function of *Nephesh* is two-fold:

1) acts as the engine of the body (instinctual),
2) insures propagation of the species (sexual).

Sigmund Freud's concept of the libido is manifested by the *Nephesh*. The libido is the emotional energy derived from underlying instincts or primitive drives found in all human and animal life. The subconscious mind belongs to the world of *Nephesh*– the animal soul of man.

The *Nephesh* takes care of all of the functions of the organism. It is the force the generates life and operates the nervous system.

The *Nephesh* also contains the personality of human beings and is the part of the being that also dies with the body. This level of the soul is in total rapport with the body, according to *ZOHAR*, and is the only element of the five that is capable of committing sin. The *Nephesh* is aware of the physical body and physical mind.

---

[203] In the *Kabalistic* Tree of Life, the *Nephesh* is that aspect of the soul which corresponds to the ninth *Sephiroth* of *Yesod*, located in third world.

[204] As given by R. Isaac Luria (1537-1572), recorded by his disciple R. Chayim Vital in *SHA'AR HA-GILGULIM* (GATES OF REINCARNATION), PAGE 19.

There are two aspects of the *Nephesh*. One is the dynamic and vivifying element of life. The Hindu call it *prana*– the electrical force that sparks life. The other part is the *Tselem*.

Kabbalists call the *Tselem* the Divine Image, similar to Carl Jung's Archetypal images. To Theosophists, this is the "astral body or the subconscious collective of all the fundamental drives and primal root impulses in humans and animals.

On the Tree of Life, the ninth *sephiroth* of *Yesod* is attributed to the *Nephesh*. The sphere of *Yesod* molds the personality which is in a constant perpetual flux of emotions, imagery, thoughts and perceptions.

The *Nephesh* is part of the *gilgul* ("cycling") process and must leave the material flesh body at the stage of death. Then, that soul without a body moves into another body where life begins once again. This is the cycling of souls, or *Giglgulim*. Once the *Nephesh* has refined itself from its own volition, then it receives aid from the evolved *Ruach*.

"The secret of creation of man [refers to] the speculative soul [ha-neshamah ha-hakhamah]– which stands forever.

And the secret of his formation [refers to] the animal soul, which does not last forever.

Emanation and creation are more spiritual than formation." [205]

---

[205] Goldreich, Pentateuch, *MEI'RAT 'EINAYYIM*. From Moshe Idel, *GOLEM*: JEWISH MAGICAL, page 110.

illustration from Zedcor Graphics collection (FEMINI08) by Dugald Stewart Walker in "Rainbow Gold" (1922), The Cloud (Percy Bysshe Shelley).

The Spiritual Soul: *Ruach*

The *Ruach* (רוּחַ) is intertwined with the *Nephesh*. This is the human spirit, expressed as the "wind" or "breath of life" [206] in the OLD TESTAMENT. This is the breath of life transmitted down to man in the form of a "wind."

A person's *Ruach* enters at the end of the 13th year when one becomes a "complete person," according to Rabbi Luria. [207] The Holy Spirit is called *Ruach Ha-kodesh*. When it rests inside of a living being, it is called *Nephesh*.

The *Ruach* survives the death of the body, but no one has been able to determine how long. No one has returned from death to confirm. The disembodied spirit that possess those afflicted with a *"dibbuk"* is the *Ruach*. According to Rabbi Meir ibn Gabbai, in his *AVODAT HA-QODESH,* when the *Nephesh* and *Ruach* are joined within a body it forms the *chayyot,* the human vitality that activates the body. [208]

---

[206] Genesis 6:17: "Behold, I am going to bring a floodwater upon the earth and destroy every living creature with the "breath of life" (*Ruach Hay-yim*) under heaven shall die."

[207] As given by R. Isaac Luria (1537-1572), recorded by his disciple R. Chayim Vital in *SHA'AR HA-GILGULIM* (GATES OF REINCARNATION), page 19.

[208] Idel, Moshe, *GOLEM,* JEWISH MAGICAL, page 131.

The Holy Soul: *Neshamah*

*"He breathed into his nostrils the breath of life
(neshamah chayyah)."*
Genesis 2:7

According to Genesis 2:7, After God formed the body of man from dust, He breathed life into its unformed body and the man became a living being.

This is the "Holy Soul," the *neshamah* (נשמא), the eternal part of the being which is possessed by both humans and animals. It is where the powers of speech, intellect and the senses are contained in humans.

According to the *ZOHAR*, a person's *Neshamah* will enter when one's complete their 20th birthday. If a person does not receive all parts of his soul, then those unrevealed parts remain hidden until the person is able to receive them. [209]

---

[209] *ZOHAR (MISHPATIM 94B),* from *SHA'AR HA-GILGULIM* (GATES OF REINCARNATION), page 19.

Gilgilim– Revolving Souls

"All souls are subject to transmigration"

The ZOHAR [210]

The soul goes through a reincarnation, or *metempsychosis*, [211] according to *Kabbalists*. This was a prominent theory chiefly in the Middle Ages and was the topic of many medieval Jewish writings. The reincarnation of a soul in Hebrew is called *gilgul* (גלגל, *GLGL),* from the Hebrew root word *GL* (גל), which means to form a circle. The ZOHAR explains that all souls must undergo transmigration and describes how the souls of man revolve as a stone slung from a sling– like a cycle. [212]

According to the theory of *Gilgulim* which first appeared in the *BAHIR,* a 12th century Jewish mystical book, living souls are said to "cycle" through "lives" or "incarnations." In Hebrew, the words *gilgul neshamot* or *gilgulei ha neshamot* means "cycling of the souls" or "turning of the souls," another term for reincarnation.

These souls attach themselves to different bodies– human and nonhuman– over time and each incarnation. This is not necessarily a punishment that the *gilgul* incurs, but often the completion of some good work that the soul was unable to accomplish while on earth is concluded in the soul's reincarnation into another body. The essential *Kabbalistic* text that discusses the idea of *gilgul* and explores the deep, complex laws of reincarnation is called SHA'AR HA'GILGULIM (THE GATES OF REINCARNATION). It was based on the earlier work of Rabbi Isaac Luria [213] and was originally compiled by his disciple, Rabbi Chayim Vital in the 16th century.

Adding a final *Mem* (ם) to the world *GL* (גל) forms the word *golem GLM* (גלם), a rounded, unshaped form. The word *golem* is often used to refer to an animated figure brought to life by a *Kabbalistic* formula.

---

[210] In PARASHAT MISHPATIM, under the title *Saba de Mishpatim* (the Old Man or the Grandfather of *Parashat Mishpatim*).

[211] *Metempsychosis*, a Greek term, is the transmigration of the soul of a human being or animal at death into a new body of the same or a different species.

[212] Abelson, Jacob, JEWISH MYSTICISM, page 164. From ZOHAR ii, 99.

[213] Isaac Luria was born in 1534 and died in 1572.

The Tree of Life

In the *Kabbalah*, the Tree of Life is a magical and numerical system that displays the design of universe. The Tree of Life (called *Eretz Chaim* in Hebrew) is also a model for the laws of physics– representing both force (energy) and form (substance).

Composed of 10 spheres (*sephiroth* in Hebrew) and 22 paths, [214] the Tree of Life symbolically represents every force and form in each of the three dimensions of Space, Time and the Soul.

The traditional model of the Tree of Life uses symbols, or signs, as a frame of reference for the correspondences between each of the three dimensions.

The 10 *Sephiroth* represent the ten major cosmic forces that control the universe. The 22 paths correspond to the 22 letters of the Hebrew alphabet (also known as the "foundation letters") and the Tarot trump cards of the Major Arcana. These are the "32 mysterious paths" described in the first sentence of the *SEPHER YETZIRAH*. [215]

The Hebrew letters are used as a pictorial glyph. As the *Kabbalist* meditates on each, the soul comes into direct with its source. A connection is made between the object in space and the specific part of the soul. "As above, so below."

Each of the 32 symbols represents a cosmic force in the Universe. When the mind concentrates on any of the symbols, it comes into contact with that force in nature. A connection is made between the two.

When the sensory processes (sight, sound, feeling...) are under control, and stimulated in unison to create to experience of each part of the Tree of Life, changes can be felt in one's soul and surroundings.

The effect of the magic rite, or ceremony, is to create in the imagination, in the senses, and from within the consciousness to produce a change in space, time and one's soul. The Tree of Life provides that framework of reference.

---

[214] *SEPHER YETZIRAH* 1: 2: "Ten *Sephiroth* of Nothingness and 22 Foundation Letters."

[215] *SEPHER YETZIRAH* 1:1: "By 32 mystical paths of Wisdom…"

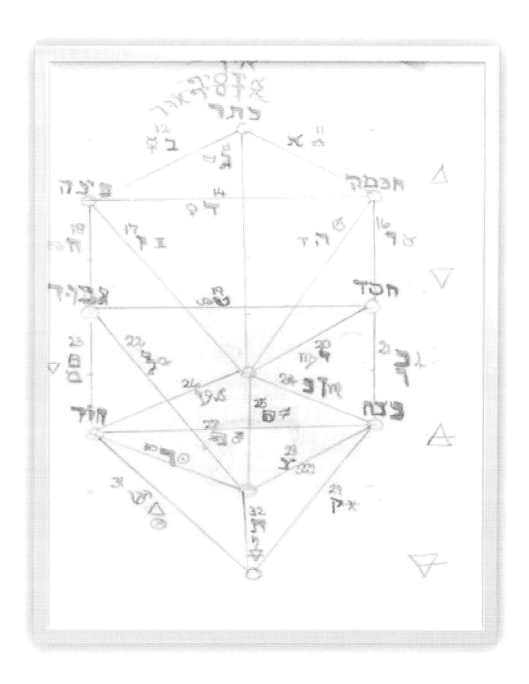

Chart of the Tree of Life with the 10 *Sephiroth* and 22 paths, drawn by Robert Zucker, 1976.

4ᵗʰ-9ᵗʰ Century (300-899)

During the classical period between the 4ᵗʰ and 6ᵗʰ centuries, very little is known about the people who played a role in transmitting the sacred knowledge. In the Geonic period (589 C.E.-1038 C.E.) the principles of the *Merkabah* and the *SEPHER YETZIRAH* were secretly circulated among small groups of Jewish scholars.

From the 8ᵗʰ century on, Hebrew was replaced by Latin and Greek. Hebrew remerged during the 10ᵗʰ century as a spoken and written language. The foundations of medieval *Kabbalah* began in Babylonia in the 7ᵗʰ and 8ᵗʰ centuries. A number of *midrashim* (commentaries on Hebrew literature) with early *Kabbalistic* references were shared among circles of followers, including the *ALPHA-BETA* OF RABBI AKIBA and the *MIDRASH KONEN*, a text on an older tradition of the mysteries of Creation and the structure of the Universe.

Several references to the *SEPHER YETZIRAH* appeared in the *BARAITA DI-SHEMU'EL HAKATAN,* a *Midrash* on astrology composed about 776 C.E., [216] in an Arabic commentary on the *SEPHER YETZIRAH* composed by Isaac ben Solomon Israeli (830-932); [217] and in a poem by Hebrew poet Eleazar ben Kalir (570-640). Kalir recited the three forms of writing, the six directions and ten words, alluded in the *SEPHER YETZIRAH*: [218]

At the turn of the 9ᵗʰ century, Baghdad Jews had more contact with Arabic philosophy, influenced by Greek rationalism. Although esoteric studies probably continued, there is no additional mention about the *SEPHER YETZIRAH* until the 10ᵗʰ century when the teachings began to emerge in Italy and Germany.

---

[216] Kaplan, Aryeh, *SEPHER YETZIRAH*: THEORY, page xxiii.

[217] This was translated into Hebrew by Nahum ha-Ma'arabi.

[218] Kaplan, Aryeh, *SEPHER YETZIRAH*: THEORY, page xxiii and Scholem, Gershom, KABBALAH, p.28.

"Then, from
eternity, with
Ten Sayings
you gouged
with scribe,
script and
scroll–
Ten, you finish
them in Six
directions,
Ten words."
Eleazar ben Kalir

Jewish shawl
graphic, from Zedcor
Graphics
(Jewish13).

91

10ᵗʰ Century (900-999)
The Rise of Jewish Mysticism

With the rise of the Golden Age of Jewish culture in Spain during the 10ᵗʰ century, interest in Jewish mysticism re-emerged.

Several prominent 10ᵗʰ century Jewish community leaders wrote extensive commentaries on the *SEPHER YETZIRAH*. Many of those that survive today in their original Hebrew still have not been fully translated into English.

Two commentaries that are still extant include the Saadia Gaon's version written in 931 with the "long" edition, and a commentary with the "short" version by Dunash ben Tamin in 955-56. There were hundreds of variations of the text circulating in the 10ᵗʰ century. They were based on either the long or short recension.

The short recension ran about 1,300 words in Hebrew and the long version was about twice the number of words. They were both available at the same time, contained similar text, but varied by letter correspondences and depth of explanation. The long version may have originally been a commentary on the short version. Jewish scholars at the time concluded that Abraham was the original author of this manuscript.

There is also a third version included in Shabbathai Donnolo's commentary, *SEPHER HAKHMONI* that provided insight into the topic not well known among the general Jewish population at the time.[219] The three mainly differ from each other in the length of the text, the organization of the material, the attributes of the letters, and they are each defective with numerous copying errors.

Centuries of transcription mistakes contributed to those discrepancies. The ignorance of many scribes who did not know Hebrew or had a poor understanding of the language degraded the accuracy of the letter correspondences. But, they provided the basis for understanding the general meaning of the book and its mystical interpretations.

It's unknown why these three commentaries were produced in different parts of Europe roughly during the same period, but they all had an impact on how we comprehend the *SEPHER YETZIRAH* and *Kabbalah* today.

---

[219] Kaplan, Aryeh, *SEPHER YETZIRAH*: THEORY, page xxv.

Jewish man graphic
from Zedcor Graphics
(Jewish13).

The SEPHER YETZIRAH Recensions

Rabbinical commentaries support the idea that a special knowledge of the Hebrew letters can accomplish great feats. Many famous rabbis published their own theories in numerous commentaries on the *SEPHER YETZIRAH* where they speculate on different techniques used to form the 231 Gates and their correspondences. But, many details seem to be either left out, not discussed in public, or have become lost to time.

There are three main recensions of the *SEPHER YETZIRAH* produced in the 10th century that are still available today. They mainly differ from each other in length of the text and organization of the material.

1. The SAADIAN recension, known through commentary of Rabbi Saadia Gaon (899-942 C.E.) was probably finished in 931. It was published six centuries later. [220] This is the most reliable version of the *SEPHER YETZIRAH* and its correspondences. He begins the Arabic preface with "This book is called 'Book of Beginnings' (*ALMBADY*) and is attributed to our father Abraham. Peace be with him." Saadiah describes the book as an authoritative text. He introduced changes and new division on the basis of the longer version which he used as his basis.

2. The DUNASH BEN TAMIM "short" recension, produced by Rabbi Tamin in Northern Africa sometime after 958. This is a defective version with errors in the correspondences. [221]

3. The SHABBATHAI DONNOLO (Italy, 913-982) "long" recension is the basis of many commentaries, but it is also a defective version. It was included in a commentary published by D. Castelli, Firenze in 1880.

In the 12th century, two leading *Ashkenazi Chasidic* leaders R. Eleazar of Worms and R. Yehuda he-Chasid wrote major commentaries on the *SEPHER YETZIRAH*. Eleazar is credited with revealing the recipes to create a *golem* and revealed great secrets about Jewish mysticism.

Most of the surviving copies of the *SEPHER YETZIRAH* are English translations of 16th-18th century Hebrew and German (Yiddish) writings. But many of them had mistranslations. The ignorance of Hebrew among the scribes also had a tendency to distort the true content.

In the late 19th and 20th century, authors like Eliphas Levi, Aleister Crowley, Israel Regardie, William Wynn Westcott published books about the *SEPHER YETZIRAH*. This brought the once

---

[220] 220 Published by M. Lambert (Paris 1891) from Ms. Oxford 1533.

[221] Published from Ms. Oxford 2250 by M. Grossberg, London 1902. Arabic fragments of the commentary published by G. Vajda in REJ CXIII (1954), p38ff; CXXII (1963), p 149ff.

secretive practice into the modern public domain.

Popular 20th Century Jewish scholars like Aryeh Kaplan, Gershom Scholem and Moshe Idel have made some sense of the *SEPHER YETZIRAH* for the Western world. Kaplan is probably best known for his work on the translation in the *SEPHER YETZIRAH*: THE BOOK OF CREATION IN THEORY AND PRACTICE. Kaplan's book is considered to be the authoritative study on the *SEPHER YETZIRAH*. This volume has relied substantially on the works and translations of Kaplan, Scholem and Idel.

But, with all of its simplicity, this cryptic manuscript has evoked speculation and controversy for centuries. The BOOK OF CREATION, or more correctly– BOOK OF FORMATION, explores deep into divine magical formation and human manipulation of the Universe. To unravel the mysteries of the book is to understand creation and know how to create something out of nothing.

Saadia Gaon's Commentary

The most popular commentary written about the *Sepher Yetzirah*, called the "Saadia Gaon" recension, was composed in Arabic by Babylonian Rabbi Saadia [222] ben Joseph Gaon [223] of Al-Fayyumi [224] in 931C.E.

In one of his earliest writings, the Gaon provided personal observation of the text's contents based on the "long version" of the *Sepher Yetzirah*. While he didn't create the "long" version of the text, he merely copied it, or modified it, along with his comments it has been referred to as the Saadia Gaon recension. [225]

In his commentary, Saadia advocated the Pythagorean view of the origin of the world. Pythagoras considered numbers to be the elements and origin of everything and that numeral symbols preceded all other forms of writing. All words were originally made up of numeral symbols or numbers. The first things that were created, he argued, are Numbers. Geometry and figures– all based on numbers.

In the Creators' universe, according to Saadia, there are 32 distinct items. Each is represented by a Number and a Hebrew Letter. These are the 32 paths– 10 numbers (which correspond to the Ten Commandments) and the 22 letters of the Hebrew alphabet.

The ten fundamental numbers represent the ten *sephiroth*, or spheres found in the Tree of Life design (next page). They are not actual entities but are the underlying principles of the existence of everything that is created in the universe.

God then carved out the shape of each letter and combined them with one to the other in order to bring everything into existence. [226]

---

[222] Also, spelled as Saadiah or Saadia.

[223] A *Gaon* is a Jewish religious leader.

[224] Saadia ben Joseph Gaon of Al-Fayyumi was born in 882 and died in 942 C.E.

[225] Hayman, Peter A., *Sepher Yesira*, page 26-28.

[226] *Sepher Yetzirah* 1:10. Using God's breath, he engraved and carved the 22 letters.

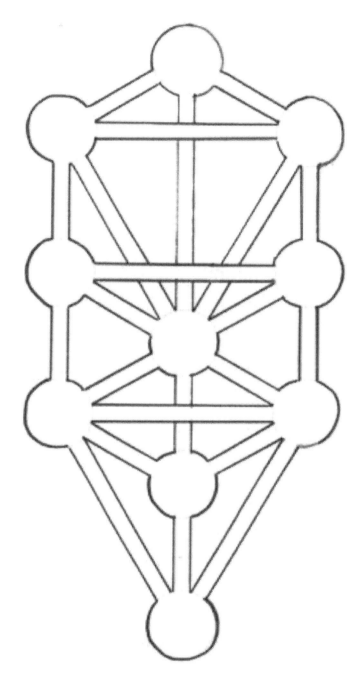

Image of the Tree of Life.

According to the *SEPHER YETZIRAH*, "their measure is ten, but they have neither beginning nor end." [227]

The letters are created in the "air" (one's mind), and formed by one's voice (breath) using five selected parts of the mouth to evoke certain sounds. Each letter has a specific vibration and location of the mouth to produce the sound, Rabbi Saadia explained.

The 22 letters are grouped together and combined into pairs to form the Holy 231 "Gates." These Gates circle or rotate "back and forth" to create, or permutate, new letter combinations. This activity can be re-created using a device called a *Kabbalah* Wheel, as described later in this volume.

Rabbi Saadia also discussed the meaning of "*creatio ex-nihilo*"– creating something out of nothing. [228] To

---

[227] *SEPHER YETZIRAH* 1:5. There are no boundaries to the ten *Sephiroth*, as they are joined to one another.

[228] *Ex-nihilo* is Latin for "out of nothing."

know the correct arrangements of the letters, he advised, is to know the code of creation.

He complained about the many variations of the *SEPHER YETZIRAH* available at the time, saying, "It is not a common book, and so many people have been careless in changing or transposing the text." [229]

The Saadia Gaon version, however, became a casualty of that carelessness over the millennia as well. Unfortunately, like the other versions, the correct letter arrangements of that sacred code have been obscured by time.

Another one of his commentaries, *TZAFSOR KTAAV AL-MABADI* (BOOK OF PRIMARY PRINCIPLES), [230] was translated into Hebrew in the 11th century. The first copy of this text became available in 1533 and is preserved in the Bodleian Library. An English translation is translated from the Hebrew and French versions. [231]

---

[229] Kaplan, Aryeh, *SEPHER YETZIRAH*: THEORY, page xxiv.

[230] "*IM PERUSH HA-GAON RABBENU SE'ADYA*," edited by Joseph Kafih (Jerusalem, 1972). A PRELIMINARY CRITICAL EDITION OF *SEPHER YEZIRA*, by Ithamar Gruenwald, page 133.

[231] The first recession of text became available in Oxford 1533. a commentary published in Hebrew at Mantua with the SEPHER YETSIRAH (Bartilocci, iv.267, ref: Waite, Lit of Kab, 175). Now preserved in the Bodleian Library. Published with French translation by Meyer Lambert, under the title, COMMENTAIRE SUR LE *SEPHER YETZIRAH*; or LIVRE CREATION PAR LE GAON SAADJA D FAYYOUM, Paris 1891. An English translation from the French and Hebrew was translated into English and published by Scott Thompson and Dominique Marson, San Francisco, 1985.

Donnolo's Commentary

Another popular commentary based on the "long" recension of *Sepher Yetzirah*, was included in a manuscript called *Sepher Hakhmoni*, authored about 946 C.E. by Italian physician and scholar Shabbethai ben Abraham ben Joel Donnolo. [232]

Donnolo's commentary was written 16 years after Saadia Gaon's and less than a decade before Dunash Tamin's commentary. It is uncertain whether Tamin was aware of Saadia's commentary since he did not speak Arabic. However, they both shared similar perspectives in their comments and may have had access to similar Judaic religious texts. [233] [234]

Although he made great contributions to medicine, pharmacology, astrology and astronomy, Donnolo also gained a reputation for his writings on cosmology and his famous Commentary on *Sepher Yetzirah*.

Donnolo's study was different from Saadia's and Tamin's versions, as he only focused on specific parts of the *Sepher Yetzirah*. [235] He expounded on Biblical exegesis, astrology, medicine and gave correspondences to the elements of the microcosm and macrocosm.

---

[232] Shabbathai ben Abraham ben Joel Donnolo was born in 913 and died sometime after 982.

[233] Published in print in 1880 *as Il commento di Sabbatai Donnolo sul Libro della creazione*, by David Castelli [Pubblicato per la prima volta nel testo ebraico con note critiche e introduzione, Firenze, 1880].

[234] Piergabriele Mancusco, "Shabbatai Donnolo's *Sepher Hakhmoni*: introduction, critical text, and annotated English translation," Doctoral thesis, UCL (University College London). 2000. ISBN: 9789004181106.

[235] Hayman, Peter A., *Sepher Yesira*, page 31.

Dunash Tamin's Commentary

Sometime before his death, about a decade after Saadia Gaon died, Abu Sahl Dunash ibn Tamin, [236] produced a "short" recension of the *SEPHER YETZIRAH*. [237] Tamin was an Arabian Jewish neo-Platonic scholar who was very interested in astronomical works.

Composed in Arabic, he added his own corrections to errors he found in Saadia Gaon's commentary and correspondences. [238] [239] Although the entire Arabic original no longer exists, enough fragments have been found to piece together a single, but incomplete, text.

Rabbi Tamin laid out a different set of correspondences than Saadia Gaon. He gives his own interpretation of the seven letters and the seven days of the week, the seven planets, the seven orifices of the body, the twelve months of the year and the twelve constellations. He may have had some influence from his teacher Isaac Israeli ben Solomon who was a contemporary of Saadia Gaon years before Dunash composed his commentary on the *SEPHER YETZIRAH*.

---

[236] Abu Sahl Dunash ibn Tamin was born in Kairouan around 890 CE and died about 955 or 956.

[237] A copy is found in National Bibliotheque of Paris (cod. hebr. 1048,2) and in the Bodleian Library (cod. Hebrew 2250,2).

[238] Gruenwald, Ithamar, A PRELIMINARY CRITICAL EDITION OF *SEPHER YEZIRA*, page 133. One version is republished in 1902.

[239] Hayman, Peter A., *SEPHER YESIRA*, page 29-30.

Other 10ᵗʰ Century Commentaries

Several other copies of the *SEPHER YETZIRAH* long version were produced either in Palestine or Egypt in the 10ᵗʰ century. [240] A commentary written by Babylonian theologian, rabbi and scholar Hai ben Sherira Gaon (969-1038) is also preserved *in SHELEET U'TSHUVOT AL SEPHER YETZIRAH* (QUESTIONS AND ANSWERS REGARDING THE *SEPHER YETZIRAH*), Vatican Ms. 181. [241]

Tenth century Gaon Aaron ben Yosef Sargado ha-Kohen in Pumbedita, Babylonia (890-960) wrote a commentary on *SEPHER YETZIRAH*. [242] [243] Sargado became the *Gaon* of Pumbedita from 943 until his death.

Rabbi Yehudah Barceloni refers to this text in later commentary on *SEPHER YETZIRAH* at the end of the 11ᵗʰ century. [244] Portions of his work were also cited by R. Moshe Botriel, a prominent Spanish scholar 300 years after that. During this time, Isaac Israeli also wrote a commentary on the *SEPHER YETZIRAH*. [245]

---

[240] Gruenwald, Ithamar, A PRELIMINARY CRITICAL EDITION OF SEPHER YEZIRA, page 136. Haberman in Sinai X in 1947, pp. 241.

[241] Kaplan, Aryeh, *SEPHER YETZIRAH*: THEORY, page 328.

[242] Ms. Vatican 299, ff 66a-71b, see A PRELIMINARY CRITICAL EDITION OF *SEPHER YEZIRA*, by Ithamar Gruenwald, page 133.

[243] Kaplan, Aryeh, *SEPHER YETZIRAH*: THEORY, page 325.

[244] Kaplan, Aryeh, *SEPHER YETZIRAH*: THEORY, page 324.

[245] A short recension of the commentary (Bodleian Ms. No. 2250) was published by Manasseh Grossberg, London, 1902.

11ᵗʰ Century (1000-1099)

The latter half of the 11ᵗʰ century were perilous times for tens of thousands of Jews who were massacred during the Crusades in Hungary, Poland and Germany. One quarter of the Jewish population in Germany was wiped out during the First Crusade (1095-1099). However, it was also a period when Jewish literature began to flourish.

For the first time, commentaries on the *SEPHER YETZIRAH* during this century included discussions on the *golem,* a creature created by the manipulation of the Hebrew alphabet combined with the Names of God.

Several famous Jewish scholars of this period were linked to creating *golems.* Rabbi and *TALMUDIST* Hananel ben Hushiel [246] wrote a commentary about the story in the *SANHEDRIN* [247] of the Rabbi's *golem.* He said, "Rava, by the [technique of] illusion, created a man, and he wanted to expose the deed of the Egyptian sorcerers, who made, by their magic, a serpent from a staff." [248]

During the Middle Ages, thousands of names of angels appeared in various magical texts. Their names were composed through letter combination techniques known as *temurah* and *gematria.*

---

[246] Chananel ben Chushiel was born 990 C.E. in Kairouan, Tunisia and died in 1053.

[247] The *SANHEDRIN* is the fourth of the four Orders of the *MISHNAH.* It deals mostly with judicial procedures, criminal law, the judges and punishments for crimes. The authority of the *SANHEDRIN* ceased when the Second Temple was destroyed in 70 C.E.

[248] See *'OZAR HA-GEONIN, SANHEDRIN,* page 557, from *GOLEM: JEWISH MAGICAL* by Idel, Moshe, footnote, page 52.

Gabirol and his maid servant

In the mid-11th century, rumors circulated about the popular Messianic poet and philosopher Solomon ben Judah ibn Gabirol, [249] known as Solomon the Sephardi.

Legends claim that Gabirol fashioned a female maid servant, a *golem*, out of wood and hinges and brought her to life by manipulating the Holy Letters. She kept house for him, and perhaps, his company. He stayed out of the public eye amidst reports that he had a serious and contagious skin disorder. [250]

After he was discovered with such a creature, he was denounced by Jewish leaders for his heathenism. When the King [251] heard about it, he ordered Gabirol to death for practicing black magic. Gabirol successfully demonstrated that she was not a full human or a complete creature. The King was satisfied when Gabirol restored her to the pieces of wood from which she had been constructed. [252]

This story circulated for centuries and was eventually published 600 years after Gabirol's death by Rabbi Joseph del Medigo [253] who said he acquired it from an earlier source. Whether it is true or not has not been confirmed by any sources other than the legend which dogged Gabirol's name for millennium.

In his short lifetime, Gabirol published over a hundred poems, biblical commentaries and other manuscripts on *Kabbalah* principles. He wrote about his depressive life, the loss of his parents, and his low self-esteem. His most famous work is *MEKOR CHAYIM* (ORIGIN OF LIFE), produced around 1049.

---

[249] Solomon Gabirol was born in Spain in 1021 and died between 1058-1060; "Solomon ibn Gabirol [Avicebron]" from Stanford Encyclopedia of Philosophy; The JEWISH ENCYCLOPEDIA, 1906, Volume 6, page 37. He was called by the Arabs as Abu Ayyub Suleiman ben Ya'hya ibn Djebirol and known as and by the acrostic from the initials of his name, RaShBaG. He is known scholastically as Avicebron.

[250] Possibly *lupus vulgarus*, from IBN GABIROL, Raphael, Loewe (1969), Cambridge University Press.

[251] Who was the king of Spain? No mention is made, but Ferdinand I. of Castile (1037-1067) ruled during this period.

[252] From R. Joseph Shelmo del Medigo, quoted in "*GOLEM*: JEWISH MAGICAL" by Moshe Idel, page 233; and THE JEWISH ENCYCLOPEDIA: Volume 6, by Isidore Singer, 1912. Page 37.

[253] From *MAZREF LE-CHOCHMAH* by Joseph Solomon del Medigo (1591-1655), and quoted in ON THE KABBALAH AND ITS SYMBOLISM, by Gershom Scholem, page 199.

At about age 28, he wrote his most notable piece translated from Arabic into Latin, *FONS VITAE* (FOUNTAIN OR SOURCE OF LIFE). It covered five tractates that deal with matter and form, and the existence of "substantiae simplicies," which he calls an intermediary between God and the physical world. The original Arabic copy is lost, but it was translated into Latin in 1150 by Abraham ibn Daud. [254]

Gabirol died young, at about age 36 or 37. He was either trampled to death by an Arab horseman or was murdered by a jealous Muslim poet who allegedly buried Gabirol under the roots of a fig tree. [255]

During his lifetime, Gabirol was more noted among the Jewish community as a poet than a philosopher. To the Christian world, he was known for his work of *FONS VITAE*. His name was eventually Latinized to Avicebron. [256]

His writings were studied in monasteries and universities for centuries without an indication of the author's real persona. In 1846, Solomon Monk exposed the author's true identity in a German novel. It wasn't until after his death that Gabirol was acknowledged for his influence on Judaism.

---

[254] "Solomon ibn Gabirol," Wikipedia.com. Abraham ibn Daud was a Spanish-Jewish astronomer, a historian, and a philosopher. He died 1180 C.E. He was known by the abbreviation Rabad I or Ravad I.

[255] ibn Gabirol, THE JEWISH ENCYCLOPEDIA.

[256] Spelling variations include Avicebron and Avencebrol.

Rashi and the SEPHER YETZIRAH

Rabbi Shlomo ibn Yitzchak [257] of Troyes, France– better known by the acronym *Rashi*– [258] was a major 11th century commentator on the *TALMUD*, the *TANAKH,* and the *SEPHER YETZIRAH*. His commentaries have been included in almost every edition of the *TORAH* since it was first printed in the 1520s by Daniel Bomberg. [259]

In his treatise, *ERUBIM, Rashi* explained how the use of the letters of the Hebrew alphabet can create magical acts. He wrote, "They used to combine the letters of the Divine Name (*Shem Ha-M*) by which the universe was created. This is not to be considered forbidden magic. For the words (works) of God were brought into being through His Holy Name." [260] *Rashi* is our main source of the letter combination techniques using the *Tetragrammaton* (The 4-Letter Name).

He compared the creation techniques discussed in the *SEPHER YETZIRAH* with the creation of man. Although the *SEPHER YETZIRAH* does not mention the actual letter combinations necessary used to create a *golem, Rashi's* view seemed to be shared among others during this time.

Rashi's name is also attributed to a 11th Century Sephardic semi-cursive typeface called *Rashi* Script, although he did not invent it or ever use it.

---

[257] Rabbi Shlomo ibn Yitzchak (Itzak) was born in 1040 and died in 1105 (4800-4865).

[258] Rabbi Shlomo Itzak– composed from the first letters of his name *Rashi*

[259] *Rashi*: Wikipedia.com.

[260] Trachtenberg, Joshua, JEWISH MAGIC AND SUPERSTITION: A STUDY IN FOLK RELIGION. Page 84.

Tetragrammaton: Four Sacred Vowels

HVHY	YVHH	VHYH	HYHV
VHHY	VYHH	YHVH	YHHV
HHVY	HVYH	HYVH	HHYV
יהוה	הווי	יהוי	ההי
יהוי	הוהי	ההוי	יההו
יההו	הויה	היוה	והוה

The permutations of the *Tetragrammaton*.

Rashi once wrote that "by means of *SEPHER YEZIRAH*, they studied the combinations of the letters of the (Divine) Name." This technique of combining the letters of the *Tetragrammaton* (the vowels) with each other is ancient.

The letters of the *Tetragrammaton* (the sacred four letter Name of God) are comprised of four Hebrew letters that are equated with the vowels *YHVH*– יהוה.

The Sacred Name was also called at an earlier time the *Shem Ha-Meforesh*. All words are comprised from the combinations of the letters when they are permutated (merged) with the *Tetragrammaton* (the vowels).

The original three letter vowels, *YHV* (יהו) are placed at the "beginning, middle and end" of a word to signify that *YHV* is God of the whole Universe.

12th Century (1100-1199)
Chasidic Kabbalah Movement

The beginning of the 12th century brought a close to the study of *Merkabah* (Chariot) mysticism and the dawn of the modern *Kabbalah*.

Persecutions against the Jews increased the 12th century. The Fourth Crusade began in 1204 and Constantinople was captured. This was also when the *Kabbalah* movement began to take root, centering around the family of Rabbi Samuel ben Kalonymus *he-Chasid* (Samuel the Pious) [261] of Speyer, Germany and one of his students, Rabbi Eleazar ben Judah of Worms (Germiza).

The students of Rabbi Judah the Pious of Speyer in Regensburg wrote down an early version of the *golem* legend regarding Ben Sira and his father Jeremiah the Prophet. The two stages of the *golem* creation included the combination of the letters of the Hebrew alphabet into "Gates" and then combining those Gates with the Divine Name, they explained.

During this time, there was an increase in the number of texts that expounded the Jewish mysticism movement. Important *Kabbalistic* works as *SEPHER BAHIR* (BOOK OF BRILLIANCE), the *ZOHAR* (BOOK OF SPLENDOR), *SEPHER HA-IYYUM* (BOOK OF INSIGHT), and several commentaries on the *SEPHER YETZIRAH* expanded the awareness among the general Jewish, and eventually the Christian populations.

---

[261] Rabbi Samuel of Speyer, Rhineland-Palatinate, Germany, 1150-1217, was the first of the *Chasidic Ashkenazi* movement and father of Judah ben Samuel of Regensburg.

The *Golem* Takes Shape

olem (גלם) began to appear as a technical term for an artificially created being in German *Chasidic Ashkenazi* literature in the 12th century.

Jewish leaders elaborated on the concept of the *golem* creation in numerous medieval commentaries on the SEPHER YETZIRAH. At the time, both Jews and Christians believed that man has the power to create human life.

In Northern France, the religious circle of the Special *Cherub* engaged in lengthy discussions about creating *golem*. Both the French and *Ashkenazi Kabbalists* were very familiar with letter combinations techniques.

Several well-known 12th century *Chasidic* rabbis were well versed in the study of the SEPHER YETZIRAH. Successful practitioners would be able to produce a *golem* as a culmination of their studies of the SEPHER YETZIRAH. The *golem* was considered an actual creature who served his master and fulfilled menial tasks, such as housework. Others believed the *golem* was essentially a symbolic spiritual experience.

A *golem* was reportedly fashioned at the time of the Crusades in France by Rabbi Judah ben Samuel, the *Kabbalist* and father of Judah *he-Chasid*, and author of the SEPHER CHASIDIM (BOOK OF THE PIOUS). He claimed he could make a *golem*, but could not make it talk. It accompanied him wherever he went as a servant and bodyguard. [262]

There is a common thread in these legends that is passed on through time. The *golem's* body is formed out of dirt and mud. Several men circle around the object and recite a secret formula.

The three sacred letters *AMT* (אמת), meaning "Truth," are inscribed on the figure's forehead. In Rabbi Judah's version, shortly after the *golem* was enlivened, it erased the first letter, *Aleph* (א), leaving the word *MT* (מת), or "Death," on its forehead. Rabbi Judah said the *golem* was destroyed because it didn't want the men to succumb to idolatry "as in the days of Enoch." [263]

---

[262] Dan, Joseph, SCHOLEM, GERSHOM AND THE MYSTICAL DIMENSION OF JEWISH HISTORY, page 121. Also, From JEWISH MAGIC & SUPERSTITION, by Joshua Trachtenberg, page 85.

[263] Manuscript of the SEPHER GEMATRIOTH, printed by Abraham Epstein, BEITRAGE ZUR JUDISCHEN ALTERTUMSKUNDE, Vienna, 1887, page 123.

Circling Objects

ircling around an object in a religious procession is a popular Jewish custom. Jews circle the groom under a wedding canopy, they circle cemetery plots on certain occasions, and there are places where a procession is made around the coffin at a funeral.

Circling is a custom found among all people of ancient times. It arose from the belief in the course of one's spiritual development that the world is full of spirits and there are many magical means to overcome them. One of the best is through the use of a circle or "magic ring."

The closed circle is even feared by the devil. The magicians of the Middle Ages would enclose themselves within a circle to keep away the evil spirits. If the spirit were to enter the circle, it would be entire helpless and would have to obey all orders.

From this practice comes the belief in the "wishing-ring," which when worn, on the hand brings fulfilment of every wish. The Hindu, Persians, Greeks, and the Romans shared the same ideas of the circle. One of the most important ceremonies of the Arabs consists of circling their sanctuary.

In the *Aggadah* of the *TALMUD* there is a story about Honi ha-Magel, a 1st century Jewish scholar who lived in Jerusalem. He was nicknamed "the circle-drawer" from his habit of making a circle around himself and telling God he would not move from the spot unless his prayer was granted. [264]

Circling an object with the recitation of specific consonant and vowel combinations produces an ecstatic experience and can mimic the act of Creation, according the Jewish mystics. To create a *golem,* one would move in a circle around molded dust. The *golem* is destroyed by reciting the original combinations backwards and circling in opposite direction.

---

[264] *TAANIT* 19A.

Rabbi Ezra's *Golem*

Sometime in the early to mid-12th century, renowned Spanish Rabbi Abraham Ben Meir ibn Ezra, [265] another notable Jewish poet, philosopher, astrologer, and commentator on the *TORAH*, was rumored to have created a *golem* to prove the power of the Holy Letters. Rabbi Ezra was strongly influenced by the *SEPHER YETZIRAH* and Saadia Gaon. He often cited the Gaon in his works.

R. Ezra was the first to mention Solomon Gabirol as a philosopher and praised his work, even repeating several passages from Gabirol's *FONS VITAE*. R. Ezra's original Commentary on *SEPHER YETZIRAH* is lost, but it may have contained the letter combination techniques he used to create his *golem*. R. Ezra possibly translated it from the original Arabic by Dunash ibn Tamin into Hebrew. [266]

In *SEPHER HA-HAYYIM* (BOOK OF LIFE), R. Ezra said the *golem* is connected to the influence of the planets. He once made a reference to animating statues in his discussion of the *teraphim* (תרפים) of Laban in the OLD TESTAMENT. R. Ezra also wrote that "The *teraphim* are built according to the forms of men and this form is made [in such a way] to receive the power of the superior [beings]." [267] A *golem* is a body without a heart, according to R. Ezra.

He also had this view in regard to the golden calf. The calf, he believed, imitated the astral form and captured the supernal glory in the absence of Moses. [268]

In the 15th century, a story of Rabbi Abraham ibn Ezra's *golem* was published. The author stated that there are "many such legends that are told by all, especially in Germany." [269] Rabbi Ezra is credited with the statement, "See what God has given by means of the Holy Letters!" [270]

---

[265] Rabbi Ezra was born in 1089 in Tuleda, Navarre, Spain and died in 1167.

[266] "Abraham ibn Ezra," STANFORD ENCYCLOPEDIA OF PHILOSOPHY, first published 2006.

[267] *SEPHER HA-HAYYIM*, from *GOLEM*: JEWISH MAGICAL by Moshe Idel, pages 86-87.

[268] Idel, Moshe, *GOLEM*: JEWISH MAGICAL, pages 86, 93.

[269] From Joseph Solomon del Medigo's *MATSREF LA-HOKHMAH*, mentioned in Scholem, Gershom, ON THE *KABBALAH* AND ITS SYMBOLISM, page 199 (1972 edition).

[270] MIMEKOR YISRAEL: CLASSICAL JEWISH FOLKTALES (1976), p.752.

The Wheel of 231 Gates

I n his book *SEPHER HA-KUZARI,* [271] [272] [273] 12th century Spanish philosopher and poet Rabbi Yehuda Halevi [274] included a commentary on the *SEPHER YETZIRAH* where he elaborated on a technique to combine the Hebrew letters by means of a "wheel" to produce 231 Gates.

Each of the 231 Gates is an opening to a specific form of creative activity, the Rabbi explained. If one combines the letters properly (through specific permutation techniques), the creative process that God used in the formation of the world can be re-enacted by humans. This whole process can be imagined as a spinning wheel.

To create this imaginary "wheel" the *SEPHER YETZIRAH* explains how to combine, or "pair," each of the 22 letters of the Hebrew alphabet with all of the other letters of the alphabet. [275] This creates 462 combinations (22 letters x 21 letters).

Eliminate the mirror images (*AG, GA*) to get 231 combinations. These are the legendary 231 Gates described by R. Eleazar of Worms. By pairing these "combinations" one can make the non-existent exist and create something out of nothing, the rabbi believed. [276]

These 231 Gates are placed on a circular wall with each two-letter combination, according to the *SEPHER YETZIRAH.* [277] The whole wall rotates as a wheel. It can spin in either direction. The combination could be forward or backward. All words arising from these combinations of these letters are then permutated with the four-letter Name of God, called the *Tetragrammaton.*

---

[271] Full Arabic title: The BOOK OF REFUTATION AND PROOF ON BEHALF OF THE MOST DESPISED RELIGION, commonly known as the BOOK OF THE *KUZARI.*

[272] Halevi, Judah, THE *KUZARI*, introduction by H. Slonimsky. Schocken Books. 1964. First published in 1905. Translated from the Arabic by Harwig Hirschfeld.

[273] "Northern France Discussions," from *GOLEM*: JEWISH MAGICAL by Moshe Idel, page 87.

[274] Rabbi Ha-Levi was born sometime in 1085 or 1086 during the conquest of Toledo (May 24, 1085) by Alfonso VI. He died in 1150. Source: JEWISH ENCYCLOPEDIA, Judah Ha-Levi (Arabic: Abu al-Hasan al-Lawi).

[275] the *SEPHER YETZIRAH* 2:5, "*Aleph* with all of them…and all of them with *Aleph.*" They repeat in a cycle and exists in 231 Gates."

[276] Halevi, Judah, THE *KUZARI*, introduction by H. Slonimsky. Schocken Books. 1964. Page 237.

[277] *SEPHER YETZIRAH* 2:4: "22 Foundation letters, placed in a circle, like a wall with 231 Gates. The circle oscillates back and forth" just like a wheel.

Among the *Kabbalists*, the sacred letters of the *Tetragrammaton* were considered vowels.

In the Appendix, there instructions to replicate of the type of Wheel device described by Rabbi Halevi that I call the *Kabbalah* Wheel.

The *Kabbalah* Wheel re-creates the structure of the 231 Gates in two simple circles that rotate up or down to form the 2 letter combinations, as instructed in the SEPHER YETZIRAH and advocated by *Kabbalists* for centuries. The instructions and diagrams to fabricate a similar device are outlined in the Appendix. Graphic by Robert Zucker.

Other 12ᵗʰ Century Kabbalists

The *Kabbalistic* concept that three Hebrew letters– הוי (*HVY*)– are the souls of other letters was widespread among members of the circle of the Special *Cherub*, especially by Rabbi Elhanan ben Yaqaar. According to Yaqaar, God blew the spirit of life into the man using those sacred Hebrew letters. [278]

In 1150, Abraham ben David ha Levi wrote *SEDER HA KABBALAH* (ORDER OF THE TRADITIONS). He followed two paths of medieval mysticism: Theosophical and Theurgical. These philosophies spread from Spain in Provence to Catalania, to Castilla to Safed, and then flourished in Germany. Theurgical operations are the methods, or rituals, used to invoke the theosophical aspects of Gods' mystical nature.

During the late 12ᵗʰ century, the mystical book *SEPHER BAHIR* was written, possibly as a reflection of earlier traditions. [279] The *BAHIR* provided elaborations on the *TALMUDIC* and the *SANHEDRIN* passages about the *golem*. This coincided with the emergence of *Kabbalah* in Provence and Spain. A small number of other works discussed the creation of a *golem* and its techniques.

At the end of the 12ᵗʰ century, there was an explosion of discussions on the *golem*. A Germanic recension of *SEPHER YETZIRAH* was written sometime between the 12ᵗʰ or 13ᵗʰ century and contained the long version of Donnolo's (913 C.E.) work. That copy is stored in the Oxford Bodleian Library. [280]

In the early 1180s, Italian mystic and theologian Joachim of Flore (1135-1202) wrote *PUGIO FIDEI* where he described the *YHVH*, the plurality of the sacred names, and attributes favoring the Christian Trinity. He did not mention any texts, but did use the word Cabala by name and mentioned his predecessor Petras Alphonsi, a rabbi who converted in 1106. [281] Joachim is the founder of the monastic order of San Giovanni and his followers called themselves Joachimites. [282]

---

[278] Dan, Joseph, COMMENTARY ON *SEPHER YEZIRAH*, pages 36-37.

[279] Scholem, Gershom, ORIGIN OF THE *KABBALAH* p. 49-198; Idel, Moshe, *KABBALAH*, NEW PERSPECTIVES, p. 122-127 and J. Dan, THE PROBLEM OF THE SOURCES OF THE *BAHIR*, THE BEGINNINGS OF THE JEWISH MYSTICISM IN MEDIEVAL EUROPE, pages 55-72, 1987.

[280] Gruenwald, Ithamar, A PRELIMINARY CRITICAL EDITION OF *SEPHER YEZIRA*. Library (Cat Neubeaur) 1531 (8) foll 95b-103b, Vellum.

[281] Kottman, Karl A., LAW AND APOCALYPSE: THE MORAL THOUGHT OF LUIS DE LEÓN (1527?–1591), page 30.

[282] "Joachim of Fiore," Wikipedia.com

Judah ben Barzillai

One of the codifiers of the Middle Ages, Catalan *TALMUDIST* Judah ben Barzillai of Barcelona [283] wrote a detailed Commentary on the *SEPHER YETZIRAH* toward the middle of the 12th century. He cited many old versions, especially Saadia Gaon's views and the passage about R. Joshua Hananiah's *golem* from the *SANHEDRIN*.

Barzillai analyzed *TALMUDIC* sayings and used them support his perspective that a "new man" can be created through spiritual achievement.

His book bore the title "Each man who looks at it [i.e., who contemplatively immerses himself in it, *tzafah*], his wisdom is beyond measure, that is, comparable to the creative wisdom of God." At the beginning and end bears the title *HILKHOTH YETZIRAH* and also ALPHABET OF OUR FATHER ABRAHAM (*OTIYYOT DE-ABRAHAM AVINU*).

While his commentary may have strayed from conventional discussion of the text, it covered over 300 pages of commentary. It was eventually published in Berlin in 1885 as *PERUSH SEPHAR JEZIRA* [284] [285] in Hebrew and several times afterwards. [286] This edition has been recently republished with its original Hebrew and commentaries.

---

[283] Judah ben Barzillai of Barcelona was born in 1070 or 1080 AD, few details of his life are known.

[284] Halberstam, Z.H., and Kaufmann, David, *PERUSH SEPHAR JEZIRA* by (1832-1900) (1852-1899), Berlin, 1995. 354 pages.

[285] For more, see *SEPHER YETZIRAH*: THEORY, by Kaplan, Aryeh, page 332; and *GOLEM*: JEWISH MAGICAL, by Idel, Moshe, page 49.

[286] Jerusalem: Makor, 1971 and in Israel in 2007.

Maimonides– the *Rambam*

Medieval Sephardic philosopher and astronomer (Moses) Moshe ben Maimonides (1135-1204), known by the acronym *Rambam* [287] for his initials, is the author of the GUIDE FOR THE PERPLEXED, a philosophical work about unity and reason. He also wrote *SEPHER HANIMTZAH* (BOOK OF THAT WHICH EXISTS) where he made some references to the *SEPHER YETZIRAH*. [288]

Nahmanides– *Ramban*

One of the most leading figures in medieval Judaism was Spanish *Kabbalist*, TALMUDIST, physician, and rabbi Moshe ben Nachman of Girondi (1194-1270), [289] known as Nahmanides ("Son of Nachman") and by the acronym *Ramban*. He wrote a commentary on *SEPHER YETZIRAH*. [290] The manuscript no longer exists, but it is mentioned one hundred years later by Rabbi Abraham Abulafia [291] and in the 17th-18th century by Rabbi Yachiel Heilpern. [292] [293]

---

[287] *Rambam* is acronym for <u>R</u>abbeinu <u>M</u>oshe <u>b</u>en <u>M</u>aimom.

[288] Fred Rosner, THE EXISTENCE AND UNITY OF GOD: THREE TREATISES ATTRIBUTED TO MOSES MAIMONIDES, pages 98-102. The book was first published in 1596 in Salonika (Thessaloniki) by Rabbi Abraham ben Solomon Akara and printed at the end of a commentary on Lamentations by Rabbi Samuel ben Chabib Di Vidash.

[289] Rabbi Moses ben Nachman Girondi was born in 1194 in Girona, Crown of Aragon (present-day Spain) and died in 1267.

[290] *Ramban's* commentary is first printed in the 1562 Mantua edition and many times afterwards. Kaplan, Aryeh, *SEPHER YETZIRAH*: THEORY, page 329.

[291] See *SEPHER HANIMTZAH*.

[292] See *SEDER HADORET*.

[293] See Kaplan, Aryeh, *SEPHER YETZIRAH*: THEORY, page 329.

Isaac the Blind's Mystic Visions

The Dean of the Provencal *Kabbalah*, French Rabbi Yitzach *Sagi Nahor* ben Ravaad (1160-1235), was known as the founder of *Kabbalah*. He was called Isaac the Blind, as he lacked visual sight. But his spiritual insights, especially on *Kabbalah,* were highly regarded.

"*Sagi Nahor*" is an Aramaic epithet that means "full of light," and alluded to his great vision despite his lack of sight. He claimed he was the inheritor of the Oral Tradition originally given to Moses on Mt. Sinai through a succession of earlier rabbis. He also wrote an extensive commentary on the SEPHER YETZIRAH. [294] [295]

R. Isaac was the first to give the names to the ten spheres, or *sephiroth,* [296] of the Tree of Life and the first to adopt the idea of metempsychosis, the transmigration of the soul– called *gilgilim* (גלגלם). [297]

The *sephiroth* are abstracts– products of human thought– that were used as a bridge to the spiritual realm, Rabbi Isaac believed.

---

[294] Yitzach Sagi Nahor, PERUSH HAR'I SAGNI NAHOR ZILLAH'H AYL SEPHER YETZIRAH, 18 pages reprinted in SEPHER YETZIRAH AM PERUSH HRASHIEEM V-HA-MEKOVLEEM. Hebr. Ms. No. 2456, 12.

[295] An English translation with notes, THE EMERGENCE OF PROVENCAL KABBALAH Rabbi Isaac the Blind's "Commentary on Sepher Yetzirah," translation and annotation, a thesis presented by Mark Brian Sendor, Near Eastern Languages and Civilizations, Harvard University, May 1994, volume 2. 185 pages. Another copy of the English translation in "Isaac the Blind - Commentary on SEPHER YEZIRA," translated by Mauch, D. R.

[296] The traditional order of the ten *sephiroth*, or emanations or "spheres*,"* are *Keter, Chockmah, Binah, Hesed, Geburah, Tefiret, Netzach, Hod, Yesod* and *Malkuth.* In his commentary, R. Isaac explains why he begins with *Chockmah* rather than the traditional *Keter,* "It does not follow the order of the directions, rather the order of the powers." He lists one order, although several manuscripts have variant orders.

[297] JEWISH ENCYCLOPEDIA, Isaac the Blind, Isaac ben Abraham of Posquires, by Kaufmann Kohler and M. Seligsohn, Isaac the Blind was "Called by Baḥya b. Asher Father of the *Kabbalah*" (Commentary on the Pentateuch, section *Wayishlaḥ*)."

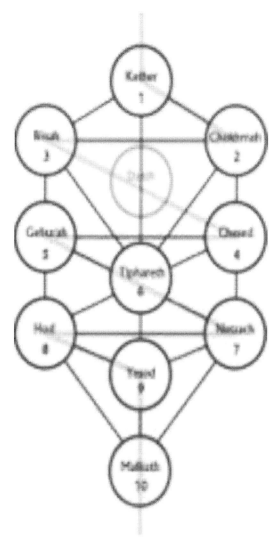

According to the *TALMUD*, the world was created with "Ten Utterances." [298]

Many rabbis believed there was a connection between the Ten Utterances (*asarah ma'amorot*) of God in Genesis and the Ten Commandments (*aseret hadibrot*) in Exodus. [299]

In the SEPHER YETZIRAH, there are ten *sephiroth*. [300] Rabbi Isaac's symbolism of the *sephiroth* and his theory of emanation has endured for centuries.

He associated each *sephiroth* with parts of the body in the lower, physical, world with their correlations in the higher, Divine, world. The human hands and feet were created with a total of 10 digits (fingers), each corresponding to a specific *sephiroth*.

---

[298] *TALMUD* - Ms. *ROSH HASHANA* 32a. Avot 5:1.

[299] Exodus 20:1-17.

[300] The first chapter of the SEPHER YETZIRAH describes the nature of the ten *sephiroth* of Nothingness.

The ten *sephiroth* are:

1. *Keter* (Crown)
2. *Chockmah* (Wisdom)
3. *Binah* (Understanding)
4. *Chesed* (Love)
5. *Geburah* (Strength)
6. *Tiferet* (Beauty)
7. *Netzach* (Victory)
8. *Hod* (Splendor)
9. *Yesod* (Foundation)
10. *Malkuth* (Kingship)

See the back cover of this volume for a representation of the Tree of Life with its color attributes.

Like Rabbi Saadia *Gaon* and others, R. Isaac explained how the 22 Hebrew letters have a body *and* a soul. The body is the shape, or vessel, of the letter. The soul is its essence, enlivened by sound.

Azriel, founder of speculative *Kabbalah*

zriel (Ezra) ben Menahem ben Solomon (1160-1238) was the founder of the speculative viewpoint of *Kabbalah*. He traveled from his home in Gerona to Southern France and became a pupil of *Kabbalist* Isaac the Blind.

After Azriel became disappointed that the French philosophers would not adhere to his mystic views, he returned to Spain to establish a school of *Kabbalah* that was attended by Nahmanides.

He wrote a commentary on the ten *sephiroth* and authored a commentary on *SEPHER YETZIRAH* called *SEPHER HA-MILLUIM* [301] espousing his speculative theory. In his commentary, R. Azriel suggested that the forward combinations of the letters create (*livnot*, "to build") and the backward combinations (*'ahor zeh din*) undo the creative effort (*listor*).

He used the term "*beri'ah*" (creation) and "*beri'ah*" (creature) in the context of doing and undoing. He followed this assumption further in his COMMENTARY ON *GENESIS RABBA*, [302] and included copies of the tables of vocalizations as they occur in R. Eleazar of Worms' *SEPHER HA-SHEM*. These tables also occur in Rabbi David ben Yehudah *he-Chasid's* writings, under influence of Rabbi Joseph. [303]

---

[301] *SEPHER HA-MILLUIM* was published in Mantua in 1719. Source: JEWISH ENCYCLOPEDIA, "Azriel (Ezra) Ben Menahem.

[302] Azriel, COMMENTARY ON *GENESIS RABBA*, p. 254-255.

[303] Idel, Moshe, *GOLEM*: JEWISH MAGICAL, Commentary on *SEPHER YEZIRAH*" in Chavel, *KITVEI RAMBAM*, vol. 2, p. 459, from p. 120-21, 125.

Rabbi Eleazar of Worms

One of the most well-known medieval *Kabbalist* was German-born Rabbi Eleazar ben Judah ben Kalonymus (1176-1238), known as Rabbi Eleazar of Worms (also spelled as Wormes). [304]

Rabbi Eleazar was also leading *TALMUDIST* and a pupil of Rabbi Samuel the Pious. He was a descendant of the prominent Kalonymus family who pioneered the *Chasidic Ashkenazi* movement. As the main inheritor of the *Ashkenazi* esoteric traditions, he fervently studied the *Kabbalah* throughout his lifetime and wrote many commentaries on Judaic mysticism.

Rabbi Eleazar obtained the instructions to create a *golem* from his teacher, R. Yehudah *ha-Chassid* (1150-1217) and from his father, Kalonymus V. "Yehudah Nathan" ben Todros. [305] His *ESER SHEMOT* is a commentary on the ten Holy Names of God.

In *SEPHER HA-SHEM* (BOOK OF THE NAME), he gave steps how to mystically combine the 22 Hebrew letters and provided a table of permutations that correspond to the limbs of the body with the Divine Name, *YHVH* יהוה.

One of the most quoted commentaries on the *SEPHER YETZIRAH* is attributed to Rabbi Eleazar from his *PERUSH AL SEPHER YETZIRAH* ("Commentary on *SEPHER YETZIRAH*"). [306] [307] This work was made public when it was first printed in Mantua in 1562. It was reprinted in Przemysl in 1889, and more recently in Israel in the early 2000s. This popular version is referred to as the Mantua edition and is still in use today.

---

[304] Rabbi Eleazar was also known as Eleazar ben Judah ben Kalonymus, Eleazar Rokeach, and Eleazar of Germiza (Worms). He was born about 1176 and died in 1238.

[305] Yehudah Nathan is the son of Rav Kalonymus *"HaZaken."*

[306] *PERUSH HA-ROQH AL SEPHER YETZIRAH* is also found in *SODEI RAZAYA* (BOOK OF SECRETS) by Eleazar ben Judah of Worms.

[307] The book is printed by Shalom HaKohen Weiss, ed, Jerusalem, Shaarei Ziv Institute in 1991. An English version, used today, *SEPHER REZIAL HEMELACH: THE BOOK OF THE ANGEL REZIAL* by Steve Savedow contains numerous translation errors but is one of the few complete English translations.

Eleazar's Book of Secrets– *SODEI RAZAYYA*

The famous medieval magical manuscript *SODEI RAZAYA* (or *RAZIEL HAMALACH*)– the SECRETS OF MYSTICISM has been attributed to Rabbi Eleazar of Worms.

In SECRETS OF MYSTICISM, the author provides a comprehensive study on creation and quotes numerous *Merkabah* traditions, *Hechalot* literature and explained the characteristics of the angels, the Divine Throne, the Chariot, and Divine Voice.

The rest of the work features discussions on God's names, the fate of the soul after death, the meaning of dreams and a practical guide for creating a *golem*. He also took extracts from Sabbathai Donnolo's commentary on the *SEPHER YETZRIAH*.

The chapter titles to the *SEPHER RAZAYA HASHEM* (BOOK OF SECRETS OF THE HOLY NAME), by Rabbi Eleazar, [308] according to my translation from my library copy, includes:

- *Ha'SkMT V'HaAyRT* (Awakening Knowledge)
- Chapter 1: *Sepher Aleph-Bayt* (Book of the Letters of the Alphabet)
- Chapter 2: *Sod HaYChod* (Secrets of the Jews), *Ha'LKot Ha'KSa* (The Laws of Knowledge)
- Chapter 3: *Sepher Ha'ZZShQ* (76 Names of Metatron, listed with descriptions)
- Chapter 4: *PYRVSh AyL Sepher Y'TziRaH* (Commentary on *SEPHER YETZIRAH*) with charts and diagrams.
- Chapter 5: *V'ZKMoT Ha-Nephesh*

---

[308] *SEPHER SODEI RAZAYA HASHEM*, by Eleazar of Worms, was published in the 1889 Przemysl edition and reprinted in Hebrew in Israel, 2004.

Subchapters of *SEPHER RAZAYA HASHEM*:

- 1: *Chochmot ha-Nephesh* (Knowledge of the Soul) This is the 5th part of *SODEI RAZAYA* that deals with psychology. Printed as a separate book 1876, Lemberg.
- 2: *Chockmat ha-Cholam* (Knowledge of Dreams)
- 3: *AyYYN ChtYYN ha-Matem* (Study of Life to the Death)
- 4: The Soul and Its Formation
- 5: Ayin TChaYYT HaMeTYM (Life and Death)
- 6: *Chockmot Nephesh v'Ruach v'LeNeshamah* (Knowledge of Soul, Breath and Spirit)
- 7: *Ayyn Nephesh v-Ruach v'Yetzirath* (Study of the Soul of the Formation)
- 8: *Shelah Shal ShMal Br'* (Drawing out the question of the Name of Creation)
- 9: *TShoVah* (Answer)
- 10: *Aynn Sod ChaTFLah* (Study of prayer)
- 11: *HaShana Blyl* (The Name in Circles)?
- 12: *Dyn Mtzoh Ray Briah* (Judgement (law) (*Zoha*) bad Creation)
- 13: *Chockmah HaZSoiot yShrebhl vTaym Pre v'rbi* (Knowledge the of Rabbi)
- 14: *Dene MaTem* (Cause of Death)
- 15: *Yitzer haRay* (Evil urge? Creation evil?)

A version of *SEPHER RAZIEL* was also published as *LIBER SALOMONIS* [309] from a 16th century Latin *grimoire*. [310] The first English printing was in 1701 in Amsterdam. Since then, dozens of editions have been printed, mostly in Hebrew.

This manuscript focused on magical practices and letter combination techniques that weren't found in rabbinical or general Jewish discussions. Christian Cabalists favored its content. This version of the book usually contained seven books:

- the *CLAVIS*: deals with astrology, the planets, Signs, and Houses;
- the *ALA*: magical virtues of stones, herbs, and animals;
- the *TRACTATUS THYMIAMATUS*: perfumes and suffumigations;
- TREATISE OF TIMES: the correct hours of the day for each operation;
- TREATISE ON PREPARATIONS: ritual purity, and abstinence;
- *SHAMAIM*: the various heavens and their angels;
- Book of Names: virtues and properties of Names.

---

[309] Ms. Sloane 3826, published in 1564.

[310] A *grimoire* is a Medieval book of magic spells and invocations.

R. Eleazar on Sepher Yetzirah

Rabbi Eleazar of Worms examined the issues revolving around the use and validation of the BOOK OF FORMATION. In his Commentary on the *SEPHER YETZIRAH*, he provided the first known written account on how to create a *golem* and then presented a letter combination technique to accomplish it. [311]

Recipes for creating a *golem,* with the use of letter combinations, are also found in R. Eleazar's *SEPHER HA-BA*, another commentary on the *SEPHER YETZIRAH* in the chapter "*Pe'ullah ha-yetsira*" (the "practice, or practical application, of the *Yetzirah*– formation"):

העוסק בספר יצירה יש לו לטהר עצמו ללבוש
בגדים לבנים ואין לו לאדם לעסוק
יחידי כי אם ב' או ג' דכתיב ואת הנפש אשר עשו
בחרן וכתיב טובים השנים מן האחד וכתיב לא
טוב היות האדם לבדו אעשה לו עזר כנגדו לכך
התחיל כי בראשית ברא . ויש לו ליקח קרקע
בתולת במקום הרים שלא חפר בה אדם שם.
ויגבל העפר במים מים ויעשת גולם אחד ויתחיל
לגלגל כאלפא ביתות של רכיב שערים כל אבר
לבד כל אבר סכמיב בלבית בספר יצירה כנגדו
ויתגלגלו כהתחלת לרב ואחיב ינגלג כמברת א
אָ אָ אָ אָ וכעולם מות הסם פתהם אָ וכל האחיב
ואחיב לָי ואחיב לָי ואחיב לָי ואחיב לָי וכן אָיו
וכן חיה כולו ואחיב יתלוך ב' וכן ב' וכל אבר
כאות שניטע בו והכל יעסוק בעתרת:

Translation: "Whoever studies *SEPHER YEZIRAH* has to purify himself [and] don white clothes. It is forbidden to study [*SEPHER YEZIRAH*] alone, but only [in groups of] two or three, as it is written: "and the souls they made in Haran." [312] And it is written: "It is not good for man to be

---

[311] *SEPHER SODEI RAZAYA HASHEM*, Hebrew reproduction of the original book, produced in Israel in 2004. This set of instructions is found on page 295. Another edition is printed by Shalom HaKohen Weiss, edited in Jerusalem, Sha'arei Ziv Institute in 1991.

[312] Genesis 12:5.

alone I will make a fitting helper (companion) for him." [313]

"Therefore, [Scriptures] begins with a "*bet, bereshit bara,*" He created. It is incumbent upon him to take virgin soil from a place in the mountain where no one has plowed. And he shall knead (*Vayigabbei he-'aafar*) the dust with living and he shall make a body [*Golem*] and shall begin to permutate the alphabets of 221 gates, each limb separately, each limb with the corresponding letter mentioned in the *SEPHER YEZIRAH.*" [314]

In this passage, R. Eleazar described how to permutate the 221 gates (instead of 231, as most widely used), "and always, the letter of the [Divine] Name with them and all the alphabets..." He explains how to use six specific vowels and how to designate each vowel to a letter to a human limb.

The translation is very close, but on closer word by word examination using an OLD TESTAMENT Hebrew Lexicon, there are even deeper meanings revealed. For example, the phrase "fitting helper" has other meanings. The dictionary definition is "a partner." The two Hebrew words *AyZR KNGDV* is defined as helpmate. Other translations use the word companion or assistant.

R. Eleazar's techniques

The Hebrew version further reveals four "systems" or methods using the letters. Each method is a different way to permutate or combine the letters. The fourth method is the permutation (*tzeruf*) of the first eleven letters from *Aleph* to *Lamed* with each of the 22 letters, often referred to in the creation of the *golem*. An example of this arrangement is described in the appendix.

Both Rabbi. Eleazar of Worms and Abraham Abulafia described two stages that are involved in the letter permutation process:

- the combinations of the 22 letters of the Hebrew alphabet with each other using the (AB-AG) *Aleph-Bayt, Aleph-Gimel* "Gate" sequence. The letters cycle through the alphabet, similar to the *Kabbalah* Wheel.
- And then, the combinations of the letters of the Divine Name with the combined "Gates." The Divine Name infuses vitality (*Chayyot*) and the soul (*Neshamah*).

---

[313] Genesis 2:18.

[314] Idel, Moshe, *SODEI RAZAYA* quoted in *GOLEM*: JEWISH MAGICAL, page 56.

R. Eleazar explained how dust is molded into the shape of a body and how the Hebrew letters are permutated according to the instructions in the 2nd chapter of the *SEPHER YETZIRAH*. He described how to combine the letters of the Hebrew alphabet into such a sequence that the combination of sounds evoke life into a lifeless body.

The instructions specify that two or three adepts, joined in the *golem* ritual, should take some virgin mountain dirt, knead it in running water, and form a *golem* with it. Over this figure they recite the combinations of the alphabet derived from the "221 gates of the Book *YEZIRAH*," which according to R. Eleazar, form 221 combinations (not the traditional 231 combinations). Each letter is combined with the *Tetragrammaton*, according to every possible vocalization.

A final step was the incision on its forehead of the name of God, or of the word אמת (*AMT*) meaning "truth." The creature was destroyed by removing the initial letter א (*Aleph*), leaving the word מת *MT*, meaning "dead."

R. Eleazar wanted to keep the pronunciation of the Divine Names secret because it may be mishandled, yet he penned numerous books revealing most of the secret formulas and drew extensive graphic charts and models. He revealed many *Kabbalistic* secrets and told the Jewish and Christian world for the first time the true ciphers of the Jewish magic. It also brought the development of Christian Cabala– a way to legitimize Jewish magical practices in the name of Jesus. This spurned a secular occult industry in magical symbols and formulas popularized during the Medieval Ages.

אך כב גג גד גה הו וו זז חח טט יי כך לל מם נן סם עע פף צץ קק רר שׁש תת

Chart of 231 Holy Gates, according to Rabbi Eleazar of Worms. This same chart is produced in Shabbathai Donnolo's HOCKMONI. For over a thousand years, *Kabbalists* have relied on this chart devised by Rabbi Eleazar of Worms that depicts the ultimate arrangement of the 22 Hebrew letters into the 231 Gates. As described in the SEPHER YETZIRAH, these 22 columns are "engraved like a garden," and "carved like a wall. "This chart can also be reconstructed using a *Kabbalah* Wheel, as explained later in this volume.

Graphic of a Medieval scholar examining a globe, from Zedcor Graphics.

The Soul of the Letters

In Northern France, during the late 12th century and first half of the 13th century, a group of Jewish *Kabbalists* in a secret mystical circle called the Special *Cherub* engaged in lengthy discussions on the human soul.

The concept that the vowels are the souls of the letters was widely believed, especially by Rabbi Elhanan Yitzchak ben Yaqaar of London, a prominent member of the Special *Cherub*. Rabbi Yaqaar [315] published a commentary on *SEPHER YETZIRAH* from the lectures of Tosafist Rabbi Abraham (Isaac the Younger) Yitzchak of Dampierre towards the end of the 12th century. [316]

According to R. Yaqaar, the three Hebrew letters– YHV הוי are actually the souls of the other letters and comprise the Divine Name. The correct positioning of the vowels, he argued, was vital to succeed in creating a *golem,* a mythical creature in Jewish mysticism that is brought to life by use of the Hebrew letters. Rumors about the Rabbi Yaqaar's ability to create a *golem* emerged after he died in 1210. [317]

The rabbi claimed that the stages in this process are similar to those outlined by others throughout the centuries:

1. combine the letters of the Hebrew alphabet; and with them,

2. combine the letters of the Divine Name *YHV* הוי .

Yaqaar followed the instructions passed on to him by previous rabbi's and learned men, although there were different variations in the arrangement of the letters to produce the desired effect. Similar to verbally passing a message from one person to another, the original message is lost.

---

[315] Rabbi Elhanan Yitzchak ben Yaqaar was born in 1150 and died in1225.

[316] Kaplan, Aryeh, *SEPHER YETZIRAH*: THEORY, page 327. It was republished in 1966.

[317] Idel, Moshe, *GOLEM*: JEWISH MAGICAL, page 91.

The Four Worlds of Kabbalah

"Every one that is called by My name,
and whom I <u>created</u> (ברא) for My glory,
I have <u>formed</u> (יצר) him, yea,
I have <u>made</u> (עשי) him."
Isaiah 43:7

R abbi Isaac ben Samuel of Acre [318] believed that there are four 'worlds,' using the acronym *ABYA* (אביא). At the turn of the 13th century, Rabbi Isaac recounted a discussion at a *Kabbalistic* seminary about the difference between Creation *(beri'ah)* and Formation *(yetzirah)*. True creation is only possible by God, he asserted.

Even though the majority of men lack the power to endow a speaking soul to an inanimate object, Rabbi Isaac believed it was possible. This particular act, accomplished with the secrets from the *SEPHER YEZIRAH* (BOOK OF FORMATION), was called Formation. He reiterated the story about Rabbi Ben Sira and the Prophet Jeremiah and "all those similar to them" who could create a speaking, wise intelligent man." [319]

---

[318] Also, called Yithak ben Shumuel d'min Akko, 1250-1340.

[319] Ms. Sassoon 919; MS Cambridge, Genizah, Taylor-Schecter, K12, 4, page 22. Referenced in *GOLEM*: JEWISH MAGICAL by Moshe Idel, pages, 112.

In *Kabbalah*, these are the four "worlds" or Universes:

- *Atzilut* (אתזלת) he highest level ("nothingness"), domain of the *Sephiroth*.
- *Beri'ah* (בריא) means "Creation"– to make "something out of nothing."
- *Yetzirah* (יצרה) means "Formation"– the world of angels.
- *Asiyah* (עשי) means "Making"– consists of the physical world.

The highest world, *Azilut*– the World of Emanation, is represented by the first letter of the alphabet, *Aleph* (א). The second level is *Beri'ah*, the World of Creation, represented by the second letter *B* (ב), and envisioned as the Divine Chariot. The third world is of *Yetzirah*, Formation, the world of angels and source of the soul, corresponds to the *Y* (י). The lower level is the World of *Asiyah*, the physical plane, represented by the final (א). *Asiyah* is the world we are all familiar with– the physical environment around us.

According to Rabbi Acre, Abraham named his book *SEPHER YETZIRAH* instead of *SEPHER BERI'AH* because few humans have access to the world of *Beri'ah* [320] which is true Creation. Only man can cause a formation, called a *yetzirah*.

---

[320] Idel, Moshe, *GOLEM: JEWISH MAGICAL*, PAGE 109.

Chart of Human Consciousness

The similarities between the 4 levels of human consciousness and the 4 levels of the *Kabbalistic* Universe became apparent when I put together this chart in 1977 to have a better understanding of the connections between the human mind and soul.

Brain Wave	Frequency	When Recorded	Level	Jewish "Soul"
BETA	12-60 cps [321]	Mental activity	*Atziluth*	*Chayyah*
ALPHA	8-12 cps	Relax, meditative	*Briah*	*Neshamah*
THETA	4-8 cps	Emotions, dreams [322]	*Yetzirah*	*Ruach*
DELTA	½-4 cps	Deep Sleep, unconscious	*Asiyah*	*Nephesh*

[321] Brain waves are measured in Hertz, CPS means cycles per second. The higher the cycles, the more awake and active is the human mind. In deep sleep, only the physical body is operating on its own. During this period, the brain is virtually silenced and void of thoughts and dreams.

[322] Sleep produced R.E.M. (Rapid Eye Movements), a characteristic of dreaming activity. When the eyes dart back and forth, as if they were awake, it is assumed that the individual is in an active dream state.

13ᵗʰ Century (1200-1299)

I n 13ᵗʰ century Germany, the *Ashkenazi Chasidism* movement expanded through Europe. Several major commentaries on the *SEPHER YETZIRAH* were written by prominent *Ashkenazi* leaders, including the "Pseudo-Saadia" version of *SEPHER YETZIRAH* printed in Jerusalem. [323]

A *Kabbalistic* treatise composed in 1200 was titled *SEPHER HA-HAYYIM* (THE BOOK OF LIFE) and attributed to Rabbi ibn Ezra, although it was probably written by an anonymous writer strongly influenced by R. Ezra. It discussed the creation of an artificial man and the two rabbis who created a man and a three-year-old calf. But, it seemed to roll together many of the loose legends into a single fantastical story. [324]

The early Provencal and Catalan *Kabbalists* were not especially interested in the nature of the *golem* or the method of its creation. Among these early Spanish *Kabbalists,* only Rabbi Abraham Abulafia discussed the topic. He was the first to put the secret teachings to writing and was condemned by many for that act.

Abulafia is the only Spaniard to produce a detail recipe to create a "creature," while R. Eleazar revealed his methods to German Jews. The Spanish *Kabbalists* mainly invested their mystical efforts in the Theurgical, or ritual, meanings of human activities.

After *Chasidic Ashkenazi* Rabbi Judah ben Samuel of Regensburg, called *He-Chasid* (the Pious), died in 1217, his students wrote down a version of the legend regarding Ben Sira in *SEPHER GEMATRIOTH*, a book on astrology. It was later reprinted in 1887. One of Rabbi Samuel's most prominent student was Eleazar of Worms. [325]

---

[323] Ms. Munich 40, fol. 56a. *KABBALAH* IN ITALY, 1280-1510: A SURVEY, by Moshe Idel, page 425.

[324] "Northern France Discussions," from Moshe Idel, *GOLEM*: JEWISH MAGICAL , pages 87-91.

[325] "Judah ben Samuel *he-Chasid* of Regensburg," Wikipedia.com.

Abulafia's Prophetic *Kabbalah*

The founder of the school of "Prophetic *Kabbalah*," Spanish Rabbi Abraham ben Samuel Abulafia, [326] was considered the master of *Tzeruf* (צרף letter combinations) during the late 1200s. Meditation performed by a human being on any of the Hebrew letters was just like meditating on the entire Creation, Abulafia often professed in his writings.

In the early 1270s, Abulafia began to study the *Kabbalah* of Names and taught this method to his students. During this time, he also made an in-depth study of the commentary of *SEPHER YETZIRAH* by Turkish Cantor Baruch Togarmi, who became Abulafia's long sought teacher.

Togarmi wrote an elaborate commentary on *SEPHER YETZIRAH* [327] and practiced *Tzeruf* (letter combinations) using the three methods of *Kabbalah– Gematria, Notariqon* and *temurah.* [328] He was most interested in the numerical manipulations of Hebrew words and the Holy Name, as explained in THIS IS THE BOOK OF THE KEYS OF *KABBALAH*, a popular handbook among his disciples.

In 1273, Abulafia was at the center of a *Kabbalastic* circle, teaching, writing and presenting his system of letter combination. The famous *Kabbalist* Joseph ben Gikatilla was also a member of Abulafia's circle.

---

[326] Abraham Abulafia was born in Zaragoza, Spain in 1240 and died about 1291.

[327] This commentary is printed by Scholem, Gershom, in *HA-KABBALAH SHEL SEPHER HA-TEMUNAH VE-SHEL ABRAHAM* ABULAFIA, edited by J. ben Shlomo (Akademon, Jerusalem, 1969), pp. 229-239. See also: *KABBALAH* IN ITALY, 1280-1510: A Survey, by Idel, Moshe, p. 373.

[328] Morlok, Eike, RABBI JOSEPH GIKATILLA'S HERMENEUTICS, pages 38-42.

Abulafia's Mystical Meditation

Abulafia's handbook on meditation was called *Or HaShekhel* (Light of the Intellect). It contained concepts from Maimonides' Guide for the Perplexed (*Moreh Nevuchim*), the ancient Book of Creation (*Sepher Yetzirah*) and Eleazar of Worms' *Sepher Ha-Shem* (Book of the Name).

Abulafia also penned *Chaye HaOlam HaBa* (Life in the Future World),[329] an influential handbook on how to achieve an ecstatic prophetic experience. As the title suggested, it covered the Judaic perspective of the afterworld and provided extensive meditation techniques, charts and instructions.

The Jewish belief in an afterlife (reincarnation, *gilguleem*, or metempsychosis) is not an ancient one. No ancient text had mentioned such a subject until the Middle Ages when it became a popular subject.

Chaye HaOlam HaBa provided an amazing insight into Rabbi Abulafia's procedures, including examples to use the two letter gates, the 231 letters and other meditative techniques not discussed in *Kabbalah* books. Life in the Future World had been quoted by many Jewish *Kabbalah* authors in discussions about the *Sepher Yetzirah* and the *golem*.

In one section of this book, Abulafia describes how to meditate on the 24 triplets of the 72 Holy Names of God. He provides explanations of the 72-letter name of God, illustrated by circular figures and explicit instructions for mystical meditation.

Abulafia explained, "It is necessary that one also learns the names of all the letters. Know that in our language, the name of each letter begins with the letter itself." Combining one letter with another to create a specific word is a deliberate act. Each word in the Hebrew alphabet was formed with serious deliberation and agreement among rabbis.[330]

One example he gives are the letters *Lamed* (L) and *Phe* (P) ף ל when combined with *Aleph* (א) to produce the word for the first letter of the alphabet *Aleph* (אלף).[331] In the *Sepher*

---

[329] Ms. Oxford, Heb. 1582, fol. 12b.

[330] Idel, Moshe, Language, *Torah,* and Hermetics in Abraham Abulafia, page 209.

[331] In Hebrew *Aleph* (א), the first letter of the alphabet, means ox. It is based on the Phoenician letter, *Alep*, which is derived from an Egyptian hieroglyphic depicting an ox's head. Source: "*Aleph*," Wikipedia.com.

YETZIRAH, the letter *Aleph* is the 'king' over the breath. [332]

Another practice of this extraordinary form of contemplation is to study a biblical phrase until the rational meaning is lost. In the disorientation following the repeated pronunciation of new meaningless phrase comes "meaning beyond meaning." Combined with specific breathing techniques and contemplation of body limbs meditation on the letters produces ecstasy almost immediately.

Abulafia called his "science of the combination of letters" *(Hochmah ha-Tzeruf)*, a methodical guide to meditation with the aid of letters and their configurations. This method utilizes letters in a certain manner to attain the divine language.

Abulafia illustrated that "…that the method of *tzeruf* can be compared to music; for the ear hears sounds from various combinations, in accordance with the character of the melody and the instrument." [333]

The continuous, monotonous repetition of letters and sounds excites the mind, rather than dulls it. This is done in combination with various bodily and breathing techniques. Abulafia's meditation method involved using head motions and controlled breathing similarly described in *OHR HA-SECHEL*.

---

[332] *SEPHER YETZIRAH* 3:7. The *Aleph* is formed in the Universe, temperate in the Year and is identified as the chest in one's Soul, male (*AMSh*) and female (*AShM*).

[333] Gershom, Scholem, MAJOR TRENDS IN JEWISH MYSTICISM, page 134.

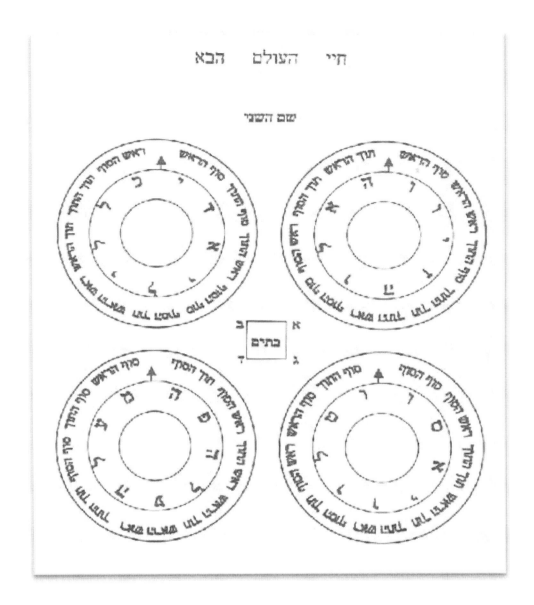

Chart of some of the circles produced in Abraham Abulafia's *CHAYE HAOLAM HABA* (LIFE IN THE FUTURE WORLD). These are the first four of 120 circles drawn out in the appendix of his book. Abulafia produced 120 circles across 30 pages. Each circle contains 9 letters for a total of 1080 letters. Start upper right, follow each circle counterclockwise from the arrow. Some claim this is a method to enliven a *golem* while others say it is merely a meditative system.

Abulafia used several methods to combine the letters. One was called "skipping," (*dillug*). He advocated the free association of ideas when using any one of the several methods of letter manipulation common in his day– such as permutations, ciphers, and *gematria*. [334]

When working within the same system (such as *gematria*), one is "skipping." When several methods are used together, it is called "jumping." Each of these meditative techniques lead to a high level of enlightenment.

Abulafia suggested that "one must completely alter his nature and personality, transporting himself from the state of feeling to intellect, from the path of imagination to one of burning fire. Otherwise, he will find his visions altered, his thought processes demolished, and his reveries will be confounded." [335] Meditation on the letters of the Hebrew alphabet can produce an ecstatic experience, according to Rabbi Abulafia. When the letters are combed with themselves, such as *Aleph* with *Bayt* (AB), *Aleph* with *Gimel* (AG), etc., one can obtain enlightenment. He borrowed techniques from Moses Maimonides and *Ashkenazi Chasidic* practices. [336]

Rabbi Abulafia agreed with R. Yaqaar, and most others, that there are two key parts to the creation process when using the 22 Hebrew letters: (1) the combinations of the letters of the alphabet with each other, and (2) the combinations of those pairs of letters with the Divine Name (the 3 sacred letters YHV.

$$\text{אב אג אד אה או אז...} \quad 1.$$

$$\text{יַא הַ בֻוַ...} \quad 2.$$

Abulafia further explained that there are three stages to complete letter permutation. These are similar to the three levels of the *Sephiroth* described in Chapter 1 of the *SEPHER YETZIRAH*.

- *MIVTA* – Articulation of the Letters. This is when the letters are <u>spoken</u> while they are being combined and transposed.
- *MIKJTAV* – <u>Writing</u> the Letters
- *MASHAV* – <u>Contemplating</u>, or meditating, on the Letters

Abulafia instructs one to start by writing (*MIKJTAV*) each of the sacred letters. Gather speed as you permutate them, speaking each combination (*MIVTA*). As you contemplate (*MASHAV*) on the different combination results, you will begin to feel a warm, glowing sensation at the heart. This is the sign of the descending *shefah* or the "divine influx." Singing certain names according to the prescribed melodies will attain ecstasy with some sensations of air, heat, rushing water, or

---

[334] *Gematria* is an alpha-numeric cipher used by *Kabbalists* to divine the secret meanings of words and formulas.

[335] Kaplan, Aryeh, MEDITATION AND *KABBALAH*, page 81.

[336] Moshe ben Maimon, 1135-1204.

oil, as described by *Merkabah* mystics. While Abulafia was mainly interested in the meditating on letter combinations to achieve ecstatic experiences, he had some interest in the creation of a *golem*. A popular meditative technique that Abulafia used to spin the Gates was linked the creation of the *golem*.

"At the beginning of the [act of] formation [*yetzirah*], the person has to be acquainted with the quality of the weight [*tuv ha-mishqal*], the combination [*tzeruf*] and the variation [*hillut*]." [337] To accomplish this, one has to be familiar with the Hebrew alphabet, the combination techniques of the Hebrew letters, and how to construct the 231 Gates.

Abulafia then instructs to "Turn the wheel in the middle, and begin to combine until the two hundred and thirty-one gates [are computed], and [then] he will receive the influx of wisdom. When he receives the influx, let him [then] recite speedily the circle of velocity, which is the divine spirit." [338]

Abulafia continues: "He has to be very cautious not to change a letter or a vowel from its place because the limb created by the means of this letter will change its natural place in your body... Know that there are three issues created in man...the head, created out of fire...the belly [created out of] water...and the torso [created out of] wind [*Ruach*]." [339]

There is an organic affinity between the letters and vital organs so that the proper pronunciation of the order of letters is strictly necessary, Abulafia emphasizes. The pronunciation of the letters is accompanied by imaging the limbs corresponding to these letters. Along with self-contemplation while the letters are being recited to each of the limbs.

There also seems to be some common content between Abulafia's book and *SEFER RAZIEL HAMELECH,* especially in the description of the 72 angelic names that are based on the 3 lines of Exodus 14:19-21. The Divine Name is derived from those three verses in Exodus and Abulafia suggests to "transpose and permutate" the letters, as described earlier in this volume, "until your heart is warmed as a result of these permutations. When you experience this feeling, the permutator gains new knowledge and is able to receive the influx (*shefa*)." [340]

---

[337] Idel, Moshe, *GOLEM*: JEWISH MAGICAL, page 97.

[338] Abraham Abulafia, quoted in "THE *GOLEM*: JEWISH MAGICAL by Idel, Moshe, pages 97-98.

[339] In Hebrew *Ruach* also means spirit.

[340] From *CHAYE HAOLAM HABA* (THE WORLD TO COME OR LIFE IN THE FUTURE WORLD). See MEDITATION AND KABBALAH, by Aryeh Kaplan, page 96-106 for more translations and several letter techniques.

Hebrew Letters & Parts of the Body

*"Know that all the limbs of your body
are combined like that of the
forms of the letters combined with one another."*

Rabbi Abraham Abulafia [341]

Abraham Abulafia was one of many *Kabbalists* who believed that there is an organic connection between the 22 letters of the Hebrew alphabet and specific parts of the human or animal body. [342]

According to tradition, when one contemplates (*kavanah*) on a certain organ or limb, and the proper pronunciation is sounded, that part of the body is stimulated and will evoke a "creative act." All 22 letters must be correctly spoken in a specific order to achieve the full results.

In Rabbi Abulafia's ecstatic experience, upon successful completion of the entire process, a spiritual human form– the double-image of the mystic– will emerge and will communicate with the mystic.

Each letter has its own form of breathing. While being pronounced, the head is moved to the left, right, up and down in accordance to each of the four directions and the particular vowel point that is required. However, there is disagreement about the correct order, even among the learned rabbis.

The first action to animate the organ, according to Yehuda Hadassi, a 12th century Jewish scholar, is to pronounce each letter (consonant) and concentrate on that corresponding body part. Then, the vowels are pronounced with a certain incantation that results in a spiritual experience.

At the end of the 20th century, psychologists theorized [343] that the brain identifies vowels and

---

[341] Abulafia, Abraham, SEPHER SITRE TORAH, from Moshe Idel, LANGUAGE, TORAH, AND HERMENEUTICS IN ABRAHAM ABULAFIA, page 7.

[342] This correlation system between the limbs of the body and the 22 letters is described in chapter 4 of the SEPHER YETZIRAH and Abulafia's CHAYYEI HA-OLAM HABA.

[343] "A selective deficit for writing vowels in acquired dysgraphia," by Robert Cubelli. NCBI, Nature.

consonants as two separate mechanisms. They observed two Italian men who had strokes that damaged the left side of their brain, leaving them with difficulties writing down vowels.

The first patient omitted all vowels when writing words and left a blank space between consonants. The second patient produced errors that involved writing vowels. It is possible that the brain might subconsciously separate words into vowels and consonants. The vowels allow the letters to be fully pronounced.

In Hebrew, the consonant letters do not have any sound by themselves. The human mouth is given the power to express them through speech and reading. The vowels were provided to indicate the sound that must be expressed with each consonant.

According the *Kabbalah*, the consonants are the vessels and the vowels are the "soul" of the letter. The *Kabbalist* needed to know how to draw out the sound of each letter as it was related to both time and space.

1991 Sep 19; 353 (6341): 258-60.

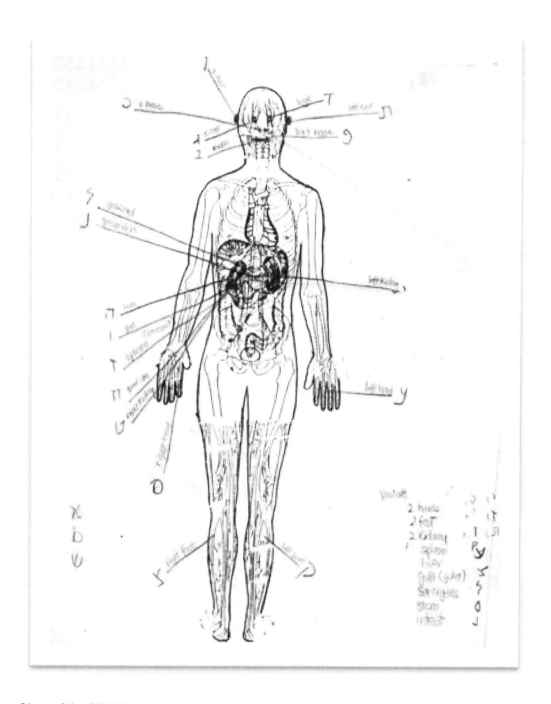

Chart of the 22 Hebrew letters matched to the limbs and organs of the human body. Drawn from Robert Zucker's personal notes, circa 1986.

The three vowels, *HWY*, are considered to be the souls of all of the other letters, according to the SEPHER YETZIRAH, the BOOK OF FORMATION.

The three circles represent each of the three vowels acting as crowns upon the letter Shin (ש).

The Hebrew Vowels

"The letter is like matter
and the vowel is like the spirit that animates it."

Abraham Abulafia, OR HA SHEKEL [344]

Vowels are considered the 'soul' of a letter or a word. The form of the letter– its vessel– is similar to physical matter, while the vowel brings it to life. Several of the 22 letters serve as vowels, indicating a specific sound that must be expressed when read or spoken out loud.

Early Hebrew did not use the dots and dashes to represent the sounds of the vowels as we know today. It wasn't until the 5th century C.E. when a group of scribes developed a system of vowel marks called *neqqudot*.

Before then, some of the consonants acted like vowel sounds, such as *Aleph* (א), *Yod* (י), *Vav* (ו).

Some believe there is a fourth vowel, *Hey* (ה), when it occurs at the end of a word.

Mystically, and spiritually, the vowels serve two functions:

- indicate the appropriate sounds in reciting the letters, and
- signal the appropriate head movements used in recitation.

---

[344] Abulafia, Abraham, OR HASHEKHEL. Source: Idel, Moshe, LANGUAGE, TORAH, AND HERMENEUTICS IN ABRAHAM ABULAFIA, page 8.

Abulafia's fortune & mystical writings

A vision Rabbi Abulafia had in the fall of 1280 [345] compelled him to personally condemn the anti-Semitic Pope Nicholas III [346] in Rome. Upon hearing this, the Christian authorities and Roman Rabbis sealed his fate with the Pope who ordered him burned at the stake.

On the Eve of *Rosh Hashana* (Jewish New Year), as Abulafia stood at the edge of Rome's boundaries, he was informed that the Pope had died during the night. His life was spared. [347]

Abulafia's *Kabalistic* writings spanned from 1273 through 1291, including his popular *PERUSH SEPHER YETZIRAH* (Commentary on *SEPHER YETZIRAH*). [348] He often mentioned Rabbi Eleazar's works on *Kabbalah*.

About 1285, Abulafia wrote *OTZAR EDEN GANUZ* ("THE HIDDEN TREASURE OF EDEN") with another lengthy discussion the *SEPHER YETZIRAH*. In 1289, he produced another commentary on the *SEPHER YETZIRAH* called *GAN NA'UL* (THE LOCKED GARDEN). [349]

Some of the dozens of *Kabbalistic* books authored by, or attributed to, Abulafia include:

- *CHAYE HAOLAM HABA* (THE FUTURE LIFE OF THE WORLD), 1280. Abraham Abulafia's masterpiece and a primer on prophetic *Kabbalah*.

- *GAN NA'UL*, a commentary on *SEPHER YETZIRAH*.
- *OR HASHEKHEL* ("LIGHT OF THE INTELLECT") is Abulafia's handbook on meditation, 1285.
- *SEPHER HA-GEULAH*, commentary to the GUIDE FOR THE PERPLEXED, 1273
- *SEPHER CHAYE HA-NEPHESH*, a second commentary to GUIDE FOR THE PERPLEXED
- *SEPHER HA -OT* ("BOOK OF SIGNS") relates his experiences and visions, some of which are really frightening. Most notable are his encounters with angels, 1285-88.
- *SEPHER HA-TZERUF* by an anonymous author attributed to Abulafia, translated into

---

[345] Reported as Hebrew year 5040 C.E.

[346] Pope Nicholas was born Giovanni Gaetano Orsini on 1216 and died in 1280.

[347] Idel, Moshe, THE MYSTICAL EXPERIENCE IN ABRAHAM ABULAFIA, page 5.

[348] "Abraham Abulafia," Wikipedia.com for a list of works and biography.

[349] Munich Ms. 58 printed in part in 1785 by Koretz. Source: *SEPHER YETZIRAH*: THEORY, by Aryeh Kaplan, p. 324. Reprinted in 1785.

Latin by Pico.

- *OTZAR EDEN GANUZ* (LOCKED GARDEN OF EDEN), commentary on *SEPHER YETZIRAH* 2, 1285-86.
- *GET HA-SHEMOT* – (DIVORCE OF NAMES) is Abulafia's attempt to describe the general ideology and cosmology that underlie the fundamental principle of *Kabbalah* - that names and letters are the essential, active, and creative elements of reality.
- *SHEVA NETIVOT HA-TORAH* demonstrates the primacy of *Kabbalah* over every other branch of knowledge. It classifies seven levels of understanding of the *TORAH*, showing what they are and how to reach them.

In about 1295, a possible disciple of Abulafia, *Ba'al Shem Tov* of Borgus, wrote a book in Hebron called *SHAAREY TZION* (GATES OF RIGHTEOUSNESS) that included discussions with Abulafia. Many copies of the book circulated and it was popular among *Kabbalists* in the Holy Land.

Over 200 years later, Abulafia's works became known by the book Shaarey Tzadek. The chief rabbi of Jerusalem at that time, Rabbi Judah Albotini wrote a book based on Abulafia's teachings called SULAM HAALIYAH (LADDER OF ASCENT) where he uses an entire chapter from GATES OF RIGHTEOUSNESS.

Abulafia: The 70 Languages

"And it is stated in the HAGGAGDAH [the angel] Gabriel came and taught him seventy languages in one night. And if you believe that [what was taught was] the actual languages, you make a foolish error. Rather, this is Gabriel, regarding whom it was written, [350] 'Then, I heard a holy one speak" i.e. he was speaking in the holy tongue... In actuality, he taught him the order of all languages, derived from the SEPHER YETZIRAH by very subtle means... so that he will recognize the order that reveals the ways of all languages— however many there may be.

And it is not meant that there are necessarily only 70 languages or [even] thousands of them.

The true tradition that we have received states that anyone who is not proficient in letter combination, and [who is not] tested and expert in it, and in the numerology of letters, and in their differences and their means of exchange, as these methods are taught in SEPHER YETZIRAH, does not know the Name [or God] in accordance with our method."

Rabbi Abraham Abulafia [351]

---

[350] Following Daniel 8:13.

[351] From *PERUSH YETZIRAH* (Commentary on *SEPHER YETZIRAH*), by Abraham Abulafia (c 1250), see Idel, Moshe, LANGUAGE, TORAH, AND HERMENEUTICS IN ABRAHAM ABULAFIA, page 9.

Combining the Hebrew Letters- *Tzeruf*

"Every word of God is permutated (tzeruf).
Proverbs 30:5

TzeRuF (צרף) is the act of letter permutation– combining and interchanging the Hebrew letters to form different words. This technique was only known among the most learned and esteemed scholars. It was expressly advocated by Rabbi Abraham Abulafia as a method to achieve spiritual enlightenment.

The process uses visualization and sound to obtain spiritual ecstasy. The repeated pronunciation of the word combinations produces a mental disorientation that leads to enlightenment. The continuous recitation evokes an altered state of consciousness where words evolve beyond their meanings.

Tzeruf comes from the Hebrew word *TzR* (צר) which mean to bind, wrap, refine or smelt together. By adding the final *F* (ף) to the word, it means joining or fusing something together.

Two of the letters *Tzadek* (צ) and *Resh* (ר) are also used in the word *Yetzirah* (יצרה) which means "formation."

In combination with specific breathing techniques, and the contemplation on body centers, meditations on the letters can produce this ecstasy almost immediately.

Similar methods to attain different levels of consciousness have been long used by Christians, Chaldeans, Muslims, Japanese, Egyptians and Hindu, among others.

When Abraham "occupied himself with the combination of letters of *Sepher Yetzirah*" [352] he was instructed how to "permutate, weigh and transform" the letters. Combining and meditating on the Hebrew letters with the Divine Name is one method of *Kavanah*, or Jewish meditation.

---

[352] Idel, Moshe, *Golem: Jewish Magical*, page 139. Translated from Rabbi Joseph ben Shalom Ashkenazi in his *Commentary on Sepher Yetzirah*, fol. 60a.

According to Jewish practice, one had to not only pronounce the combinations in a strict manner, but also had to construct the combinations as part of the ritual.

In rabbinical literature and *TALMUDIC* statements, the world was created by the combination of letters, possibly using the letters of the Divine Name. In the *TALMUD*, every letter in the alphabet has a symbolic meaning.

The Babylonian *TALMUD*, compiled around the 4th Century C.E., made a reference to Bezalel, the son of Uri of the tribe of Judah, who knew how to join together (*le-tze-ref*) the letters "by means of which the Heavens and the Earth were created." [353]

According to Exodus, Bezalel was "filled with the spirit of God, with wisdom and understanding, and in knowledge, and in all manner of workmanship." [354] Bezalel [355] [356] [357] was the chief architect of the Tabernacle in the desert since he had the sacred knowledge of letter permutation (joining together, *le-Tzeruf* צרף). That expertise also charged him with authority to build the Ark of the Covenant. [358]

The practice of combining and permutating letters with the Divine Name occurred especially during the time of R. Eleazar of Worms in the 12th century, Rabbi Abulafia in the 13th century, and among the *Ashkenazi* Jews in Europe.

While R. Eleazar wanted to keep the correct pronunciation of the Divine Name secret because it might be mishandled, Abulafia sought to reveal it, believing that the *Messianic* era arrived.

An anonymous author wrote that one can "pronounce the Holy Names or the names of the angels in order to be shown [whatever] he wishes, or to inform him of a hidden nature, and then the Holy Spirit reveals itself to him, and his flesh trembles because of the strength of the Holy Spirit." [359]

---

[353] Babylonian *TALMUD, TRACTATE BERAKOTH 55A.*

[354] Exodus 31:1-6 and chapters 36-39. "And He hath filled him with the spirit of God, in wisdom and in understanding, and in knowledge."

[355] Bezalel is described in the genealogical lists as the son of Uri, the son of Hur, of the tribe of Judah (I Chron. ii. 18, 19, 20, 50), from "Bezalell, by Jastrow, Morris Jr., Charles Foster Kent and Louis Ginsberg, JEWISH ENCYCLOPEDIA (unedited full-text of the 1906 Jewish Encyclopedia).

[356] TB *Berachoth*, 55a. Referenced: Abelson, Joshua, JEWISH MYSTICISM. Page 100.

[357] Idel, Moshe, ABSORBING PERFECTIONS: *KABBALAH* AND INTERPRETATIOn, page 32.

[358] Exodus 31:1-6 and chapters 36 to 39.

[359] Idel, Moshe, *KABBALAH* NEW PERSPECTIVES, page 98; from *SEPHER HA-HAYYIM*, MS Cambridge, Add 643, fol. 19a; Ms. Oxford 1547, fol. 34b; MS Vatican 431, fol 39.

The first step of *tzeruf* is the act of permutation. The Hebrew letters are combined and interchanged to form different words in order to obtain spiritual ecstasy. The repeated pronunciation of the word combinations produces a disorientation that leads to enlightenment. Out of that comes "meaning beyond meaning."

Israel Eliyahu *Ba'al Shem Tov*, [360] the father of *Hasidism* and a well-known Jewish mystical rabbi of the 18th century, believed that when the *Messiah* comes, he will interpret the entire *TORAH* from beginning to end, according to all of the combinations within each word. This will reveal the true secrets of the *TORAH*. [361] *Baal Shem*, means Master of the Divine Name.

The characteristic feature, described in the *SEPHER YETZIRAH*, is the combinations of each set of letters (or "Gate") with a vowel of the *Tetragrammaton*, according to every possible vocalization. This produces 231 Gates.

By pairing these "combinations" with the appropriate vowels, and meditating or chanting each of the 231 Gates, the non-existent can be made to exist and something can be created out of nothing. The assumption is that if one combines the letters of the alphabet properly, the creative process used by God in the formation of the world can be re-enacted.

A quote from the late 13th or early 14th century in a manuscript called THE GATES (*SHE'ARIM*) reveals the secrets of *tzeruf* [combination of letters]:

---

[360] R. Israel, the *Ba'al Shem Tov*, was born in 1698 and died in 1760 in Ukraine.

[361] Sears, Dovid, THE PATH OF THE *BAAL SHEM TOV*: EARLY *CHASDIC* TEACHINGS AND CUSTOMS, page 99.

"Great is the power of the tzeruf."

He answered to us, "You know that by the combination of the letters of His names, God created everything.

And our ancestor, blessed be his memory, out of the combination of the letters which he was taught...

he achieved the entire gist of His unity and the strength of all the formations, and he almost reached that degree that he knew how to form excellent formations of thought [yezirot mahshaviyot].

This is the reason he called his excellent book by the name "SEPHER YEZIRAH." [362]

---

[362] From THE GATES (*SHE-ARIM*) OF THE OLD MAN (*ha-zaqen*)," a late 13th or early 14th century *Kabbalistic* text. edited from "*GOLEM*: Jewish Magical," by Moshe Idel. Page 112.

Creation of the World by the Letters

YTz. The word comes from the two Hebrew root letters: *Tzaddick* and *Resh* (Tz R) which means "to shape, to form."

YTzR. When a *Yod* (Y) is added the word before Tz R, it means "to form."

YTzH. The Hebrew word *yetzir* (Y Tz R)

YTzRH. The Hebrew word *yetzirah* (Y Tz I R H) means "a formation, such as a work of art– an object that is formed. It can also mean "the act of creating." This is also the Hebrew spelling to the Hebrew name of the BOOK OF FORMATION– *SEPHER YETZIRAH.*

Harkavah– Grafting Letters

The act of combining letters was known to the sages by a tradition from the prophets as "grafting" (הרכבה *harkavah*) of one letter to another, a new word to another, or one Divine Name to another, according to Rabbi Abulafia." [363]

Harkavah is similar to grafting one tree branch to another to morph into a single branch, or cross-breeding animals to merge two species into one.

Grafting letters involves joining two separate letters to form one word, also called a "Gate." Advanced grafting techniques included using the Divine Name in every permutation possible. When all of these letter combinations are correctly "grafted" wisdom is given to the one who "gazes, sees and understands."

In an example, to graft the first two letters of the Hebrew alphabet, join them together so that the two independent letters for a single set, or "Gate."

$$אב = ב + א$$

$$AB = B + A$$

---

[363] Idel, Moshe, MYSTICAL EXPERIENCE IN ABRAHAM ABULAFIA, page 21.

5 Steps of Letter Permutation

According to Chapter 2:2 of the *SEPHER YETZIRAH*, there are five steps necessary to properly construct the alphabets. It involves using the voice, breath and imagination to mentally form, and arrange, the letters.

1. Engrave   חקק   engrave (hew) with voice   imagine each letter as it is spoken

2. Hew   חצב   carve with breath   express sound in 5 places of the mouth

3. Permutate   צרף   combine letters   (*"Aleph with aleph…"*)

4. Weigh   שקל   balance one letter against the other with the vowels

5. Transform   צור   cycle the letters, with the vowels, to form new words

To begin the process: rid all imagery from the mind, except for a single letter, such as the first letter of the Hebrew alphabet– *Aleph* (א). Then, carve out the image of the letter in your imagination.

Hewing & Carving the Letters

The 22 Hebrew letters can become visible, tangible, entities that are carved in the mind's imagination and "hewn" from the breath. The sound of the letter, produced by the breath, "hews" each letter, one by one, according to instructions in the *SEPHER YETZIRAH*. [364]

To "hew, or engrave" (חק *ChK*) and "Carve" (צב *TzV*) and are the two processes to depict the letters in the mind. [365]

This is similar to molding a shape from a lump of clay. One way to hew an image is to surround the letter with pure white or black. The form of the letter is filled with the opposite shade of color. Hewing implies separating the image from the others.

To engrave the letter means to fix an image in the mind's eye so it does not waver or move. The engraved image remains no matter whatever other thoughts or images arise in the mind. This meditation technique becomes an easy process once mastered and is a critical step to next process.

As an example, concentrate on the letter *Aleph* (א) until the entire letter fills your entire mind. Then, carve the shape of the letter from out of that darkness. Imagine the letter shaped in white with a black background. Or, imagine the letter in black protruding out of the blinding white light. This is the act of hewing and carving.

The correct pronunciation of each letter, the position of the tongue, shape of the mouth, and the proportion of inhalation and exhalation are necessary to form, or carve, these letters into "vessels." Use either of the five spots in the mouth to produce each specific sound– the throat, that palate, the tongue, the teeth and the lips. [366]

Combine each letter of the alphabet with another and rotate through the alphabet from *Aleph* to

---

[364] *SEPHER YETZIRAH* 2:3 "With the 22 letters– engrave with voice, carve with the breath and set in the mouth in five places."

[365] *SEPHER YETZIRAH* 2:3 "Engrave them with voice and hew (carve) them with breath."

[366] *SEPHER YETZIRAH* 2:3. The five places in the mouth are the throat to produce the "guttural" letters (*Aleph, Chet, Heh, Ayin*); the palate to sound out the "palatal" letters (*Gimel, Yud, Kaf*); using the tongue to pronounce the "lingual" letters (*Daleth, Tet, Lamed, Nun, Tav*); and the "dentals" (*Zayin, Samech, Shin, Resh, Tzadik*) through the teeth; and producing the "labial" letters (*Bayt, Vav, Mem, Peh*) through the lips.

Tav, using the "*Aleph* with *aleph…* method to form 231 pairs, or "Gates."

The three vowels (Y, H, V) are added to "balance" or "weigh" each Gate. The exact order of the vowels, however, has been the most coveted secret among *Kabbalaists*.

The letters are exchanged with each other (permutated) and engraved on a "wall (carved on a blank canvass of the mind)," as described in SEPHER YETZIRAH 1:11. They are represented in the chart of the 231 Holy Gates (2-letter combinations) used by R. Shabbathai Donnolo hundreds of years earlier, and, later by Rabbi Eleazar of Worms.

The 231 Gates are just half of the combination of the letters, Rabbi Isaac the Blind explained, since there are actually 462 alphabet combinations– twice as many. Half of them are "above" the horizon line on the "wall" and the other half are "below." The use of the word "wall" is a descriptive way to imagine the entire 462 Gates side by side in columns, like a "wall with 231 Gates." [367] Rabbi Isaac the Blind's vision helped transform Geonic mysticism into the concepts of *Kabbalah* that have become accepted practices over the next centuries.

---

[367] SEPHER YETZIRAH 2:4. The 22 letters are placed in a circle, like a wall, with 231 Gates. The circle rotates back and forth. This activity can be demonstrated with the *Kabbalah* Wheel, a hand-made device that spin the circles like wheels.

Letter Permutation Techniques

*"A permutator (tzeruf צרף) for silver
and the furnace for gold.
But, God tests the heart."*

Proverbs 17:3

There are several secret methods of letter permutation (*tzeruf* צרף) that divide the Hebrew letters into groups according to specific criteria.

These techniques were used to reveal the Wisdom of letter permutation. Through meditation, the continuous recitation of sounds, produced from the word combinations, eventually induces an altered state of consciousness and a spiritual experience. Some of these techniques were advocated by Rabbi Abraham Abulafia.

While there are dozens of different methods, some of the more popular permutation techniques include *ALBM, AYQBKR,* and *ATBASh.*

'AL-BM' Method

AL-BM (אל—במ also called *Albam*) is the one of the most well-known forms of letter substitution, where the alphabet is divided into two equal groups of eleven letters. The two groups are paired, like columns. The name, *AL-BM* refers to the first two of these transformation pairs (gates).

א *Aleph* (A)   ל *Lamed* (L)

ב *Bayt* (B)   מ *Mem*(M)

ג *Gimel*   נ *Nun*

ד *Daleth...*   ס *Samech*, etc...

The permutation (*tzeruf*) of the first eleven letters from *Aleph* to *Lamed* with each of the 22 letters of the entire alphabet, often mentioned the creation of the *golem*.

The key to the *Aleph-Lamed* (ל א) *AL* technique is to avoid the repetition of the same letters twice. The *AL* method is often mentioned when constructing the 231 Gates.

'AYQ BeKer' Method

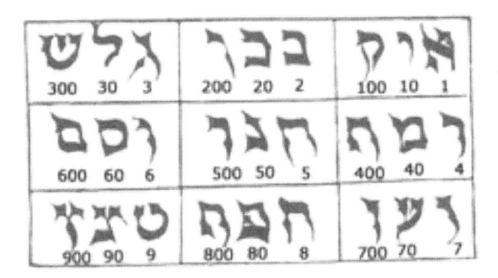

This letter combination technique is known as the "*Qabalah* of 9 Chambers." The *AYQBKR* (בכר—איק) arrangement is used in the formation of symbols or sigils. The name is taken from the first two chambers: *AYQ, BChR.* Three chambers containing three letters each are stacked in three rows:

איק בכר גלש

דמת הנך וסם

זען חפף טצץ

'AT-BASH' Method

A T-BASh (אב—שׁ) is a common letter transformation method where first letter is substituted for the last letter of the alphabet, the second for the second to the last, etc. basically reversing the alphabet.

This method consists of 11 pairs of letters. The first row represents one gate and the second row is the other gate. Using this process, the English word "HOB" can be "at-bashed" into the word "*SLY*" as an example in English:

First 13 letters: A|B|C|D|E|F|G|H|I|J|K|L|M

Last 13 letters: Z|Y|X|W|V|U|T|S|R|Q|P|O|N

Julius Caesar communicated with his generals using a similar encryption technique known as the Caesar Cipher. The device operated like a wheel within a wheel. Each wheel could be adjusted to fit the cipher being used. Numerous alphabets can be devised depending on which two core letters are used.

The Caesar Cipher device is similar to the *Kabbalah* Wheel, described in the Appendix. This was the inspiration to create a *Kabbalah* Wheel.

Over the centuries, there were dozens of other permutation exercises to achieve a variety of spiritual results.

Abracadabara! "I create as I speak"

אברא כדברא

A medieval drawing of a magician teaching the basic principles of the occult using the *Abaracadabara* formula. Image from Zedcor Graphics.

ne of the most well-known magical charms is the *Abaracadabara* chant. It has mistakenly been associated with Jewish mysticism, especially during the Middle Ages. Many of the medieval magical formulas were often attributed to Jewish magic, although they may have been actually devised by non-Jews who practiced a corrupted form of magic.

In a 3rd century medical manuscript called *LIBER MEDICINALIS,* [368] written by physician Quintus Serenus Sammonicus, [369] the incantation was reportedly used among the Greeks to dispel malaria. Sufferers wear an amulet around the neck inscribed with the words in the form of a descending triangle.

Sammonicus explained that the power of the amulet makes the disease dissolve away. As the letters gradually disappear, so does the affliction.

The phrase *Abaracadabara* originally may be Aramaic (meaning, "I create as I speak"). In Hebrew, it could translate as "it came to pass as it was spoken."

The syllables of *A bara cada bara* contains the Hebrew word *bara* (ברא which means to "create") twice. [370]

The letters of *Abracadabara* are written out in rows. The final letter is dropped with each line until only the first A remains.

---

[368] Vollmer, Friedrich, *QUINTI SERNI SAMONICI DE MEDICINA*, Leipzig: Teubner, 1916. Chapter LII (52), page 150. The chapter title is *Hemitritaeo depellendo* (Tertian Fever- a fever that lasts 36 hours).

[369] Quintas Serenus Sammonicus was the physician to the Roman emperor Caracalla. He died in 211 C.E.

[370] The remaining letters add up to 26, the numerical value of the *Tetragrammaton*. Kaplan, Aryeh, *SEPHER YETZIRAH*: THEORY, page 348, footnote 106.

A B A R A C A D A B A R A
A B A R A C A D A B A R
A B A R A C A D A B A
A B A R A C A D A B
A B A R A C A D A
A B A R A C A
A B A R A
A B A R
A B A
A B
A

אבראכדברא
בראכדברא
ראכדברא
אכדברא
כדברא
דברא
רא
א

In another perspective, the letters *DABRA* (דבר) translates as "thing." The phrase *Abaraca-dabara* could also mean "a created thing" in Hebrew.

The incantation was later used by 16th century English navigator Capt. Edward Fenton who described that one is healed of fever by "hanging *Abaracadabara* around the neck." [371] It appeared again in a passage by Daniel Defoe in 1722 as he ridiculed the use of charms and amulets to ward off the plague. [372]

Now, the phrase is only uttered by stage magicians to impress the audience as they attempt an illusionary feat and has no place in Jewish mysticism.

---

[371] Edward Fenton died in 1603. Cited in Eva Rimington Taylor's THE TROUBLESOME VOYAGE OF CAPT. EDWARD FENTON.

[372] Defoe, Daniel, JOURNAL OF THE PLAGUE YEAR, 1722. From THE WORKS OF DANIEL DEFOE, Volume 5, page 37, edited by Howard Maynadier, C.T. Brainard, 1904.

Medieval Mystic Writings

Late in the 13th century, the *BAHIR* and the *ZOHAR* became exposed outside closed circles. This is also when the concepts of *Kabbalah* were introduced to the secular world.

Spanish *Kabbalist* and Rabbi Joseph ben Shalom *Ashkenazi* wrote a commentary on *SEPHER YETZIRAH*. Rabbi Joseph claimed he was a descendant of Judah ben Samuel *he-Chasid* and was revealing ancient secrets passed down to him. He was heavily influenced by Rabbi Eleazar of Worms and provided a unique recipe for creating a *golem,* including using color visualization as part of his meditative technique. [373]

Rabbi Joseph also mentioned the *Kabbalistic* formulas from Isaac ben Samuel of Acre who was an expert in composing sacred names using the Hebrew alphabet (*tzeruf*). [374] In 1305, he fled the Crusader-controlled town of Acre and went to Spain where he composed several commentaries [375] on *Kabbalah.*

In Joseph's Commentary on the *SEPHER YETZIRAH*, he follows Rabbi Eleazar's instructions to initiate a creative act. Rabbi Joseph suggested one technique to assemble the 231 Gates and

divide the Hebrew alphabet into the *AB* (אב) to *AK* (אכ) arrangement for 'creation' (*mizad ha-hesed livriy'ato*).

אב, אג , אד, אה... (*AB, AG, AD, AH...*)

There is a one order of the letters for the process of creation, and one arrangement for its reversal, he explained. [376] The first half of the combinations of the letters form the creative process of the 231 Gates, and the remaining half forms the destructive process. Those combinations are laid out Rabbi Eleazar's chart of Gates.

Italian Rabbi Menahem ben Benjamin Recanati (1250-1310) produced two manuscripts called

---

[373] Ms. Sassoon 290, *GOLEM: JEWISH MAGICAL*, by Idel, Moshe, page 118.

[374] Kaufmann Kohler, M. Seligsohn, ISAAC BEN SAMUEL OF ACRE, JEWISH ENCYCLOPEDIA (1918).

[375] One major book was *MEIRAT ENAYIM*, a *Kabbalistic* commentary on Nahmanides' commentary to the Pentateuch.

[376] Idel, Moshe, *GOLEM: JEWISH MAGICAL*, page 120. The work is published in Mantua, 1562.

PERUSH HA-TEFILLOT (COMMENTARY ON PRAYERS) and *TA'AME HA-MIẒWOT*. These included the shorter version of *SEPHER YETZIRAH* and commentaries on *SEPHER YETZIRAH* by R. Azriel of Gerona, R. Dunash Ibn Tamin, an anonymous *Ashkenazi* text, and content from Nahmanides and D. Abrams (as written by R. Yaaqov *ha-Kohen*). He also quoted mystical observations of Rabbi Judah *he-Chasid* of Regensburg and Rabbi Eleazar of Worms.

In 1263, *SEPHER YETZIRAH* version Z [377] was produced. The Hebrew compared with a copy in the National Library of Jerusalem's microfilm and proved to be an almost faultless original of Saadia Gaon recension published 300 years later in 1531 and then by Meyer Lambert in 1891.

THE BOOK OF LIFE (*SEPHER CHAYIM*), attributed to R. Abraham Ezra, appeared in 1268 with a similar story about the creation of a man with earth as its basic element. It also connected the *golem* with the influence of the planets and astrology. [378]

---

[377] Oxford Bodleian Library, 1533 (L) Paper. Adina-Baghdad. Also, see Ithamar Gruenwald, A PRELIMINARY CRITICAL EDITION OF *SEPHER YEZIRA*, page 135.

[378] Translated by Scholem Gershom, Ms. Munich 207, Fol. 10d-11a, and Cambridge, Add 643, Fol. 9a in ON THE *KABBALAH* AND ITS SYMBOLISM, by Scholem, Gershom, page 183.

The Brilliance of the ZOHAR

Spanish Rabbi Moses de Leon [379] revealed a manuscript in 1290 called the *ZOHAR* (זהר "Brilliance"), the literary foundation of the Jewish *Kabbalah*. It contained a commentary on the mystical view of the *TORAH* and scriptural interpretations on Jewish mysticism.

Although de Leon, a known *Kabbalist,* said he found the manuscripts in a cave in Israel, suspicion swirled that he was actually the author and not the claimed Shimon bar Yochai, the 2nd century *Tannatic* sage and disciple of R. Akiba.

The *ZOHAR* outlined the four levels of understanding, called *Pardes*, which are necessary when studying the *TORAH*. The Hebrew letters *PARDES* (פרדס) are taken from the first letter of each of the four levels:

- פ *Peshat* ("simple")– the direct meaning of the TORAH.

- ר *Remez* ("hint')– the allegorical meaning.

- ד *Deresh* ("inquire")– the Rabbinical meaning (*Midrash*).

- ס *Sod* ("secret")– the esoteric, metaphysical meaning (*Kabbalistic*).

Each level provides an extended meaning to the level above it. Everyone who is familiar with the words of the *TORAH* understands its direct meaning– whether in English or Hebrew. The allegories, myths and legends that have been tied to certain passages (many cited in this volume) reveal the hidden, or symbolic meaning behind the words in the *TORAH*.

The two other levels are only comprehended by learned rabbis and *Kabbalists*. Because of the *ZOHAR's* intense popularity, many other mystical manuscripts were not published and became lost or destroyed. However, the *ZOHAR* had little mention of meditative techniques so many of those practices became obscure.

---

[379] R. Moses de Leon was born in 1240 and died in 1305 in Spain. He was known in Hebrew as Moshe ben Shem-Tov.

Christian Cabala– 13th Century

Kabbalah came into contact with Christianity during the 13th century. Numerous *Kabbalistic* and *TALMUDIC* texts were translated into Spanish. Alfonso X of Castile, [380] who ruled Spain from 1252 until his death in 1284, had fostered a Judeo-Christian Muslim atmosphere.

This is when Christian scholars took a curious interest in the mystical practices of the Jewish people and developed the Christian Cabala. To distinguish their version of the practice Christian Cabalists spelled it as Cabala– using a C in place of a K for the word *Kabbalah*

An anonymous Italian commentary in the 13th century described how to create a creature [*"livro' beri'ah"*] using the 24 circles, vocalization and formation. [381] This became one of many instances where the creation of a being is connected with Hebrew letter combination techniques and many legends about the Jewish people were perpetuated.

Jewish philosopher, Christian apologist and Spanish Cabalist Abner de Burgos (1270-1347) interpreted his own dreams in a Cabalistic perspective as a sign of the truth of Christianity. He wrote about the Divine Names and their plurality and several apologetic works in Hebrew under the Christian name Alfonso de Valladolid. His *MOREH ZEDEQ/MOSTRADOR DE JUSTICE* was used to convert Jews who did not read Hebrew well. [382]

---

[380] Born on November 23, 1221 in Toledo, Spain and died April 4, 1284 in Seville, Spain.

[381] Ms. Parma 2784, Catalogue de Rossi 1390, Italy, *KABBALAH IN ITALY, A SURVEY* 1280-1510, Idel, Moshe, page 91.

[382] Abner of Burgos, Wikipedia.com.

14ᵗʰ Century (1300-1399)

The plague graphic. Zedcor Graphics.

The 14th century was filled with persecutions, expulsions and scapegoating of the Jews—even blaming them for the plague. During this century, several notable works attributed to Jewish magic were produced by anonymous authors. These books included THE KEY OF SOLOMON THE KING: *CLAVICULA SALOMONIS*, and THE BOOK OF THE SACRED MAGIC OF ABREMELIN THE MAGE (1458). They were translated into English in the 20th century by S.L. MacGregor Mathers.

Several versions of the *SEPHER YETZIRAH* were also produced in the 14th century.

- *SEPHER YETZIRAH* version "G" [383] written sometime during this period using Franco-German square writing. It included the Donnolo long recension of 913 and was full of mistakes, but preserved some old and important readings.
- *SEPHER YETZIRAH* "K," a short version of Tamin's work from the 9th century, was produced about 1316-1317. [384]
- *SEPHER YETZIRAH* "L," a short recension was produced in Italian. [385]
- *SEPHER YETZIRAH* "M," a short recension in Spanish. [386]
- *SEPHER YETZIRAH* "N" was written in Spanish (maybe in North Africa) between 1365 and 1393. [387]

In addition, a comprehensive commentary on *SEPHER YETZIRAH* was written by R. Joseph ben Shalom Ashkenazi in Spain, but it was erroneously attributed to R. Abraham ben David. [388]

Another commentary on *SEPHER YETZIRAH,* written in 1331 by Spanish *Kabbalist* Meir ben Solomon ibn Sahula (1251-1335), criticized Nahmanides writings and argued over the mystical account of creation. [389] R. Jacob ben Shalom, who came to Barcelona from Germany, wrote in 1325 that, in regard to the destruction of a *golem,* the laws of destruction are nothing more than

---

[383] Stored in the British Museum (Cat, Margoliouth) 752 (5), foll. 79b-81a. Vellum, A PRELIMINARY CRITICAL EDITION OF *SEPHER YEZIRA*, by Ithamar Gruenwald, page 135. The lettering attributed to each version is provided by Gruenwald.

[384] Parma De Rossi, foll 36b-38b. Italy, 1316/7.

[385] 802 (4), foll. 57b-59b. Vellum, A PRELIMINARY CRITICAL EDITION OF *SEPHER YEZIRA*, by Ithamar Gruenwald, page 136.

[386] "M" Paris 726 (2), foll. 44b-46b. Vellum, A PRELIMINARY CRITICAL EDITION OF *SEPHER YEZIRA*, by Ithamar Gruenwald, page 136.

[387] Paris 764 (1), foll. 1a-3a. Paper. A PRELIMINARY CRITICAL EDITION OF *SEPHER YEZIRA*, by Ithamar Gruenwald, page 136. ,

[388] Scholem, Gershom, ,KABBALAH, page 29.

[389] Sahula, Meir Ben Solomon Abi, ENCYCLOPEDIA JUDAICA. Angelica Library of Rome, (DeCaua 53), Ms. Or. 45.

a reversal of the laws of creation. [390]

The tales of the Egyptians were similar to the *golem* creation process, according to Arab Muslim historian Ibn Khaldun (1332-1406) who described an enchantment he witnessed in Muslim Egypt by the Nabatean sorcerers of the Lower Euphrates.

"We saw with our eyes one of these magicians fashion the image of the person he desired to bewitch," he wrote. "The images were composed of materials whose properties bear a certain relation to the intention and design of the operator and which represent symbolically, for the purpose of uniting and of separating, the names and characteristics of him who must be the victim." [391]

Nehunya ben ha-Kaneh (c. 1350-1390) copied the whole passage about Jeremiah the Prophet and Ben Sira in the *Kabbalistic* book SEPHER HA-PELI'AH, a commentary on the first section of the TORAH. [392] [393] But, one change is made using the phrase "*YHWH Elohim AMT.*" The other instructions remain the same. The first letter of the word *AMT* (meaning "truth") is crossed out leaving the Hebrew word for death, *MT* to destroy the creation [394]

Moroccan philosopher Yehudah ben Nissim ibn Malka wrote (c. 1365) in his Arabic Commentary on SEPHER YETZIRAH called *PIRKE DE-RABBI ELIEZER* (THE CHAPTERS OF RABBI ELEAZAR) that students of the book are given a magical manuscript named *SEPHER RAZIEL* that consisted of seals, magical figures, secret names, incantations and prayers. [395]

---

[390] Trechtenberg, Joshua, JEWISH MAGIC AND SUPERSTITION, page 85-86.

[391] Al-A'raaf 7:116. SEMITIC MAGIC, ITS ORIGINS AND DEVELOPMENT, by Reginald Campbell Thompson, page 144.

[392] de Herrera, Abraham Cohen, GATE OF HEAVEN, page 375.

[393] Scholem, Gershom, ON THE MYSTICAL SHAPE OF THE GODHEAD: BASIC CONCEPTS IN THE KABBALAH, page 305.

[394] Scholem, Gershom, ON THE *KABBALAH* AND ITS SYMBOLISM, page 180. cf. ed. Koretz, 1786, 36a.

[395] Oxford Ms. 1536. *SEPHER YETZIRAH*: THE BOOK OF CREATION IN THEORY AND PRACTICE, by Kaplan, Aryeh, page 341. Edited by Georges Vajda, *PHILOSOPHE JUIF MAROACIAN*, Paris, 1954, p171. Reprinted in 1974, Bar Ilan University.

Color and the *Kabbalah*

Since it was forbidden to visualize the ten *Sephiroth*, colors were substituted by the *Kabbalists*. Colors are the "covering" of the *Sephiroth*. This may have been the "world of lights" which emanated from the *Sephiroth*, according to the authors of *TIKKUNEY ZOHAR* and *RA'YA MEHEIMMA*.

While color-based meditation became a popular part of *Kabbalah* during the lifetime of Isaac the Blind, color attributes to the ten *Sephiroth* were first proposed by one of the founders of the *Chasidic* movement, Spanish *Kabbalist*, Rabbi David ben Yehudah *he-Chasid*, in the late 13th early to early 14th century. [396]

In the earliest text that explicitly refers to the use color as a mystical technique, Rabbi Yehuda remarked that we are "not allowed to directly visualize the ten *Sephiroth*." He suggested to imagine each sphere according to its respective color. [397] The imaginary "colors" are the "covering" or "vessel" of the *sephiroth*.

In the late 13th century, R. Joseph ben Shalom Ashkenazi included the visualization of colors as part of his meditative technique. [398] The relation between colors and the *Sefiroth* occurred several times in his Commentary on *SEPHER YETZIRAH* and Commentary on *GENESIS RABBAH*. [399]

R. Chayim Vital mentioned the use of color visualization in his *SHA'AREY KEDUSHAH* and ended with the ascent to *'Aravot*, where "one should visualize the firmament with a great white curtain upon which the *Tetragrammaton* is inscribed in [color] white as snow in Assyrian writing in a certain color." He copied this passage from R. Joseph Ashkenazi. [400]

R. Mohe Cordovero wrote in his 16th century *PARDES RIMONIM* (ORCHARD OF POMEGRANATES) that "it is good and fitting if he wishes to visualize these *havayot* [that is, the different vocalizations of the *Tetragrammaton* according to their color, as then his prayer will be very effective, on the condition that his [mystical] intention is that there is no other possible way to represent the activity of a certain attribute [but] the certain [corresponding] color. And as the colors in the gate of colors are many, we shall not discuss here the colors. But when he is

---

[396] Ms. Cambridge, Add. 505, fol. 8a, from Moshe Idel, NEW *KABBALAH*.

[397] Ms. Cambridge, Add. 505, fol. 8a, from Moshe Idel, *KABBALAH*: NEW PERSPECTIVES, page 104.

[398] Ms. Sassoon 290 from Idel, Moshe, *GOLEM*: JEWISH MAGICAL, p. 123, 126

[399] Idel, Moshe, *GOLEM*: JEWISH MAGICAL, p. 122

[400] Ms. British Library, 749, fol. 14b, 18a.

interested to direct his prayer behold that gate which is before [the eyes] of the disciple."

While there are some variations between the colors attributed to each *Sephiroth*, these are the most agreed upon:

Keter	White
Chochmah	Grey
Binah	Black
Chesed	Blue
Geburah	Red
Tiphereth	Yellow
Netzach	Green
Hod	Orange
Yesod	Purple
Malkuth	Brown or a combination of colors

These colors are represented on the Tree of Life diagram on the back cover of this volume.

15ᵗʰ Century (1400-1499)

Before the Expulsion from Spain in 1492, German *Chasidic Ashkenazi* scholars and *Kabbalists* introduced the concept of the *golem* as a way to demonstrate their superiority over Greek science and philosophy. An interest in the *golem* tale among Christian authors further developed during the Renaissance period, especially in Italy where Jewish culture flourished during the diaspora.

After the hand-operated metal movable type– the printing press– was devised in 1440 by Johannes Gutenberg, [401] the spread of the *Kabbalah* spawned hundreds of printed versions, and variations, of the *SEPHER YETZIRAH*. The first Jewish prayer book was published in Venice, Italy in 1486. [402]

Rabbi Yehuda (Judah) Albotini (1453-1519), a *TALMUDIC* scholar and author of a commentary of Maimonides, was best known in the *Kabbalah* community for writing *SULAM HAALIYAH* (LADDER OF ASCENT).

Albotini taught Jewish meditation (*kavanah)* and its connection with Abulafia's mystical methods. He was well versed in letter manipulation techniques (*tzeruf*). Albotini also supported the notion that continuous recitation of the letters produced an altered state of consciousness and a spiritual ecstasy. Combining the Hebrew letters with the Divine Name was another, more sacred, method of *kavanah*.

In LADDER OF ASCENT, Albotini explained that "the other prophets and pious men in each generation, by means of the combination and permutation of letters and their movement, used to perform miracles and wonders and turn about the order of Creation such as we find it explained in our *TALMUD* that Rava created a man and sent him to R. Zera." [403]

Italian Rabbis Yhanan Alemanno, [404] David Messer Leon, [405] and Abraham de Balmes [406] studied together in one group. Alemanno, who taught that *Kabbalah* was divine magic, compiled

---

[401] Born in 1398 and died in 1468.

[402] Isidore Singer, The JEWISH ENCYCLOPEDIA: Philipson-Samoscz, page 172.

[403] Idel, Moshe, MYSTICAL EXPERIENCE IN ABRAHAM ABULAFIA, page 37.

[404] Rabbi Yhanan Alemanno was born in Constantinople in 1435 and died after 1504.

[405] Italian physician, writer and rabbi David Messer Leon was born in 1470 and died in 1526.

[406] Abraham de Balmes was born in Italy in 1440 and died in 1523 in Italy. He was a Jewish physician and translator. He wrote *MIKNEH AVRAM* [THE POSSESSION OF ABRAM] in 1523.

a list of animals that can be created by the combinations of letters using the instructions in the *SEPHER YETZIRAH*. [407] He was a Hebrew teacher to Pico della Mirandola, one of the first Christians to introduce Jewish *Kabbalah* to the Christian world.

In R. Leon's *Kabbalistic* work, *MAGEN DAVID*, he quoted Greek and Arabic philosophers. Their exposure to the earlier forms of medieval and Jewish philosophy had an effect on their religious training and often brought them into conflict with more conservative views of *Kabbalah*. [408]

In the 1480s onward, certain Jewish intellectuals interpreted the *Kabbalah* in line with philosophical concepts that were widespread at the time. When the Jews were expelled from Spain in 1492, many relocated to Poland and the town of Safed in the Galilee and took their *Kabbalah* teachings with them.

---

[407] Ms. Paris (BN) 849, fol. 6b: "ox, sheep, and a calf." From *GOLEM: JEWISH MAGICAL*, by Moshe Idel, page 281.

[408] Idel, Moshe, JUDAH MOSCATO: A LATE RENAISSANCE JEWISH PREACHER.

15th Century Editions of SEPHER YETZIRAH

Spanish scholar and astronomer Rabbi Moses Botarel Farissol wrote a commentary on *SEPHER YETZIRAH* in 1409. He quoted earlier authors and cited false quotations from his predecessors. His commentary was later printed at Mantua in 1562 and republished in 1745 (Zolkiev), 1806 (Grodno), and 1820 (Vilna). [409]

Two short recensions of Tamin's work were produced during the 15th century, both with Spanish characters– *SEPHER YETZIRAH* "P" [410] and *SEPHER YETZIRAH* "Tz." [411]

In Italy, a copy of *SEPHER YETZIRAH* "D" [412] was produced with the long recension of Donnolo.

In the late 15th or beginning of the 16th century, *SEPHER YETZIRAH* "Q" is produced in Germany with both of the Tamin and the Saadia Gaon versions. [413]

---

[409] Moses Botriel, Wikipedia.com.

[410] Cincinnati 523. Gruenwald, Ithamar, A PRELIMINARY CRITICAL EDITION OF *SEPHER YEZIRA*, page 136.

[411] British Museum, Gaster 415, foll. 29a-32a. Gruenwald, Ithamar, A PRELIMINARY CRITICAL EDITION OF *SEPHER YEZIRA*, page 136.

[412] Firenze Mediceo-Laurentiana Pluteo II codex V (8), foll. 227a-229b.

[413] Moscow Ginzburg collection 133, foll. 198a-199a. Gruenwald, Ithamar, A PRELIMINARY CRITICAL EDITION OF *SEPHER YEZIRA*, page 136.

Christians *Cabalalists*

One of the Christians who further introduced Jewish *Kabbalah* to Christian scholars was Italian Giovanni Pico della Mirandola. [414] In 1486, Mirandola had his massive personal library of Hebrew books on *Kabbalah* translated into Latin by Sicilian Jewish convert Flavius Mithridates. He provided the manuscripts to the Vatican Library in Rome where they remain today.

Mirandola's aim was to confirm the truth of the Christian religion through the Jewish *Kabbalah*. Mirandola argued that "no science can make us more certain of Christ's divinity than magic and *Kabbalah*." [415] He believed that this type of magic was acceptable and advocated that "natural magic" is the link between heaven and earth. Mirandola described four types of Cabala practices:

1) mystical manipulation of the letters
2) the three worlds
3) the world of the stars and astrology, and
4) the world of the angels.

Jewish *Kabbalists* use the secret Names of God and the names of angels and combine them with the Hebrew alphabet to invoke magical acts, Mirandola explained. [416] [417]

---

[414] Pico Della Mirandola Giovanni was born in 1463 and died in 1494.

[415] "Pico Della Mirandola Giovanni," from Jewish Virtual Library.

[416] Goodrick-Clarke, Nicholas, D. Phil. PICO DELLA MIRANDOLA AND THE CABALA.

[417] In 1487, according to APOLOGY by Pico della Mirandola.

The *Golem* in Christian Cabalah

Recipes for creating *golems* were collected throughout Northern Italy, translated into Latin and Italian, and become part of the Christian Cabala.

German physician, scholar and occult author Heinrich Cornelius Agrippa von Nettesheim (1486-1535) was acquainted with the Jewish creation of a *golem* and the mystical interpretation of Abraham and Sarah who "created souls" in Haran. He wrote, "But who can give soul to an image, life to stone, metal, wood or wax? And who can make children of Abraham come out (*HZV*, carve) of stones?" [418] Agrippa is legendary for his THREE BOOKS OF OCCULT PHILOSOPHY.

Christian Cabalist and Italian humanist and poet Lodovico Lazzarelli (1447-1500) composed the first complete edition and translation of Hermetic writings of his time near the end of the 15th century.

This was an important contribution to Christian Hermetic literature. In his *CRATER HERMETIS*, he described the creation process of the *golem*. Lazzarelli explained, similar to Abulafia, that Abraham was taught from a book called *SEPHER IZIRA* ("*Yetzirah*") to "form new men" out of virgin, undistributed, earth. [419]

Johann Goethe's SORCERER'S APPRENTICE later developed from these Jewish traditions as the source for "The Sorcerer's Apprentice" in 1797, and then became the inspiration from composer Paul Dukas, and Mary Shelley's FRANKENSTEIN.

---

[418] DE OCCULTA PHILOSOPHIA, II.

[419] Idel, Moshe, *GOLEM*: JEWISH MAGICAL, page 176.

Old World Jewish refugees, Zedcor Graphics (Jewish10).

16th Century (1500-1599)

A s Jews dispersed from Spain and resettled in new locations, the *Kabbalah* re-emerged. The community of Safed in the Galilee became the center for Jewish mystical and legal studies and retained its popularity as a Jewish community through the 16th century. From Safed, the *Kabbalah* spread to Asia, Africa and the European centers of the Jewish diaspora.

Golem legends were very popular in the 16th century among German Jews. The topic was widely discussed among the notable rabbis of the period– Rabbi Judah Loew, Moshe Cordovero, Isaac Luria, and Eliyahu of Chelm. *Golem* stories became more widespread among non-Jews as well. Rumors tied to Rabbi Loew, the *Maharal* of Prague and the Rabbi of Chelm became entrenched in tradition.

Nehemiah Brull published one of the earliest reports of a *golem* in the 16th century. He came across a story about Samuel the Pious, (father of Judah the Pious) who "created a *golem*, that could not speak but accompanied him on his long journeys through Germany and France and waited on him," like a servant. [420]

The printing of the Latin version of the *SEPHER YETZIRAH* by Guillaume Postellus in 1552 fueled the curiosity among the non-Jewish communities, especially in Italy. Except for Paracelsus, Jewish and Christian authors limited themselves to merely repeating past traditions.

In Venice, Daniel Bomberg's printing shop, the largest Hebrew book printer of the time, collected and printed the first complete edition of the *TALMUD* between 1520-1549, including *RASHI'S* commentaries in four editions. [421] The *ZOHAR*, originally produced by Moses de Leon in the 13th century from possibly earlier sources, was first printed in 1558 in Mantua. [422]

---

[420] Scholem, Gershom, *KABBALAH* & SYMBOLISM, pages 198-199.

[421] A. Rosenthal, editor, THE *TALMUD* EDITIONS OF DANIEL BLOOMBERG, Jerusalem.

[422] The *ZOHAR* is printed again in 1560 in Cremona, at Lublin in 1623, and a 4th edition in 1684.

1516. A scholar holding a replica of the Tree of Life, from the title page of "*PORTAE LUCIS: HAEC EST PORTA TETRAGRAMMATON, IUSTI INTRABUNT PER EAM,*" (The gates of the Light: This is the gate of *Tetragrammaton*, but the righteous shall enter into it) a Latin translation of Joseph ben Abraham Gatatilla's work by Paulus Ricius (Paulo Riccio, 1480-1541) in *SHA'AREI ORAH*. [423]

---

[423] Scholem, Gershom, *KABBALAH*, front plate. Public domain from Wikimedia Commons.

Cordovero's view of the golem

One of the greatest *Kabbalists* was rabbi and Jewish mystic Moshe ben Jacob Cordovero (1522-1570), known as the *Ramak* [424] of Safed. Cordovero, a widely respected *Talmudic* scholar, began his *Kabbalah* studies in 1542 when he heard a Divine Voice urge him to study the *Kabbalah* with his brother-in-law, Rabbi Shlomo Alkabetz, the author of the *L'cha Dodi* prayer. [425]

By 1548, he systemized the *Kabbalah* in his *PARDES RIMONIM* (ORCHARD OF POMEGRANATES), one of the most important *Kabbalistic* texts ever produced. He used concepts from Abulafia's *OR HASHEKHEL* (LIGHT OF THE INTELLECT). [426] *PARDES RIMONIM* was published in Cracow in 1591. An English edition was published 400 years later. [427] Cordovero founded a *Kabbalah* academy in Safed in 1550.

Like his predecessors Cordovero believed that there are two stages of spiritual enlightenment, they include:

1. combining of the letters of the alphabet (into "Gates"); and
2. the combination of those letters with the Divine Name.

The *Ramak* did not attribute his methods directly to Abulafia, but rather to an obscure manuscript called *SEFER HANIKUD* (BOOK OF DOTS).

Cordovero wrote *SEPHER SHIUR KOMASH,* a treatise dealing with the esoteric structure of the worlds and *sephiroth*. In it, he mentioned the "combinations of letters" and the "particulars of letters" numerous times. [428] Just as tradition implied, Cordovero agreed that the *golem* was activated by the mystical letters combinations. As man blew the spirit of life into the *golem* using the permutated Hebrew letters, this caused the formation (or the animation) of the limbs, and infused a soul (*Nephesh*) into the *golem*.

With the inscription of the letters *AMT* (*AMT*) or "truth" on its forehead, Cordovero concurred,

---

[424] See Idel, Moshe, *GOLEM*: JEWISH MAGICAL, pages 196-203 for a detail discussion in Cordovero's views.

[425] *L'cha Dodi* is recited on (Sabbath) Friday nights at dusk. See article on "Rabbi Moshe Cordovero," from *Chabad*.org.

[426] Kaplan, Aryeh, MEDITATION AND *KABBALAH*, page 87.

[427] Republished in 2007. ISBN: 1-897352-17-4. Translated by Elyakim Getz, Providence University.

[428] Idel, Moshe, STUDIES IN ECSTATIC *KABBALAH*, page 168.

the *golem* was enlivened. When the *Aleph* was removed, the word spelled *MT* ("dead") and the creature collapsed. The power that gives life to the *golem* is "vitality" (*chayyut*), Cordovero believed. But, the *golem* lacked a soul or the type of spirit that is endowed in humans.

Rabbi Luria– The Ari

Rabbi Isaac ben Solomon Luria of Safed (1534-1572), known as the *Ari* ("The Lion"), wrote a commentary on his perspective of the *SEPHER YETZIRAH*. [429] The *Ari* demonstrated how letter combinations in the *ZOHAR* were to be used as meditative devices.

His teachings, compiled by his disciples, are known as the Luriatic *Kabbalah* and was quite popular. His students copied and circulated his instructions, although the *ZOHAR* still overshadowed most mystical works at the time.

The *Ari's* methods were practiced by only a few groups, as most *Kabbalists* were devoted to theory instead of practice. The *Kabbalistic* writings of Cordovero, the printing of the *ZOHAR* and the study of the *Kabbalah* among Christians caused the *Ari* to tighten the secrecy of his circle.

Between 1560-1630, Rabbi Isaiah Horowitz, a Jewish Law specialist, spent ten years in the Holy Land where he became familiar with the teaching of The *Ari* and the Safed School of *Kabbalah*.

Rabbi Chayim Vital collected notes from Luria's disciples and produced numerous works, including the eight-volume *ETZ CHAYIM* (TREE OF LIFE). It remained unpublished, under direction of Luria's students, so copies would not circulate in public. One copy eventually made its way to Europe and was published in 1772. [430] His works are now widely available.

---

[429] It was printed two hundred years later. Idel, Moshe, *GOLEM*: JEWISH MAGICAL, page 333. First printed in 1719 (Constantinople), in 1745 (Zolkiev), in 1884 (Warsaw edition), and other editions. [429]

[430] "Isaac Luria," Wikipedia.com.

Rabbi of Chelm's golem

Polish Rabbi Eliyahu (1550-1583) was the Jewish leader of the community of Chelm in eastern Poland. He was known as *"Ba'al Shem"*– Master of the Divine Name– because of his knowledge of the Holy Names.

The young rabbi was familiar with the mystical techniques of letter combination and is credited to have created the '*Golem* of Chelm.' This was supposedly how he earned the moniker.

A hundred years after his early death at age 33, his great-grandson Rabbi Zev *Ashkenazi*, a noted *Halakhist*, wrote that his ancestor (Rabbi Eliyahu) created a *golem*. Zevi passed on the story to his son, German Rabbi Jacob Emden who wrote about it a generation later. [431]

Rabbi Jacob Emden (1697-1776) [432] elaborated the story [433] in 1748. He wrote that the *golem* was created by the great *"Ba'al Shem"* after he inscribed the *Shem* (Name of God) on its forehead and recited certain letter combinations that were constructed from instruction in the *SEPHER YETZIRAH*. Emden wrote that the *golem* served the rabbi, but it grew larger and larger.

The rabbi became afraid it would get so large and dangerous it could destroy the world, so he decided to destroy it first. When the Rabbi removed one of the letters from its forehead, the *golem* returned to dust. In the process, the *golem* fell on the master and the rabbi escaped with only scratches and bruises. In some versions, he was crushed to death. After it was turned back into a lump of clay, the *golem's* remains were stored in the attic of the Old Synagogue and no one was allowed to enter, but everyone knew that the *golem* of *Ba'al Shem* laid there. [434]

---

[431] Although Moshe Idel argues that Zevi was born in 1660 and it is doubtful that R. Elijah, who died in 1583, was his grandfather, but instead was the father of his grandfather. See Moshe Idel, *GOLEM: JEWISH MAGICAL*, page 229, footnote 21.

[432] Jacob Emden, also known as Ya'avetz. He might have also acquired this story from Rabbi H.Y.D. Azulai in SHEM HA GEDOLIM, No. 163. See Isidore Singer in *GOLEM* OF HOHE RABBI LOW, JEWISH ENCYCLOPEDIA.

[433] In his autobiography *SEPHER MEGILLAT* (Warsaw, 5656).

[434] Jewish Life and Work in Chełm chapter of the COMMEMORATION BOOK OF CHEŁM (Poland) (*YISKER-BUKH CHEŁM*).

Rabbi Loew's golem

Another famous rabbi who lived at the time of Eliyahu of Chelm was Judah Loew ben Bezalel of Prague (1520-1609). During the reign of Emperor Rudolph II, Prague was the center for arts and sciences, alchemy and the occult.

Known as the *Maharal*, Rabbi Loew was a leading rabbi in Prague and a Jewish mystic. He was a great *TALMUDIC* scholar and a *Kabbalist* who was also credited to have created a *golem*. This famous legend became known as the *Golem* of Prague. But it shared many of the same plots as the *Golem* of Chelm. Over time, the story of Rabbi Eliyahu of Chelm's *golem* morphed into the *golem* of Rabbi Loew of Prague, leaving the Rabbi of Chelm in historical dust.

Loew wrote numerous books on Jewish law and philosophy. He was called to an audience with Holy Roman Emperor Rudolf II [435] on February 23, 1592, but the details of this meeting are only in legend. According to the story, Rabbi Loew demonstrated to the Emperor the creation of a *golem* and revealed other *Kabbalistic* secrets ("*nistarot*"). [436] Other accounts say that the *Maharal* was able to secure protection of the Jews against the blood libel during this meeting.

Although Loew is credited to having inspired the *Golem* of Prague legend, its origin might actually have been with the Rabbi of Chelm. About the beginning of the 19th century, Loew's name started to appear in place of the Rabbi of Chelm who lived during the same period about 550 miles west of Prague. Through this visibility, Rabbi Loew became the symbol of the modern-day *golem* legend. However, not until 20 years after Loew's death was there any mention of his involvement with the *golem*. [437]

The story about the *Maharal's golem,* gathered from oral traditions, was written down in 1847 by Leopold Weisel in DER *GOLEM*, part of a collection of Jewish legends called *GALERIE DER SIPURIM* by Jewish Austrian publisher Wolf Pascheles. [438]

---

[435] Rudolph II was born on July 18, 1552 and died January 20, 1612.

[436] Peter Demetz, PRAGUE IN BLACK AND GOLD: SCENES FROM THE LIFE OF A EUROPEAN CITY, page 211.

[437] Edan Dekel, and David Gannt Gurley, HOW THE *GOLEM* CAME TO PRAGUE, "The Jewish Quarterly Review," Vol. 103, No. 2 (Spring 2013), 241-258.

[438] Pascheles was born in 1814 and died in 1857.

A *golem* story that named Rabbi Loew was related by Rabbi Yehuda Yudl Rosenberg in 1909. [439] His version became the standard account of the *Maharal's* deeds. Rosenberg claimed this was an account by an eyewitness. Some critics, however, questioned Rosenberg's story of the *Maharal's golem* as a hoax.

According to the Rosenberg's version, [440] in a quest to wage a fight against a priest who was his antagonist, Rabbi "Liva" received a divine message in a dream. He revealed the secret to his son-in-law, Isaac ben Sampson *ha-Cohen*, and to his pupil Jacob ben Khaim-Sasson *ha-Levi*.

Rosenberg related that on a chilly, early morning in February 1580 (Jewish year of 5340 in the month of Adar), the three men walked to the nearby shores of the Moldau River. They drew out the form of a man in the sand three cubits long. The three stood at its feet face-to-face with the *golem*.

The Rabbi commanded Isaac ben Sampson to circle the figure seven times from the right to the head and then to the left side, then back to its feet. He recited the formula as he circled seven times. The *golem* turned red with fire. Then Khaim-Sassoon circled the figure citing a different formula provided to him by the rabbi. The fire flamed out and a wisp of vapor rose from the body. The rabbi circled the body seven times. They concluded the ceremony with the recitation of "And the Lord God formed man of the dust of the ground and breathed into his nostrils the breath of life, and man became a living soul." [441]

The *golem* opened his eyes and stared at the three men who stood above him. The rabbi called him Joseph and said it would be his servant and protect the Jews from harm. The *golem* could not speak, but it could understand simple commands. Joseph was dressed in clothes and stayed close to Rabbi Loew. The towns folk considered Joseph to be another follower of Rabbi Loew and his servant, albeit a little dimwitted.

The *Maharal's* main use for the *golem*, however, was to stalk the Jewish ghetto in disguise and seek out anything suspicious. He made several successful attempts to thwart adversaries, according to stories related by Rosenberg.

One particular wives-tale that arose was about the *golem's* wayward actions was similar to earlier tales about the sorcerer's apprentice and the out of control broom. Once the Rabbi's wife disobeyed his prohibition from using the *golem* for menial tasks. While the rabbi was gone, she

---

[439] Shnayer Z. Leiman, THE ADVENTURE OF THE MAHARAL OF PRAGUE IN LONDON: R. Yudl Rosenberg and the Golem of Prague."

[440] As told by as told by Yudel Rosenberg, in THE GOLEM OR THE MIRACULOUS DEEDS OF RABBI LIVA, from GREAT TALES OF JEWISH OCCULT AND FANTASY, compiled by Joachim Neugroschel, 1991, pages 162-225.

[441] Genesis 2:7: "God formed a man from the dust of the ground and breathed into his nostrils the breath of life, and the man became a living being."

gave Joseph instructions to fetch water from the river on the day before Passover. Joseph complied, but he repeatedly kept returning to the river to fill the buckets and the room became flooded.

When the Rabbi returned, he discovered what was happening and took the buckets away from the *golem* and told him to sit down. This apparently is the meaning of the Yiddish proverb that accompanies this story, "You know as much about watchmaking as Joseph the *Golem*." [442] The term *golem* became popularized as a reference to someone who was slow-witted, a "blockhead," or an automaton.

Similar to the *Golem* of Chelm story, the *Golem* of Prague was supposedly stored in the attic of the Old Synagogue and no one was allowed to enter.

The original "Sorcerer's Apprentice" was inspired in a poem called "Der Zauberlehrling," composed by Johann Wolfgang von Goethe [443] in 1797. The lesson was the inherent danger of the power to invoke magical acts. That scene was played out in the famous 1940 Walt Disney Company film animation "FANTASIA."

Cartoon character Mickey Mouse [444] portrayed the sorcerer's understudy who used a magical formula to enliven a broom to fetch water while the sorcerer was gone. The broom got out of hand, running back and forth, and the room was flush with water. The apprentice couldn't stop the broom and he tried to chop the broom in half with an axe. But, the two separate pieces began fetching water. It continued until the sorcerer returned and cancelled the spell.

---

[442] "The Golem or The Miraculous Deeds of Rabbi Liva," from GREAT TALES OF JEWISH OCCULT AND FANTASY, compiled by Joachim Neugroschel, 1991, page 174.

[443] Johann Wolfgang von Goethe was born on August 28, 1749 and died on March 22, 1832.

[444] Mickey Mouse is the official mascot of the Walt Disney Company and was created by Walt Disney in 1928.

SEPHER YETZIRAH Versions in 16th Century

Yaakov ben Naftali Gazolo published the first printed edition of *SEPHER YETZIRAH* in 1562 [445] called the Mantua version. This edition had both the long and short recensions. It is different from Saadia Gaon's recension.

Version I had 600 words and version II has 1800 words. Version II was riddled with errors. The Mantua edition commentaries are attributed to *Raavad*, *RAMBAN* B, Rabbi Moses Botriel, Saadia B, Eleazar of Worms. [446]

The author had little or no concept of Hebrew or knowledge of the *SEPHER YETZIRAH*. He considered it to be only a cosmology based on the letters of the alphabet. A Latin version of Gulielmus Postellus' work preceded it by ten years. After that, over a hundred manuscripts of *SEPHER YETZIRAH* followed in various forms– most full of errors.

The most popular version used today is reprinted in the 1884 Warsaw edition. Two manuscripts are reproduced in this edition, one at the end of the volume and the other among different commentaries. They differ in two ways– one is repetitious while the other has abbreviations; one combines what the other separates; and one is more explicit than the other in both words and meanings. This copy is archived in the Microfilm Institute of the National and University Library in Jerusalem.

---

[445] Said to be in 1592 by A.E. Waite, DOCTRINE OF THE *KABBALA*, page 172.

[446] Kaplan, Aryeh, *SEPHER YETZIRAH*: THEORY, page 319.

Rabbi Galante's Instructions

An *Ashkenazi* technique to create a *golem* using the instructions from the SEPHER YETZIRAH was preserved by Rabbi Abraham ben Mordecai Galante, [447] a 16th century *Kabbalist* from Safed, and a disciple of R. Moshe Cordovero. [448] His views were quoted by R. Abraham Azulai in his commentary on the ZOHAR, 'OR HA-HAMAH:

"The creation of all the worlds was [accomplished] by the
22 letters, and so also the creation of man by the 22 letters.
The father, when he engenders his son,
engraves the 22 letters which his father engraved in him...
at the time of his [own] engendering.

By the virtue of these 22 letters the foetus emerges and develops.
Likewise, the existence of the creature created by the ancients, as it is
indicated in the Gamara that R. Oshaya created a man, and
similar things, [these] were by means of the 22 letters.

And they were doing it in the following way:
They took new dust, which was not wrought,
and spread it on the earth in a homogeneous way [besgaveh].

---

[447] Abraham ben Mordecai Galante died in 1560.

[448] "Views on the *Golem*," from by Idel, Moshe, GOLEM: JEWISH MAGICAL, page 69.

Then they engraved in this dust the name
of the thing they wanted to create,
and with each and every letter they were
combining all the alphabets.

How [was it done]?
[In the case of the creation of] a man ['Adam]
they were combining the letter 'A (א) with all the alphabets,
then the letter Daleth (ד) with all the alphabets and likewise with
the letter Mem (מ) with all the alphabets,
all this together with other conditions that they were doing.
Then that thing was created."

From Abraham Azulai[449]

---

[449] "Views on the *Golem*," from by Idel, Moshe, *GOLEM: JEWISH MAGICAL*, page 69. Idel quotes this from Abraham Azulai's ''*OR HA-HAMAH*, 1886, vol. 1, fol 62d.

Writing the names on the ground and pronouncing the letters of alphabet implies a creative power inherent in the letters. Both Galante and Rabbi Joseph Ashkenazi, the *Tanna* of Safed believed that the creation of world and the creation of man was accomplished through the 22 letters.

According to Rabbi Joseph Ashkenazi (1525-1572), there is a relationship between the expression of a name and the lower soul (*Nephesh chayyot*) and the higher soul (*Neshamah hayyim*).

"A man can make a *golem* which possess a living soul [*Nephesh hayyah*] [450] by the power of his speech, but the [higher] soul [*Neshamah*] cannot be conferred by man because it is from the divine speech. Behold, [you can] understand the issue of the higher souls [*neshamoh*] which are in the body [*guf*]. [Abraham] combined [the letters] and was successful [in creating] a creature, as it is said, "The souls they made in Haran" [451]

Italian physician and *Kabbalist* Abraham von Hananiah Yagel [452] (1553-1623), of Italy, was interested in the 'meaning' of the creation of the *golem*. Was it witchcraft? He believed it was natural magic. It did not involve demonic methods, Yagel suggested. He commented on the *SANHEDRIN* account about the creation of a third-year calf and agreed that is was an acceptable practice. [453]

---

[450] Genesis 2:7.

[451] "Views on the *Golem*," from by Idel, Moshe, *GOLEM*: JEWISH MAGICAL, pages 70-71.

[452] See more on Abraham Yagel in Idel, Moshe, *GOLEM*: JEWISH MAGICAL, pages 180-182.

[453] Idel, Moshe, *GOLEM*: JEWISH MAGICAL, pages 180-181.

16ᵗʰ Century Christian Cabala

As the Jewish community circulated tales about *golems* and the superhuman powers of *Kabbalah*, the Christian community took notice. They adapted some of the *Kabbalah's* teachings to their own perspective and gave it religious approval.

In 1517 Christian Cabalist Johannes Reuchlin (1455-1522) published *DE ARTE CABALISTICA* (ON THE ART OF THE *KABBALAH*) with a discussion on the *golem* and a section on the *SEPHER YETZIRAH*. [454] This copy was more widely available than other books about the *Kabbalah* and the *golem*.

Reuchlin, a contemporary of Lodovicio Lazzarelli, was one of the architects of the Christian *Cabala* movement who also defended attacks against Jewish scholars. He retold the ancient story about Jeremiah the Prophet and his son Ben Sira and attributes it to Tannaite Judah ben Bathyra– one of the Elders of Bathyra during the Destruction of the 2ⁿᵈ Temple.

He wrote that Jeremiah would busy himself with the *SEPHER YETZIRAH* and a voice told him to find a companion to help study. His son Sira and him studied it for three years. They eventually create a man (*golem*) with the letters *YHYH Elohim Ameth* ("God is truth") on his forehead and erase the *Aleph* from the word *AMT* to destroy it. [455]

The first Latin edition of *SEPHER YETZIRAH* of Christian scholarship was printed in 1552 by Gulielmus Postellus (Postel) [456] of Paris, France. He translated the *SEPHER YETZIRAH* from Hebrew to Latin ten years before the first Hebrew edition was printed.

A second Latin version was printed 25 years later under the title of ABRAHAM, PATRIARCH, BOOK OF *YETZIRAH*: "Abrahami Patriarchae Liber Jezirah, sive Formationis Mundi, Patribus quidem expositus Isaaco, et per Proetarum manus posteritati conservatis, ipsis autum 72 Mosis auditoribus in secund divine veritatis loco, hoc est in ratione, quoe est posterior authiritate, habitus. Vertebat ex Hebrais et commentaris illustrabad 1551, ad Babylonis ruinam et corrupti mundi finem, Gulielmus Postellus, Restitutus. Paris, 1552. ("The SEPHER YETZIRAH of the Patriarch Abraham; or the creation of the world, revealed by the ancients in the time of Abraham expounded to Isaac, and which was conserved in the caring hands of posterity…Translated from the Hebrew and accompanied by commentaries… William Postel(lus) Restored (Gulielmus?)")

---

[454] Johann Reuchlin, ON THE ART OF THE *KABBALAH*. Translated and reprinted in 1993, U of Nebraska Press.

[455] Ms. Halberstam, 444 (in the Jewish Theological Seminary in New York).

[456] Gulielmus Postellus died in 1583.

[457] [458] A.E. Waite used Postel's translation in his edition in 1902.

German physician and theologian Heinrich Cornelious Agrippa of Nettesheim (1486-1535) published a three-volume study in 1533 on Hermetics, *Kabbalistic* and occult philosophy called *DE OCCULTA PHILOSOPHIA LIBRI* III (THREE BOOKS OF OCCULT PHILOSOPHY). [459]

These books, still available today, provide a comprehensive study of astrology, Hermetics, *Kabbalah*, the angels and the various names of God. Agrippa proposed the concept of a *homunculus* (Latin for "little man"), an artificial being.

Swiss German philosopher, occultist, botanist and physician Phillippus Aureolus Theophrastus Bombastus von Hohenheim better known as Paracelsus (1493-1541) believed that natural philosophers could create life. He detailed how to create a *generatio homunculi* ("little man")– a body without a soul– in his book *DE HOMUNCULUS* (c 1529-1532) and in *DE NATURA RERUM* (1537) where the Latin word *homunculus* first appeared in writing. [460]

The *homunculus* has been compared to the *golem* in Jewish folklore, although Paracelsus didn't make use of known *golem* instructions. Instead, he had his own method.

Paracelsus believed that alchemy can be used to create a *homunculus*– a fully formed human being developed from a fetus using sperm that is putrefied for forty days, or until it begins to move on its own. [461] [462] The *homunculus* was brought to life through an alchemical process, while the *golem* receives its spark of life through the recitation of permutated letters.

Homunculi-type characters eventually appeared in 20th century animations, books, film, television and fantasy role-playing games such as Dungeons & Dragons (1974).

Around the same time, German historian and occultist Johannes Pistorius Niddanus (the Younger, 1546-1608) published a second Latin version of the Christian Cabalah in 1587– the first and only volume of *ARTIS CABALISTICAE SCRIPTORES*. [463] A third Latin translation was made

---

[457] Kaplan, Aryeh, *SEPHER YETZIRAH*: THEORY, pages 336-337.

[458] Available in the public domain at archve.org.

[459] Idel, Moshe, *GOLEM*: JEWISH MAGICAL, page 179.

[460] Paracelsus, DE NATURA RERUM, volume 1.

[461] Waite, A.E. editor, THE HERMETIC & ALCHEMICAL WRITINGS OF PARACELSUS, Vol. II. Shambhala Publishing. A BOOK CONCERNING LONG LIFE, Chapter 4, pages 120, 121, 334. Originally published in 1894.

[462] Hartmann, Dr. Franz, THE LIFE OF PARACELSUS, pages 302, 303. Kegan Paul, Trench, Trübner, 1896. Reprinted in 1985, Wizards Bookshelf.

[463] Waite, A.E. *ARTIS CABALISTICAE SCRIPTORES*, by Johannes Pistorius, published by Baseileae Sebastianum Henricpetri, 1587. See BOOK OF FORMATION OR *SEPHER YETZIRAH*: ATTRIBUTED TO RABBI

about 60 years later. This differed from Postellus's version published 35 years earlier. Some say either Paolo Ricco or Johann Reuchlin actually wrote it.

SEPHER RAZIEL– Medieval Grimoire

A version of the medieval *grimoire* attributed to Rabbi Eleazar of Worms in the 12th Century, the *SEPHER RAZIEL* – BOOK OF *RAZIEL*– was translated from an unidentified Latin version and was dated November 2, 1564. [464] The Hebrew writing was extremely poor and it contained many errors.

The seven sections of this version of the *SEPHER RAZIEL* included:

- the *CLAVIS*– deals with astrology and its use in magic including precise interactions between planets, signs, and the Houses;
- the *ALA*– outlines the magical symbols of stones, herbs, and animals;
- the *TRACTATUS THYMIAMATUS*– determines perfumes and suffumigations (the act of burning of substances, like herbs, to produce fumes used in the magical arts);
- a TREATISE OF TIMES– details the correct hours of the day for each operation;
- a TREATISE ON PREPARATIONS on ritual purity and preparations;
- *SAMAIM*– covers the different heavens and their angels;
- a BOOK OF NAMES and their properties, includes the seven *Shem ha-foresh* Holy names) of Adam and seven *Shem ha-foresh* of Moses.

AKIBA BEN JOSEPH, page 1.

[464] This copy is preserved in the British Library, Ms. Sloane 3826.

17ᵗʰ Century (1600-1699)

After Rabbi Eliyahu of Chelm passed away in 1583, and Rabbi Judah Loew of Prague died in September 1609, the famous *Golem* of Prague legend spread across Europe. Originally attributed to R. Eliyahu of Chelm, the story's character morphed into Rabbi Loew ben Bezalel sometime before the 18ᵗʰ century.

Italian-Jewish doctor, scientist and scholar Rabbi Joseph Solomon del Medigo (1591-1655) wrote during his journeys through Germany, Poland and Lithuania in 1625 that "many (*golem*) legends of this sort are current, particularly in Germany." He quoted the story about Abraham ibn Ezra and mentioned the 11ᵗʰ century poet and Rabbi Solomon ibn Gabirol (1021-1069) who created a *golem* and was denounced by the government. Del Medigo commented that there are numerous traditions [*shemu'ot*], especially among the *Ashkenazi*. [465]

The gender of the *golem* was not discussed in writing until R. del Medigo brought it up in 1625, and by R. Isaiah ben Abraham ha-Levi Horowitz (1635-1640's) in his *SHENEI LUHOT HA-BERIT*. Some texts of the *SEPHER YETZIRAH* give the exact order of the vocalizations to produce a male or a female. But, the *golem* had to be created without any sexual instinct, it is argued. If he had such a desire, no woman would be safe from him.

Another one of the earliest known written legends of a contemporary figure creating a *golem* was published in 1630. It did not mention R. Loew, but recounted the story of R. Eliyahu of Chelm who both used the *SEPHER YETZIRAH* to create a *golem*. The *golem* continued to grow that, as common in all legends, the rabbi had to destroy it by erasing the "A" (א *Aleph*), first letter from the word *emet (AMT)* (אמת truth). Other similar legends dated as late as 1660. [466]

An account by two of Jewish *Halakhists* (scholars of Jewish religious laws) who were R. Eliyahu of Chelm's descendants– Rabbi Zevi Hirsh ben Ya'aqov *Ashkenazi* [467] and his son Rabbi Jacob Emden [468] discussed the legal status of the *golem*. In a paper from in 1630, they speculated if a *golem* could be counted in a *minyan* (the quorum of ten men required for prayer).

---

[465] Idel, Moshe, *GOLEM*: JEWISH MAGICAL, page 233.

[466] Idel, Moshe, THE *GOLEM*: AN HISTORICAL OVERVIEW, also see Wikipedia: Elijah *Ba'al Shem* of Chelm.

[467] Zevi Hirsh ben Ya'aqov *Ashkenazi* (1656-1718) the great-grandson of Rabbi Eliyahu of Chelm was also *known* as Chacham Zvi.

[468] Rabbi Jacob Emden, also known as *Ya'avetz*, was born in 1697 and died in 1776.

"Human form and modicum of understanding were not enough to make something human," they argued. Also, according to Emden, the destructive potential of the *golem* could destroy the world. [469] Emden and Zevi acknowledged that their ancestor, the Rabbi of Chelm, did create a *golem*. They also further popularized the story about the Rabbi of Chelm's *golem*.

Kabbalist R. Naphtali Hertz ben Jacob Elhanan Bacharach of Frankfurt published EMEK HA-MELEKH (VALLEY OF THE KING) in 1648. He included a set of incomplete instructions on *golem* creation in his Luriatic *Kabbalistic* text. [470] Levi ben Kalonymos published a folio edition of the ZOHAR at Lublin in 1623.

Six versions of the SEPHER YETZIRAH were collected and printed at Lemberg in 1680. [471]

---

[469] Idel, Moshe, GOLEM: JEWISH MAGICAL, pages 217-219.

[470] Scholem, Gershom, ON THE KABBALAH AND ITS SYMBOLISM, page 185.

[471] Kaplan, Aryeh, SEPHER YETZIRAH: THEORY, page 319. Attributed to Westcott.

Cabalists Perpetuate the Legends

A nti-Jewish writer and Christian convert Samuel Friedrich Brenz reported in 1614, that Jews had a magical device "called *Hamor Golem*; they make an image of mud resembling a man, whisper or mumble certain spells in his ears, which makes the image walk." [472] The book was published in Nuremburg from an earlier 1601 version where he denounced Jewish religious literature.

Zalman Zevi of Aufenhausen published his rebuttal to the apostate Brenz about the legend of artificial creations. A year later he wrote, "The apostate said that there are those among the Jews who take a lump of clay, fashion it into a man, and whisper incantations and spells, whereupon the figure lives and moves. In the reply which I wrote for the Christian, I made the turncoat look ridiculous, for I said that he himself must be fashioned from just such kneaded lumps of clay and loam, without any sense or intelligence, and that his father must have been such a wonder worker, for as he writes, we call such an image a *homer golem* [an unshapen, raw mass of material], which may be rendered "a monstrous ass" [a really good pun], which I say is a perfect description of him. I myself have never seen such a performance, but some of the sages possessed the power to do this, by means of the BOOK OF CREATION. We German Jews have lost this mystical tradition, but in Palestine there are still to be found some men who can perform great wonders through the *Kabbalah*. It can be done, but not by us any longer by us." [473]

A third Latin edition of *SEPHER YETZIRAH* with Hebrew translation in Amsterdam was published in 1642 by Johann Stephen Rittangelius (1606-1652), called *LIBER JEZIRAH QUI ABRAHAMO PATRIARCHAE ADSCRIBITUR*, with commentary by Rabbi Abraham F. ben Dior, Amsterdam, 1642. [474]

This version was used by A.E. Waite in his 1932 edition of BOOK OF FORMATION. The 32 Paths are given in Hebrew and Latin, followed by part of the commentary by R. Abraham (about the Paths of Wisdom), in Latin and Hebrew and an explanation by Rittangelius quoting many authorities including the *ZOHAR* and Supplements. After the Path discussion is the *SEPHER YETZIRAH* text in Latin and Hebrew. The first edition was published in 1551 by Postellus.

In 1664, a Latin version of Rabbi Cordovero's *PARDES RIMONIM* (ORCHARD OF POMEGRANATES) by Joseph Ciantes was translated by Bartolocci in *DE SANCTISSIMA TRINITATE CONTRA JUDAEOS*. It was again published by German Christian Hebraist, Christian Cabalist and

---

[472] Scholem, Gershom, ON THE *KABBALAH* AND ITS SYMBOLISM, page 199.

[473] Trachtenberg, Joshua, JEWISH MAGIC AND SUPERSTITION: A STUDY IN FOLK RELIGION, page 86.

[474] Beitchman, Philip, ALCHEMY OF THE WORD: CABALA OF THE RENAISSANCE, page 184.

composer Christian Knorr von Rosenroth (1631-1689) in 1677. [475] A Latin version of the 1562 edition of *SEPHER YETZIRAH* was also published in 1644 with a commentary by Willem Henricus Vorstius (d. 1652), titled *CAPITULA R. ELIESER.* [476]

Another Christian Hebraist, Johann Christoph Wagenseil,[477] wanted to prove that the Polish Jews practiced sorcery. In 1674, he reprinted a letter written in Latin by amateur astronomer Christoph Arnold. [478] The letter told the story about R. Eliyahu of Chelm and how his *golem* helped protect the Jews in the community.

The *golem* was animated by an amulet inscribed with the word Truth (the 3 Hebrew letters *Aleph, Mem* and *Tav– AMT*) inscribed across its forehead. After the *golem* was deactivated (by removing the first letter to spell Death) by the Rabbi *Ba'al Shem*, it remained in the attic of the Old Synagogue and no one was ever allowed to enter. The *golem* laid there as a heap of clay. [479] [480]

This was the first Central European report on the tradition connected with the Rabbi of Chelm. Arnold, a Polish *Kabbalist*, generalized how Polish Jews could bring life to a man of clay after they recite certain prayers, fast, and say the *Shem ha-Meforesh* over the prostrate form. After the image came to life, it did all kinds of housework, according to Arnold, but it couldn't leave the house.

Arnold then tells another story he heard about Rabbi Elias (Elijah), a *Ba'al Shem Tov* (Master of the Divine Name) in Poland who could no longer reach his *golem's* forehead to erase the first letter to destroy it. Threatened by the creature's daily growth, the Rabbi tricked the *golem* by commanding him to bend over and remove his master's boots. It worked and enabled the rabbi to remove the *Aleph* when the *golem* stooped down. But, when the *golem* began to crumble, the resulting pile of mud fell on his creator and crushed him.

Johann Steidner published *Judische ABC Schul im Buch Yezirah* ("The Jewish ABC School on the Book *Yetzirah*"), a Catholic interpretation of Rittangelius' work, in 1665. [481]

---

[475] *Pardes Rimonim*, Wikipedia.com.

[476] Reprinted in 2009, Kessinger Publishing.

[477] Johann Christoph Wagenseil was born in 1633 and died in 1705.

[478] Christoph Arnold was born in 1650 and died in 1695.

[479] Gelbin, Cathy S., THE *GOLEM* RETURNS: FROM GERMAN ROMANTIC LITERATURE TO GLOBAL JEWISH CULTURE, pages 8-9.

[480] Idel, Moshe, ON THE *KABBALAH* AND ITS SYMBOLISM, page 200.

[481] Ibid.

German Hebraist and Christian Cabalist Knorr Rosenroth [482] published numerous books on Cabala from the Christian perspective and devoted his studies to Oriental languages, especially Hebrew. His 1684 *KABBALAH DENUDATA* [483] included a version of the *SEPHER YETZIRAH* and sections from *EMEK HA-MELEKH* (1648). A partial English translation of *KABBALAH DENUDATA* was made by S.L. MacGregor Mathers in 1887 and is published today under the title of THE *KABBALAH* UNVEILED. [484]

Johann Wulfer wrote in 1675 that in Poland there are "excellent builders who can make *mute famuli* ("mute servants") from clay inscribed with the Name of God." [485] However, he could not find any eyewitnesses. [486]

German, anti-Semitic Orientalist Johann Jakob Schmidt (1664-1722) wrote in 1682 that these creatures "perform all sorts of human activities for forty days and carry letters like messengers wherever they are sent, even a long way. But, if after forty days the parchment is not removed from the forehead, they inflict great damage upon the person or possessions of their master or his family."

German philologist Johann Georg Wachter (1663-1757) published *DER SPINOZISMUS IM JUEDENTHUMB* in Amsterdam in 1699. His work interpreted the theology of the *Kabbalah* in a more populist view. [487]

---

[482] Christian Knorr Rosenroth was born in Poland in 1631 and died in Germany in 1689.

[483] Kaplan, Aryeh, SEPHER YETZIRAH: THEORY, page 365.

[484] Christian Knorr von Rosenroth, Wikipedia.com.

[485] Winkler, Gershom, MAGIC OF THE ORDINARY: RECOVERING THE SHAMANIC IN JUDAISM, page 80.

[486] See ON THE *KABBALAH* AND ITS SYMBOLISM, by Idel, Moshe, page 200.

[487] Idel, Moshe, ON THE *KABBALAH* AND ITS SYMBOLISM, page 200.

18ᵗʰ Century (1700-1799)

The ancient grammatical lessons attributed to Rabbi Akiba, THE ALPHABET OF RABBI AKIBA BEN JOSEPH, was published in 1708 in Amsterdam. As a *Midrash* on the names of the letters of the Hebrew alphabet [488] it recounted how each of the Hebrew letters competed to be the first letters to form the beginning of creation (*bereshith*). Italian Rabbi and philosopher Moshe Chaim Luzzatto (*Ramhal*, 1707-1746) joined a *Kabbalistic* group in 1727 and devoted his life to mystical studies after he claimed to hear a voice who revealed itself as a "*maggid*," a divine messenger who shared heavenly secrets. [489] His followers practice Luria's influence. Some of his *Kabbalistic* works include and *KELALUT HA-ILAN* (ESSENTIALS OF THE TREE) and *KELA PITHEI HOKHMAH* (138 GATES OF WISDOM).

In 1714 or 1718 German, anti-Semitic Orientalist, Johann Jakob Schudt (1664-1722) wrote *JUDISCHE MERKWURDIGKEITE* (JEWISH MARVELS). This became the source for Jakob Grimm's story about the *golem* published almost 100 years later. [490] "The present-day Polish Jews are notoriously masters of this art, and often make the *golem*," Schudt wrote, "which they employ in their homes, like *Kabolds* (*homunculus*), or house spirits for all sorts of housework."

About mid-18ᵗʰ century, the *golem* legend about R. Chelm shifted to Prague and became connected with the "Great Rabbi" Loew of Prague instead of the Rabbi of Chelm. In the Prague legend, certain special features of the Sabbath are mentioned. The 16ᵗʰ century works of Rabbi Isaac Luria's *ETZ CHAYIM* (TREE OF LIFE) were published in Zolkiev in 1772 by Isaac Satanow. This further helped revive Luranic *Kabbalah* principles based on the *ZOHAR*. The corrupted Medieval incantation *Abaracadabara* appeared in a passage by Daniel Defoe in 1722 where he explained how it is used to ward off the plague or evil spirit. [491] At the end of 18th century, Czech Rabbi and Talmudist Pinchas HaLevi Horowitz [492] composed the *SEPHER HA-BERIT*, a work on *Kabbalah* and science. He described the creation of a *golem* by the manipulation of Divine Names and holy letters as explained in the *SEPHER YETZIRAH* and in the book *BEIT HA-YOZER*. [493]

---

[488] "ALPHABET OF AKIBA BEN JOSEPH," JewishEncyclopedia.com and Wikipedia.com.

[489] "Moshe Chiam Luzzatto," Jewish Virtual Library.

[490] Herzog, Hillary Hope and Todd Herzog, Benjamin Lapp editors, REBIRTH OF A CULTURE: JEWISH IDENTITY AND JEWISH WRITING IN GERMANY, page 21.

[491] Daniel Defoe, JOURNAL OF THE PLAGUE YEAR, 1722.

[492] His name is also spelled as Hurwitz, 1731-1805.

[493] Idel, Moshe, GOLEM: JEWISH MAGICAL, page 238. From *SEPHER HA-BERIT*, 1799.

The Gra Commentary

The Ari recension of the *SEPHER YETZIRAH*, with comments by R. Luria (The *Ari*) was further edited by the 18th century Gaon of Vilna, Rabbi Eliyahu of Chelm. [494] This is known as the *Gra-Ari*, or simply the Gra version, and is considered the most authoritative source among *Kabbalists*.

The *Ari* edited his work from Rabbi Moshe Cordovero's collection on the *Kabbalah* compiled around 1550. [495] The Gra version was later edited by the 18th century Gaon of Vilna. It is still considered to be the most authoritative source among *Kabbalists* and is a popular commentary in use today.

SEPHER YETZIRAH Republished

In the 1700s, a slew of versions of the *SEPHER YETZIRAH* circulated throughout Europe. The Hebrew texts, however, usually followed the early-century short or long recensions along with old commentaries and very little new perspective.

An edition of *SEPHER YETZIRAH* was published in 1713, with a preface by one of the most influential Jewish leaders in Amsterdam, *TALMUDIC* scholar, *Kabbalist* and Rabbi Moshe ben Yaakov Hagiz (1671-1750). [496] This was the second Amsterdam edition. [497]

Yonah ben Yaakov and Yeshiah Ashkenazi published a version of *SEPHER YETZIRAH* in Constantinople in 1719. This edition included abridged commentaries from *Raavad*, *Ramban* B, and the *Ari*. The document is stored in the British Museum. [498] The same edition was

---

[494] *Gra* is the nickname for Rabbi Eliahu, the Gaon of Vilna. *Ari* is the nickname for Rabbi Yitzchak (Isaac) Luria.

[495] Kaplan, Aryeh, *SEPHER YETZIRAH*: THEORY, page xxv.

[496] Kaplan, Aryeh, *SEPHER YETZIRAH*: THEORY, page 319.

[497] 1642 was the first edition published in Amsterdam.

[498] Kaplan, Aryeh, *SEPHER YETZIRAH*: THEORY, page 319.

republished in 1724 in Constantinople. [499] An edition of *SEPHER YETZIRAH* was published in Zolkiev in 1745 with all of the commentaries from the Mantua and Ari recensions. [500]

Moses ben Yitzchak of Kiev in 1779 produced another edition of *SEPHER YETZIRAH* in Korzec (Koretz) and included a commentary on *OTZAR HASHEM*. [501]

Nearly the entire Commentary on *SEPHER YEZIRAH* by Abraham Abulafia (Munich Ms. 58) was published in 1784 in the *SEPHER HA PELLIAH*, by an anonymous *Kabbalist*, although it was attributed to Rabbi Nechunyah ben Ha-Kaneh. [502]

In 1797, Rabbi Elijah ben Solomon Zalman (1720-1797), the Gaon of Vilna of the Lithuanian rabbinical authority, confided about a frightening event to his student Rabbi Chayim Volozhin, the founder of the *Talmudic* academy of Volozhin. He told his student that when he was a young boy under the age of 13 he undertook the making of a *golem*. In the middle of his preparations some unshaped form or apparition passed over his head. It scared him enough that he stopped the process and never continued again. He wrote an extensive commentary on *SEPHER YETZIRAH* called *KOL HATOR*, where he is probably the only rabbi to claim to have created a *golem*. [503]

One of the founding fathers of the *Chabad* movement, Shneur Zalman of Liadi, published the *TANYA*, first anonymously published in 1797 as *LIKKUETI AMAR*. It is the fundamental work on the *Chabad* philosophy and its approach to *Chasidic* mysticism. It took a more intellectual view than focus on the emotional, expressive contemplation among the *Chasidic*.

In the same year, an edition of *SEPHER YETZIRAH* was published in Grodno, including a commentary on *SEPHER YETZIRAH* by Rabbi Yitzchak Isaac ben Yetutiel of Mohelov. [504]

---

[499] Ibid.

[500] Ibid.

[501] Ibid.

[502] Kaplan, Aryeh, *SEPHER YETZIRAH*: THEORY, page 325. Published in Koretz (Korzec).

[503] Nicolas Kraushaar, THE ESOTERIC CODEX: CZECH LEGEND AND FOLKLORE, page 17.

[504] Kaplan, Aryeh, *SEPHER YETZIRAH*: THEORY, page 319.

Goethe's "Sorcerer's Apprentice"

German author and statesman Johann Wolfgang von Goethe [505] wrote a poem called "The Sorcerer's Apprentice" in 1797. He retold the old wives-tale about an autonomous creature that becomes uncontrollable.

In Goethe's story, the old sorcerer leaves his apprentice alone at his workshop. The lazy apprentice enchants a broom to fetch water for him, but it gets out of hand. The broom continues to bring buckets of water back to the house and the floor becomes flooded. The apprentice can't stop the magical broom, so he splits the broom in half with an axe.

But each piece becomes a whole new broom and grabs a pail of water at twice the speed. Each time he splits the broom in half, each half goes to collect more water. Later, the sorcerer returns and breaks the spell. The poem ends with the sorcerer warning that these powerful spirits should only be used by the sorcerer himself.

The ballad provided the inspiration for Mary Shelley's book FRANKENSTEIN two decades later. One hundred and forty years later, the 1940 Disney film "FANTASIA" brought this story to the big screen.

---

[505] Goethe was born in 1749 and died in 1832.

19ᵗʰ Century (1800-1899)

At the same time many old texts were reprinted and circulated throughout Europe, the teachings of the *Kabbalah* and traditional Jewish folktales crossed the Atlantic as millions of Jews began to emigrate from Europe and other countries to populate New World. Major rabbinical commentaries were translated into English from Hebrew, German, and Latin.

One of the most influential books among the *Chabad* movement, was the *TANYA*. [506] The TANYA explains Jewish mysticism, psychology, and the theological approach towards *Chasidic* life.

The 1814 version contained five sections, including *SHA'AR HA-YACHUD VE-HE'EMUNAH* (THE GATEWAY OF UNITY AND BELIEF) which explained how "life flows...through combinations and substitutions of the letters which are transpose into the" 231 Gates either in direct or reverse order as that life-force descends through the 10 *Sephiroth* ("Utterances," as they are called in the text) until the soul inhabits the created object to give it life. [507]

---

[506] First published in 1797 as *LIKKUETI AMARIM*, republished in 1814.

[507] *SHAAR HAYICHUD*, chapter 1, page 287-288.

19th Century SEPHER YETZIRAH

Several editions of SEPHER YETZIRAH were printed in its original Hebrew during the 19th century.[508]

- 1806 at Grodno, with vocalized text and all commentaries from the Mantua edition including commentaries of Ari and R. Eliahu Gaon of Vilna.
- 1812 edition printed in Dyhernfurth.
- 1820 edition printed at Vilna-Grodno all commentaries of the Mantua and Gra recensions, and was edited by Menachem Mendel of Sklav.
- 1831 edition printed at Salonica (Salonika, Thessalonica), Greece.

---

[508] Kaplan, Aryeh, *SEPHER YETZIRAH*: THEORY, page 319.

The *Golem* in the Secular World

The Hebrew and Yiddish *golem* legends continued to be a favorite literary subject among 19th century German Jews and non-Jews. In the late 19th century, visual artists brought the *golem* into the public realm throughout Germany and America.

The tales that began in medieval Germany were modified throughout the decades. Often, they dealt with the *golem's* ability to save the Jews from persecution of the libelous accusations placed by their enemies to arise fears. These legends were probably remerged after the resurgence of accusations of ritual murder in the 1890s.

Jakob Grimm [509] published one of the first *golem* stories in the ZEITUNG FUR EINSIEDLER (Journal for Hermits) on April 23, 1808. His tale was derived from the 1714 version by Johann Jakob Schudt, adapted from the 1674 account by C. Arnold about R. Eliyahu, the Rabbi of Chelm. This story by Grimm influenced many people and shaped the contemporary image of the *golem*.

In Grimm's account, after certain prayers the Polish Jews make a figure out of a man out of clay and pronounce the Holy Name of God, the *Shemhamaphoresh* (the sacred Name) over it. The rabbi would inscribe the letters *AMT* (אמת) on its forehead and it would come to life. Every day, it grew larger and larger. To destroy the creature, the first letter inscribed on his forehead (*Aleph* א) was removed from the other letters (*MT* מת). This transformed the word from *MT* (truth) to *MT* (he is dead), Grimm explained in agreeance to earlier accounts.

But, according to the tradition, the *golem* grew so tall that the letter could not be reached. However, when the creature bent over, the rabbi was able to erase the letter and the creature crumbled into a heap of clay. But, when it fell, it accidently crushed the rabbi to death. [510] This story related by Grimm is consistent with the way a *golem* is animated and destroyed in past accounts.

Over the next decades, numerous German novels, poems and plays were written about the Prague *golem*. Those interpretations formed the basis of the *golem* legend that survived today.

---

[509] Jakob Grimm was born in 1785 and died in 1863.

[510] Cathy S. Gelbin, THE GOLEM RETURNS: FROM GERMAN ROMANTIC LITERATURE TO GLOBAL JEWISH CULTURE, 1808-2008. The University of Michigan Press, 2011. Page 13, 24, 28. Also, see HOW THE GOLEM CAME TO PRAGUE, by Edan Dekel and David Gantt Gurley. The "Jewish Quarterly Review," Vol. 103, No. 2. Spring 2013, 241-258.

Influenced by Grimm's tale of the *golem*, German poet and novelist Ludwig Achim von Arnim [511] published a tale in 1812 about *Golem* Bella called *ISABELLA VON AGRPTEN* (Isabella of Egypt) in *KAISER KARLS DE FUNFTEN ERSTE JUGENDLIEBE* (Novelle). [512] This is the first use of the *golem* as a *doppelganger*. [513]

The popular monster-based novel, FRANKENSTEIN OR, THE MODERN PROMETHEUS was published in 1818, authored by Mary Wollstonecraft Shelley and Clair Bampton. Shelley incorporated several sources to create her creature– including the characteristics of the *golem* brought to life by a human and eventually turned against its creator. FRANKENSTEIN was later published under Shelley's name in 1823. FRANKENSTEIN becomes a popular character portrayed in theatre and, later, in film.

The German edition of Ernst Theodor Amadeus Hoffmann's [514] *DIE GEHEIMNISSE*, (THE CONFUSIONS/THE SECRETS), published in 1822, used the Jewish *teraphim* [515] in his story about the Rabbi who created an artificial man named Theodore. He alluded to Rabbi Shabbathai Zevi as the *golem's* creator. Hoffman's *golem* was probably borrowed from Arnim's 1812 "Isabella." [516] [517]

Christian theologian Johann Friedrich von Meyer, D.D. [518] published a 36-page Hebrew text German translation of *SEPHER YETZIRAH* in Leipzig, called *DAS BUCH YEZIRAH: DIE ALSTER KABBALISTISCHEN URUNDED DER HEBRAER* in German with his explanatory notes in 1830. [519] [520]

---

[511] Arnim was born in 1781 and died in 1831.

[512] ROMANTIC PROSE FICTION, edited by Gerald Ernest Paul Gillespie, Manfred Engel, Bernard Dieterle, page 209.

[513] A *doppelganger* is the German word for an apparition or double of a living person.

[514] He was known as E.T.A. Hoffman, born in 1776 and died in 1822,

[515] *Teraphim* are the primitive Semitic house-gods. They were human shaped small clay figurines who may have had the power of gods (Genesis 31:30: regarding Rachel's theft of the *teraphim*). From "*Teraphim*," by the Executive Committee of the Editorial Board, "Jewish Encyclopedia."

[516] *KABBALA UND DIE LITERATUR DER ROMANTIK: ZWISCHEN MAGIE UND TROPE*, edited by Eveline Goodman-Thau, Gert Mattenklott, Christoph Schulte. Page 119.

[517] Cathy S. Gelbin, THE GOLEM RETURNS: FROM GERMAN ROMANTIC LITERATURE TO GLOBAL JEWISH CULTURE, page 35 and 50.

[518] Meyer was born in 1772 and died in 1849.

[519] Isidor Kalisch, Knut Stenring, *SEPHER YETZIRAH*: THE BOOK OF CREATION, page 5-7.

[520] Kaplan, Aryeh, *SEPHER YETZIRAH*: THEORY, page 3336.

In 1834, Joseph Kohn [521] published *DER JUDISCHE GIL BLAS,* a story about the *"golam"* created by Rabbi "Liva" and how it was animated with a special paper inscribed with God's name on it and placed in the creature's mouth. There was one formula for weekday and one for the Sabbath (*"Shabbot"*) when the *golem* would be inactive. One Friday night, he forgot to remove the paper. It interrupted services just after Psalms 93 was finished. After the "weekday" prayer was inserted into its mouth, it calmed down. Its remains were locked in the Old Synagogue attic with other relics from the Rabbi's time. [522]

DIE VOGELSCHEUCHE (THE SCARECROW), [523] a story about a grotesque scarecrow puppet who established a secret society that defended bourgeois values, was penned in 1835 by German poet and philosopher Ludwig Tieck. [524] Although it wasn't about the usual image of a *golem,* the animated scarecrow had its own vision of a utopian society.

The 1836 publication of German poet and essayist Christian Johann Heinrich Heine's [525] analysis of Adolf Henrich von Arnim-Boitzenburg [526] greatly enhanced the *golem's* popularity. The story told about Achim von Arnim's Gypsy Princess Isabella– a soulless figure of clay shaped like a *golem.* [527] German author Berthold Auerbach (1812-1882) published "the first Jewish novel," titled *SPINOZA: EIN HISTORISCHER ROMAN,* and connected the *golem* to Rabbi Loew in 1837. [528] [529]

Non-Jew journalist and folklorist German Franz Klutschak (1814-1886) published several accounts of the *golem.* In 1838, he published a series of pieces called THE OLD JEWISH CEMETERY IN PRAGUE AND ITS LEGENDS. Three years later in 1841, he published his story *DER*

---

[521] Joseph Seligmann Kohn (1803-1850). He wrote the book anonymously but would use the name Frederick Korn, among others.

[522] *GOETHE UNIVERSITÄT FRANKFURT AM MAIN,* freeman-Sammlung Universitätsbibliotheck.

[523] Printing and publishing by Georg Reimer. Berlin, 1854.

[524] Johann Ludwig Tieck was born in 1773 and died in 1853.

[525] Heine was born in 1797 and died in 1856.

[526] The first Prime Minister of Prussia 1803-1868. Read more about Von Arnim in GENDER AND GERMANNESS: CULTURAL PRODUCTIONS OF NATION, by Patricia Herminghouse, Magda Mueller, 51-62. *DIE ROMANTISCHE SCHULE* (THE ROMANTIC SCHOOL)

[527] Edan Dekel and David Gantt Gurley, HOW THE *GOLEM* CAME TO PRAGUE. The Jewish Quarterly Review, Vol. 103, No. 2. Spring 2013, 241-258.

[528] M. Cornis-Pope and John Neubauer, HOW DID THE *GOLEM* GET TO PRAGUE? in HISTORY OF THE LITERARY CULTURES OF EAST-CENTRAL EUROPE: Junctures and Disjunctures in the 19th and 20th Centuries, vol. 4, Types and Stereotypes (Amsterdam, 2010), 296–307.

[529] John Neubauer, HISTORY OF THE LITERARY CULTURES OF EAST-CENTRAL EUROPE: JUNCTURES, edited by Marcel Cornis-Pope, page 303.

GOLEM DES RABBI LOW (THE GOLEM, RABBI LOEW). [530]

Gustav Philippson published DER GOLEM EINE LEGENDE in ALLEGEMEINE ZEITUNG DES JUDENTUMS [531] in 1841. He retold the legend of the Maharal's *golem* in German verse, similar to Auerbach. [532] In this story, the golem is a ghost, not a clay figure. He can speak and is aware of his identity. The *golem* become belligerent on Yom Kipper rather than on Shabbot, as described in an earlier version a few years prior.

Abraham Moses Tendlau (1802-1878) published a narrative of the *golem* story and Rabbi Loew titled DER GOLEM DES HOCH-RABBI-LOB in his DAS BUCH DER SAGEN UND LEGENDEN JÜDISCHER VORZEIT IN 1842. He attested his knowledge about the *Maharal's golem* was based on oral tradition. [533] His story also followed Auerbach's version of the tale.

The same year, German Daniel Uffo Horn (1817-1860) wrote DER RABBI VON PRAG (Novelle), [534] in Prague, about a functionless carved wooden *golem* with a clockwork in his head. [535] German Otto von Skepsgardh (1818-1845) produced a satirical story about *golems* called DREI VORREDEN, ROSEN UN GOLEM-TIECK in 1844. [536] German educator and writer Gustav Philippson [537] published a ballad called DER GOLEM UND DIE EHEBRECHERIN (THE GOLEM AND THE ADULTERESS) in 1843. [538]

German writer and composer Annette von Droste-Hulshoff (1797-1848), penned the poem *"DIE*

---

[530] Hillel J. Kieval, LANGUAGES OF COMMUNITY: THE JEWISH EXPERIENCE IN THE CZECH LANDS, page 106.

[531] *ALLEGEMEINE ZEITUNG DES JUDENTUMS 5*, no. 44: 629-31 (Gedicht) from "THE GOLEM RETURNS: FROM GERMAN ROMANTIC LITERATURE TO GLOBAL JEWISH CULTURE," By Cathy S. Gelbin, page 202.

[532] See "*Golem*" in JEWISH ENCYCLOPEDIA (1906).

[533] Stuttgart, page 16-18 (Gedicht), See "*Golem*" in Wikipedia.com.

[534] John Neubauer, HOW DID THE GOLEM GET TO PRAGUE? in Cornis-Pope, Marcel, and Neubauer, J. HISTORY OF THE LITERARY CULTURES OF EAST-CENTRAL EUROPE, John Benjamins, 2010.

[535] HISTORY OF THE LITERARY CULTURES OF EAST-CENTRAL EUROPE: JUNCTURES, edited by Marcel Cornis-Pope, John Neubauer, page 302.

[536] Otto von Skepsgardh, Friedrich Rückert, DREI VORREDEN, ROSEN UND GOLEM-TIECK: EINE TRAGI-KOMISCHE ..., Volume 2, Issue 2. Berlin.

[537] Philippson was born in 1814 and died in 1880.

[538] Sulamith: eine Zeitscrift zur Beforderung der Cultur und Humanitat unter den Isrealiten (1843), Issue 2, Pg. 254-257. Cathy S. Gelbin, THE GOLEM RETURNS: FROM GERMAN ROMANTIC LITERATURE TO GLOBAL JEWISH CULTURE, page 202.

GOLEMS" the following year and was reprinted in 1976. [539] The poem, as follows:

"It's is a legend from the East
Of ways, dead flounder forms giving
Beloved forms that knows longing,
And the magic words are invigorating;
The Golem converts with known steps
He talks, he smiles with a known touch,
But it is not a beam in his eye,
It proposes no heart in his breast center." [540]

After it was printed in 1846, German Leopold Weisel (1804-1873) produced *DER GOLEM,* an influential collection of Jewish tales that become the standard *golem* story for the rest of the century. It was published in Prague by Wolf Pascheles *in GALLERIA DER SIPURIM EINE SAMMULUNG JUDISCHER SAGEN MARCHEN UND GESCHICHTEN ALS EIN BEITRAG ZUR VOLKERJUNDE."* [541] Wiesel spent the 1830s through 1840s involved in collecting and distributing Jewish folklore. Weisel was a friend of Franz Klutschak, according to *SIPPURIM: EINE SAMMLUNG JUDISCHER VOLKSSAGEN (1847).* [542] [543] [544]

German poet and writer Theodor Storm (1817-1888) wrote a poem called *"Ein Golem" ("A*

---

[539] *KABBALAH* AND THE ROMANTIC LITERATURE: BETWEEN MAGIC AND TROPE, edited by Eveline Goodman-Thau, Gert Mattenklott, Christoph Schulte. Page 130.

[540] Portion of poem "THE *GOLEMS*," by Annette von Droste-Hulshoff.

[541] John Neubauer, HOW DID THE *GOLEM* GET TO PRAGUE? in Cornis-Pope, M., and Neubauer, J. HISTORY OF THE LITERARY CULTURES OF EAST-CENTRAL EUROPE, John Benjamins, 2010.

[542] John Neubauer, "How did the *golem* get to Prague?" in Cornis-Pope, M., and Neubauer, J. HISTORY OF THE LITERARY CULTURES OF EAST-CENTRAL EUROPE, John Benjamins, 2010.

[543] Abraham Moses Tendlau, *DAS BUCH DER SAGEN UND LEGENDEN JÜDISCHER VORZEIT,* edited, 1873.

[544] Hillel J. Kieval, LANGUAGES OF COMMUNITY: THE JEWISH EXPERIENCE IN THE CZECH LANDS, page 106.

Golem") in 1851: [545] [546]

> *"A Golem. You say it was a eunuch, A beautiful state Kalenderer;*
> *But because it does not see any that he stitched leather? If only the*
> *right rain drip.*
> *And washes the number off his head So certainly calls each one:*
> *Lord, a fellow of leather!"* [547]

Another German poet and dramatist, Christian Freidrich Hebbel (1813-1863), produced a libretto in 1858 for Anton Rubenstein's musical drama *EIN STEINWURF ODER OPFER UM OPFER.* In it, the *golem* became R. Loews' servant. [548] [549]

Jakob Grimm published a *golem* story in the *ZEITUNG FUR EINSIEDLER* (JOURNAL FOR HERMITS) in 1808 (April). The tale was derived from the 1714 version by Schudt and was adapted from the 1674 account by C. Arnold about R. Eliyahu of Chelm. Grimm's story was a huge influence in the modern development of the *golem* legend. [550]

The creation of the *golem* was explained using the three letter *AMT* to instill life into the object in *ENTSTEHUNG*, (formation origin, rise) *DER VERLAGSPOESIE* (publishing poetry), a publication of poetry and verse was published in 1869 from *KLEINERE SCHRIFTEN (Short Writings) VON*

---

[545] DER GOLEM - HANDBUCH JÜDISCHE KULTURGESCHICHTE, "MANUEL JEWISH CULTURAL HISTORY: THE GOLEM, by Tanja Karlsbock and Armin Eidherr. C.VII.3

[546] *KABBALAH* AND THE ROMANTIC LITERATURE: BETWEEN MAGIC AND TROPE, edited by Eveline Goodman-Thau, Gert Mattenklott, Christoph Schulte. Page 13.

[547] Theodore Storm from *STAATSKALENDER*. Poems from the State Calendar. Chapter 59, 2. Available in Gutenburg Project.

[548] Eveline Goodman-Thau, Gert Mattenklott, Christoph Schulte, *KABBALA UND DIE LITERATUR DER ROMANTIK: ZWISCHEN MAGIE UND TROPE*, Appendix, page 134.

[549] COMPANION TO LITERARY MYTHS, HEROES AND ARCHETYPES, edited by Pierre Brunel, page 447.

[550] "THE NEWSPAPER FOR HERMITS," Issue 7, April 23, 1808. "Origin of Publishing Poetry," related by Jacob Grimm, Sp. 58. Published by Heidelberg University. Published April-August 1808. See also THE GOLEM RETURNS: FROM GERMAN ROMANTIC LITERATURE TO GLOBAL JEWISH CULTURE, by Cathy S. Gelbin.

JAKOB GRIMM.

German-Jewish novelist Ludwig Kalisch (1814-1882) wrote *DIE GESCHICHTE VON DEM GOLEM* (romanzen) in 1872. [551]

DAS BUCH DER SAGEN UND LEGENDEN JÜDISCHER VORZEIT, edited by Abraham Moses Tendlau, was published in 1873 and contained the story of the *golem* among other Jewish legends. [552]

In 1880 Mortiz Gudermann (1835-1918) published *Gescgichte des Erziehungswesens und der Cultur der abendländischen* (History of education and culture of the Occidental) from Ms. Munich (1268) where he discusses the creation of a man using earth as its basic element.

Leopold Kompert [553] penned DER *GOLEM* (THE *GOLEM*) (Gedicht) in 1882. [554] The following year, Austrian author Moritz Bermann (1823-1895) wrote *DIE LEGENDE VON GOLEM* (THE LEGEND OF THE *GOLEM*) (Erzahlung). [555]

A *golem* creation technique of possible *Ashkenazi* source was preserved by Rabbi Abraham Galante, a 16th century Safed *Kabbalist* and a disciple of R. Moses Cordovero. His views were quoted by Rabbi Abraham Azulai [556] in his commentary about the creation of a *golem* in 'OR HA-HAMAH. In 1886, he wrote that "creation of all the worlds was [accomplished] by the 22 letters, and so also the creation of man by the 22 letters." He cited the feats of Rabbi Hoshaya (Oshaya) who "created a man, and similar things, [these] were by means of the 22 letters." [557]

In his explanation, he said the mystics would spread a layer of "new" dust on the ground or floor and inscribe the name of the being they want to create. They would combine each letter of the object's name with every letter of the Hebrew alphabet. To destroy their creation, they would

---

[551] Eveline Goodman-Thau, Gert Mattenklott, Christoph Schulte, *KABBALA UND DIE LITERATUR DER ROMANTIK: ZWISCHEN MAGIE UND TROPE*, appendix, page 134.

[552] [552] Abraham Moses Tendlau, *DAS BUCH DER SAGEN UND LEGENDEN JÜDISCHER VORZEIT*, edited 1873. Page 364.

[553] Kompert, a Bohemian Jewish writer, was born in 1822 and died in 1886. He was brought to Vienna court for publishing ideas contrary to the Catholic faith. This became known as the Kompert Affair. See Wikipedia, "Leopold Kompert."

[554] Eveline Goodman-Thau, Gert Mattenklott, Christoph Schulte, *KABBALA UND DIE LITERATUR DER ROMANTIK: ZWISCHEN MAGIE UND TROPE*, appendix, page 134. November 1882," in Sa¨mtliche Werke in zehn Ba¨nden, ed. S. Hock (Leipzig, 1906). Wikipedia, "Leopold Kompert."

[555] Ibid.

[556] Rabbi Azulai was born in 1570 and died in 1643.

[557] Idel, Moshe, "Views on the *Golem*," from GOLEM: JEWISH MAGICAL, page 69 and footnote page 79.

reverse the pattern, according to the story of R. Hanina. [558]

William Wynn Westcott (1846-1925) published SEPHER YETZIRAH, THE BOOK OF FORMATION in 1887. He translated it from the Hebrew into English and followed Golden Dawn principles to explain the concepts. Westcott was the Supreme Magus of the Rosicrucian Society of England. His work was collated with the Latin versions of Johannes Pistorius, Postellus (Postel) and Rittangelius. [559] This translation was a primary source for the rituals and Knowledge lectures of the Golden Dawn. It was reprinted in 1893 and 1911 and is still one of the most popular versions of the SEPHER YETZIRAH in circulation today.

Abraham Epstein [560] published BEITAGE ZUR JUDISCHEN ALTERTUMSKUNDE in Vienna in 1887. It was a reprint of Rabbi Judah the Pious (d. 1217) of Speyer in Regensburg who wrote down a version of the legend regarding Ben Sira from SEPHER GEMATRIOTH. [561] [562]

Czechoslovakian artist and painter Mikolas Ales, [563] a non-Jew, rendered a pencil drawing in 1897 depicting Rabbi Loew of Prague conjuring a *golem* with Hebrew letters that spelled out his last name, "Ales," dancing in the air in front of him in place of the letters *AMT* ("truth"), as traditionally shown. The drawing was on display during an exhibit at the Jewish Museum in New York in 1988. [564]

---

[558] Ibid.

[559] Kaplan, Aryeh, SEPHER YETZIRAH: THEORY, page 335.

[560] Abraham Epstein was born in 1841 in 1918.

[561] Abraham Epstein, BEITRÄGE: ZUR JUDISCHEN ALTERTHUMSKUNDE, 1887.

[562] Scholem, Gershom , ON THE KABBALAH AND ITS SYMBOLISM, page 179.

[563] Mikolas Ales was born in 1852 and died in 1913.

[564] ABOUT THE ARTS: THE GOLEM - AS MEDIEVAL HERO, FRANKENSTEIN MONSTER AND PROTO-COMPUTER, "*New York Times*," December 4, 1988.

19ᵗʰ Century SEPHER YETZIRAH

The book *YETZIRAH* was published in 1860 in Lemberg with commentaries from Saadia Gaon, Rabbi Abraham ben Dior Halevi, Rabbi Moses ben Nachman, Elieser of Germisa, Moses Botriel, and Rabbi Eliah Wilna. This was an update to the 1830 edition by Johann Friedrich von Meyer, D.D. [565]

That same year, a printed edition of *SEPHER YETZIRAH* was also published by Benjamin Bischko in Lvov. It contained commentaries from the Mantua, Ari and *Gra* recension. [566]

German politician Frieherr Albert von Thimus, (known as Albert of Thimus, 1806-1878), wrote an analysis of the *SEPHER YETZIRAH* in 1868 in *DIE HARMONIKALE SHMBOLIK DES ALTERTHUMS.* [567] Thimus argued that the SEPHER YETZIRAH probably originated from the period shortly before the end of the Babylonia exile. [568]

A three-volume edition of *SEPHER YETZIRAH* was published in 1874-1875 in Jerusalem. It had commentaries of Gra, edited by his disciple Rabbi Moshe Shlomo of Tulchin, and the commentary on Gra by Rabbi Yitzack ben Yehudah Leib Kahana. [569]

The Gra version of the *SEPHER YETZIRAH* from Elijah ben Solomo Zalman (the Ari, 1720-1797), the Gaon of Vilna, was published in 1974 with some corrections by his disciple Moshe Shlomo of Tolichin. It included a lengthy super-commentary, *TOLDOTH YITZCHAK* by Yitzchak Kahana with a foldout Kabbalistic chart at the end depicting the 231 Gates according to the interpretations of the Ari. Although the title is 1874, the approbations are dated 1875. [570] The Gra-Ari version is considered the most authentic.

The first English translation of the *SEPHER YETZIRAH* was published in 1877 by American Reform Rabbi and author Dr. Isidor Kalisch (1816-1886) titled *SEPHER YETZIRAH*, A BOOK ON CREATION OR THE JEWISH METAPHYSICS OF REMOTE ANTIQUITY, WITH ENGLISH TRANSLATION, PREFACE, EXPLANATORY NOTES AND GLOSSARY BY REV. DR. ISIDOR KALISCH.

---

[565] Kalisch, Isidor, Knut Stenring *SEPHER YETZIRAH*: THE BOOK OF CREATION, page 8.

[566] Kaplan, Aryeh, *SEPHER YETZIRAH*: THEORY, page 319.

[567] (Cologne), p 370-395 from Kaplan, Aryeh, *SEPHER YETZIRAH*: THEORY, page 336.

[568] Rosh-Pinnah, Eliyahu, *SEPHER YETZIRAH* AND THE ORIGINAL TETRAGRAMMATON, Berlin.

[569] Kaplan, Aryeh, *SEPHER YETZIRAH*: THEORY, page 320.

[570] Kestenbaum & Company auction item #60, Lot 109.

In it, he reproduced many of Meyer's annotations. Hebrew is set side by side with the English translation. He says the book "contains nothing but a medley of arbitrary, mystical explanations and sophisticated distributions of scriptural verses, astrological notions, oriental superstitions, a metaphysical jargon, a poor knowledge of physics..." in reference to the book *YETZIRAH*, published 1860. Mentions about Rittangelius, Postellus, Saadia, etc. Some material was courtesy of Manley P. Hall's SECRET TEACHINGS OF ALL AGES. [571]

A third commentary on *SEPHER YETZIRAH* was published in 1880 by David Castelli, in Firenze, *called II COMMENTO DI SABBETAI DONNOLO LIBRO DELLA CREAZIONE.* It contained text from 10th century Donnolo's works with a comprehensive introduction. Andrew Sharf's 1976 book on THE UNIVERSE OF SHABBETHAI DONNOLO contained critical discussions from this work. [572]

In 1882, Jewish convert to Christianity Alfred Edersheim (1824-1889) published a translation of the *SEPHER YETZIRAH* with a commentary in his piece titled "THE LIFE AND TIMES OF JESUS THE MESSIAH," which combined an in-depth study of first century Jewish life and customs with Christian orthodoxy. He strongly advocated that Jesus' teachings are derived from Judaism. [573]

In Warsaw, Poland, the most popular version of *SEPHER YETZIRAH* containing two editions within one was published in 1884. The first section included nine commentaries from the Mantua edition, *OTZAR HASHEM,* and the *CHAKAMONI* commentary by Shabbethai Donnolo.

The second section contains *PRI YITZCHAK,* commentaries from Gra and Ari, and the Long Version at the end. Most of today's circulated sources are no earlier than this version. Gershom Scholem believed this version is distorted and contained many typographical errors. [574] While the actual text of the variant version of *SEPHER YETZIRAH* may contain errors, it is the commentaries of famous rabbis that hold value to this edition.

In Berlin Shlomo Zalman Chaim Halberstam [575] published *PERUSH SEPHER YETZSIRAH* in 1885. It contained the work of 12th century Spanish Talmudist Judah ben Barzillai of Barcelona (often called *Al-Bargeloni*– "the Barcelonian"). [576]

---

[571] Rev. Dr. Isidor Kalisch, SEPHER YETZIRAH, A BOOK ON CREATION; OR, THE JEWISH METAPHYSICS OF REMOTE ANTIQUITY, 1877, New York. L.H. Frank & Co.

[572] Gruenwald, Ithamar A PRELIMINARY CRITICAL EDITION OF SEPHER YEZIRA, page 224.

[573] Magdalena Maczynska, THE GOSPEL ACCORDING TO THE NOVELIST: RELIGIOUS SCRIPTURE AND CONTEMPORARY FICTION, 2015.

[574] Kaplan, Aryeh, SEPHER YETZIRAH: THEORY, page 320.

[575] Shlomo Zalman Chaim Halberstam was born in 1832 and died in 900.

[576] Schechter, Solomon and Louis Ginsberg, JUDAH BEN BARZILLAI, Jewish Encyclopedia.

Paris doctor and occultist Gerard Encausese, [577] better known as Papus, published a 1888 French edition of *SEPHER YETZIRAH.* [578] He added the 32 Paths of Wisdom and 50 Gates of Intelligence. His work followed Pistorius, Postellus, Rittangelius, the Golden Dawn, and Rosicrucian teachings. Encausese was a student of the French occultist Eliphas Levi (Alphonse Louis Constant, 1810-1875) and founded the Masonic Order of Martinists. [579]

PERUSH AL SEPHER YEẒIRAH, a commentary on the *SEPHER YETZIRAH* with extracts from Eleazar ben Judah of Worms and Shabbathai Donnolo's commentary was printed in Przemysl in 1889. It contained the 221 Gates of Rabbi Eleazar prescribed to create a *golem*. Parts are included in the popular late 20th century work of *SEPHER YETZIRAH* THE BOOK OF CREATION IN THEORY AND PRACTICE by Aryeh Kaplan. [580]

Rabbi Meyer Lambert [581] published a 1891 French version of Saadia Gaon's work *TZAFSOR KTAAV AL-MABADI* (931), under the title of *COMMENTAIRE SUR LE SEPHER YETZIRAH PAR LE GAON SAADYA.* It was republished with a Hebrew translation by Yosef ben David Kapach in 1972. [582] The work was translated into French and printed in Paris from the Ms. Oxford 1533 Mantua edition and is on display in Bodleian Library.

A medieval *grimoire* called THE SWORD OF MOSES, was published by Dr. Moses Gaster [583] a prominent linguist who had a vast library of over two thousand manuscripts. He translated it from a 13th or 14th century manuscript in his library [584] that described the world of angels, provided prayers and obscure incantations that the student was required to perform in order to use this "sword." Gaster believed the text predated the 11th century. Gaster's book was republished in 1997. [585]

---

[577] Gerard Encausese was born in 1865 and died in 1916.

[578] Kaplan, Aryeh, *SEPHER YETZIRAH*: THEORY, page 320.

[579] "Papus," Wikipedia Spain.

[580] Kaplan, Aryeh, *SEPHER YETZIRAH*: THEORY, page 303. The charts are on pages 304-309.

[581] Rabbi Meyer Lambert was born in 1863 and died in 1930.

[582] Kaplan, Aryeh, *SEPHER YETZIRAH*: THEORY, page 330.

[583] Moses Gaster was born in 1856 and died in 1939. In 1954, his library collection was purchased by the John Rylands Library. Gaster composed dozens of works in many subjects, including books for the Romanian Jewish community. See Moses Gaster, Wikipedia.com.

[584] This manuscript was formerly called Ms. Faster 78, now London. British Library Ms. Or. 10678.

[585] "The SWORD OF MOSES," Wikipedia.com.

Hebrew scholar Phineas Mordell [586] published *SEPHER YETZIRAH* in an 1894 translation. But, it is not accepted by *Kabbalistic* scholars in Philadelphia, PA. He published a similar version in 1914. [587]

Peter Davidson [588] published an 1896 English version of *SEPHER YETZIRAH* and added the 50 Gates of Intelligence and 32 Paths of Wisdom. [589]

---

[586] Phineas Mordell was born in 1861and died in 1934.

[587] Kaplan, Aryeh, *SEPHER YETZIRAH*: THEORY, page 335.

[588] Peter Davidson was born in 1837 and died in 1915.

[589] Printed at Loudsville, GA. "THE *SEPHER YETZIRAH*," by William Wynn Westcott.

19ᵗʰ Century Secular Versions

English translations of the *SEPHER YETZIRAH*, were published under the titles of BOOK OF CREATION and THE BOOK OF FORMATION began to circulate in the 19ᵗʰ century.

When the popular handbook on all magic acts, THE MAGUS, was published by occultist Francis Barrett in 1801, it sparked an interest among non-Jews and English-only speaking American Jews.

THE MAGUS was a handbook of ceremonial magic and contained charts, diagrams from ancient Hebrew mystical texts. He reproduced the chart of 72 Angels "bearing the name of God *Shemhamphora*." [590]

SEPHER YETZIRAH, THE BOOK OF FORMATION, by William Wynn Westcott, MB, JP is reprinted in English in 1893 from the 1887 Warsaw edition with additional notes as part of *COLLECTANES HERMETICA* by Samuel Weiser, York Beach, ME., and once again in London in 1911. [591]

Christian theologian Lazarus Goldschmidt [592] published a text in 1894 of Isaac Luria (Loria) *in SEPHER JEZIRAH— DAS BUCH DER SCHOPFUNG* (Frankfurt am Mein). [593] [594] He says the *SEPHER YETZIRAH* originated in the 2ⁿᵈ century BCE. [595] According to the "Jewish Quarterly Review," Goldschmidt constructed a poor text from four existing versions instead of any one version.

---

[590] Barrett, Francis, THE MAGUS, PAGE 243.

[591] Kaplan, Aryeh, *SEPHER YETZIRAH*: THEORY, page 335

[592] Lazarus Goldschmidt was born in 1871 and died in 1950.

[593] Kaplan, Aryeh, *SEPHER YETZIRAH*: THEORY, page 342.

[594] Arthur Edward Waite, THE DOCTRINE AND LITERATURE OF THE *KABBALAH*, page 172.

[595] Giulio Lepschy, HISTORY OF LINGUISTICS VOLUME I: THE EASTERN TRADITIONS OF LINGUISTICS, 2014, page 155 from "Jewish Quarterly Review," 19:1928.

The century ended with Detlev von Liliencron's [596] ballad in 1898 titled *"Der Golem."* [597] A portion follows:

Der Golem

Prag, das alte sagenreiche,

Barg schon viele Menschenweisheit,

Barg schon viele Menschentorheit,

Auch den hohen Rabbi Löw.

Rabbi Löw war sehr zu Hause,

In den Künsten, Wissenschaften,

Und besonders in der schwarzen,

In der schweren Kabbala.

So erschuf er einen Golem, Einen holzgeschnitzten Menschen, Tat belebend in den Mund ihm Einen Zauberspruch: den Schem.

Roughly translated: The *Golem*. Prague, the old saying already many people wisdom, already many people foolishness, even the Great Rabbi Loew who was very at home in the arts, sciences, and particularly in the black arts, in the heavy *Kabbalah*. So, he created a *golem*, a wooden carved person. In the mouth was placed a spell: the *Shem (*Holy Name*)*.

---

[596] Detlev von Liliencron was born in 1844 and died in 1909.

[597] Goodman-Thau, Eveline, *KABBALA UND DIE LITERATUR DER ROMANTIK: ZWISCHEN MAGIE UND TROPE*, edited by Gert Mattenklott, Christoph Schulte, Appendix, page 134.

20ᵗʰ Century (1900-1999)
Kabbalah Comes to America

Throughout the 20ᵗʰ century, the *SEPHER YETZIRAH* and *golem* were popular cultural topics across Europe and America. Nearly every year some form of media was produced that featured either topic.

The *SEPHER YETZIRAH* continued to be circulated in both long and short recensions with the ancient commentaries, original errors, and new perspectives by 20ᵗʰ century *Kabbalists*. While the study of the *SEPHER YETZIRAH* was limited to students of *Kabbalah*, the *golem* took a life of its own.

The *golem* became a familiar cultural icon in the arts, theatre, film and television. Hundreds of authors, poets, and movie producers produced their twists on the legend of the *golem*. Rabbi Loew, however, remains the central figure over the original Rabbi of Chelm.

Austrian playwright Rudolf Lother [598] published a volume of stories about the *golem* and Rabbi Loew in 1900 (and in 1904) called *DER GOLEM, PHANTASIEN UND HISTORIEN* (THE *GOLEM*: FANTASIES AND MYSTERIES). [599]

Under the auspices of the Theosophical Publishing Society, [600] Dr. S. Karppe, published *ETUDE SUR LES ORIGINES ET LA NATURE DU ZOHAR PRECEDE D'UNE ETUDE SUR L'HISTORIE DE LA KABBALE* in Paris the following year. [601] Dr. Karppe explored the origins of the *ZOHAR* and its relation to *Kabbalah*. Occultist A.E. Waite read his work and commented about him in his own writings.

American-born British poet and well-known mystic Arthur Edward Waite (A.E. Waite) [602]

---

[598] Rudolf Lother Spitzer was born in 1865 and died in 1943.

[599] Goodman-Thau, Eveline, *KABBALA UND DIE LITERATUR DER ROMANTIK: ZWISCHEN MAGIE UND TROPE*, edited by Gert Mattenklott, Christoph Schulte, Appendix, page 134. See also the Jewish Virtual Library, from ENCYCLOPEDIA JUDAICA.

[600] See an in-depth discussion of Karppe and Waite in THE DOCTRINE AND LITERATURE OF THE KABBALAH by Arthur Edward Waite, page xviii.

[601] Kaplan, Aryeh, *SEPHER YETZIRAH*: THEORY, page 335. Public domain document.

[602] A.E. Waite was born in 1857 and died in 1942.

published the popular volume of DOCTRINE AND LITERATURE OF THE *KABBALAH* in 1902. His chapter on *SEPHER YETSIRAH* gave a good overview, but he labeled the book as an "arbitrary doctrine of a virtue inherent in words and letters" which "can only be scandalized (sic) at the childish nature of *Yetziratic* tabulations." [603] Waite wrote extensively on occult subjects, including several books on the *Kabbalah*.

Manasseh Grossberg published THE *YESIRA* in 1902. It was a version of Dunash ben Tamin's work with a commentary apparently based on the lectures of Isaac Israeli, Abu Sahl's instructor in London. [604] An edition of *SEPHER YETZIRAH* was printed in London with a commentary by Donash ibn Tamin that year. [605]

In 1902, German industrialist, politician and writer Walther Rathenau (1867-1922) published RABBI ELIESERS WEIB. AUS DEM JERUSALEMITISCHEN *TALMUD*, a piece about Rabbi Eleazar and the *TALMUD*. [606]

Prague German-language poet, lyricist and writer Hugo Salus (1866-1929) published a verse in 1903 on "Der hohe *Rabbi* Low" (Ballade) which gained popularity by World War I. [607]

Joshua Eisenbach of Prystik published *OTOT U-MO'ADIM* in Przystyk, with commentaries on *SEPHER YEZIRAH* from Elijah ben Solomon and the Gaon of Vilna (1847) in 1903. [608]

Karl Baron von Torresani (1846-1907) published *"Der Diener"* (The Servant)in *Deutsches Skizzenbuch,* (German Sketch Book) Volume 2 in Charlottenburg in 1904. [609]

Two German translations of the ALPHABET OF RABBI AKIBA were published in Leipzig in 1907 by August Wünsche in his *AUS ISRAELS LEHRHALLEN, VI*. Both have similar content, but vary on length. It also includes an explanation on the use of the *ATBASh* and *ALBM* letter permutation methods.

In 1908 German novelist and playwright Arthur Holitscher (1869-1941) produced THE *GOLEM*

---

[603] Waite, A.E., DOCTRINE AND LITERATURE OF THE *KABBALAH*, London: Theosophical Publishing Society. 1902.

[604] Bodleian Ms. No. 2250.

Kaplan, Aryeh, *SEPHER YETZIRAH*: THEORY, page 320.

[606] Published in in *GESAMMELTE SCHRIFTEN*, 305-7, Berlin: S. Fischer Verlag." (Legende). From THE *GOLEM* RETURNS: FROM GERMAN ROMANTIC LITERATURE TO GLOBAL JEWISH CULTURE, By Cathy S. Gelbin, page 202.

[607] From the Jewish Virtual Library, from ENCYCLOPEDIA JUDAICA.

[608] Scholem, Gershom, LA CABALA, page 37.

[609] John Neubauer, HISTORY OF THE LITERARY CULTURES OF EAST-CENTRAL EUROPE, edited by Marcel Cornis-Pope, page 687.

GHETTO LEGEND in three acts [610] It was performed at the Deutsches Theatre as a psychological interpretation of the *golem* legend. However, the play was rejected after several changes. It was later adapted to by Gustav Meyrink's novel, THE *GOLEM*, in 1914. [611] [612] Holitscher later accused film director and actor Paul Wegener of plagiarizing his story. Also, that year Georg Munzer (1866-1908) published *DER MARCHENKANTOR* (Roman). [613]

Rabbi Yudel Rosenberg (1859-1935) published *NIFL'OS MAHARAL* (WONDERS OF THE MAHARAL) in 1909, a legend of the *golem* created by Rabbi Loew. Rosenberg said he had an original letter from a manuscript written by R. Loew's and a manuscript by his son-in-law that described the feat of the Rabbi. One of the *Maharal's* deeds was rescuing the Jews from a blood libel. During Rosenberg's time, false accusations and blood libels became a real threat again during the Hislner case in Czechoslovakia in 1899, so the topic was a current interest. Rosenberg published the tales in Hebrew and Yiddish and they become one of the most important modern literary works produced at the time. They formed the basis of Chayim Bloch's version that was published a decade later. [614] [615]

In a 1911 letter to Carl Jung (1875-1961) from Sigmund Freud (1856-1939), he mentioned the *doppelganger*, an apparition or a double of a living person. He wrote, "If there is such a thing as a phylogenetic memory in the individual, which unfortunately will soon be undeniable, this is also the source of the *uncanny* (Freud's italics) aspect of the *doppelganger*." [616]

Phineas Mordell published his thesis THE ORIGIN OF LETTERS AND NUMERALS ACCORDING TO THE *SEPHER YETZIRAH* in the Jewish Quarterly Review, 1912-1913." [617] The book version is published by the Dropsie College in Philadelphia, PA. and it is republished by Samuel Weiser, Inc. in 1975. [618] Mordel said the two versions of *Sepher Yetzirah* commentators of 9th century

---

[610] Arthur Holitscher, *DER GOLEM; GHETTOLEGENDE IN DREI AUFZÜGEN*, 1908. Publisher S. Fischer, Berlin. Also read "HISTORY OF THE LITERARY CULTURES OF EAST-CENTRAL EUROPE: JUNCTURES," edited by Marcel Cornis-Pope, John Neubauer, pages 310-311.

[611] Wikipedia, Germany.

[612] From the Jewish Virtual Library, from ENCYCLOPEDIA JUDAICA.

[613] Georg Munzer, *DER MARCHENKANTOR,* Berlin, Marquardt & Co., 1908.

[614] Emily D. Bilski and Idel, Moshe, THE GOLEM: AN HISTORICAL OVERVIEW.

[615] See more in *GOLEM*: JEWISH MAGICAL, by Idel, Moshe, page 252.

[616] Freud, Sigmund, THE FREUD-JUNG LETTERS: THE CORRESPONDENCE BETWEEN SIGMUND FREUD AND C.G. JUNG, By William McGuire, Ralph Manheim, Richard Francis Carrington Hull, Alan McGlashan. Page 200. Written in Vienna on October 13, 1911.

[617] April 1912, vol. II, and April 1913 vol. III. JEWISH QUARTERLY REVIEW," New Series 2:557-583 (1912), 3:517-544 (1913). Published separately in 1914, see *SEPHER YETZIRAH: THEORY* by Kaplan, Aryeh, page 335.

[618] Kaplan, Aryeh, *SEPHER YETZIRAH: THEORY*, page 335.

mixed the original *Sepher Yetzirah* with an early commentary, referred to as *Sepher Yetzirah* II. As it was handed down, it was probably re-written to fit with the culture of the time. All commentaries written since the beginning of the 10th century are based on this commentary on *Sepher Yetzirah* and not the original. The shorter and longer version (the longer version is printed as an appendix) existed in 10th century, and its earliest written form in the 11th century.

Freemason British occultist, and one of the founders of the Hermetic Order of the Golden Dawn, Samuel Liddell MacGregor Mathers (1854-1918) translated Christian Knorr von Rosenroth's 1684 edition of KABBALAH DENUDATA (THE *KABBALAH* UNVEILED in 1912. It contained portions from the ZOHAR, THE BOOK OF CONCEALED MYSTERY and THE GREATER AND LESSER HOLY ASSEMBLIES. This popular book was reprinted many times.

Mathers also translated the works of THE KEY OF SOLOMON THE KING: *CLAVICULA SALOMONIS* (anonymous 14th century), THE *GOETIA*: THE LESSER KEY OF SOLOMON THE KING, *LEMEGETON – CLAVICULA SALOMONIS REGIS*, Book 1 (anonymous 17th century), The BOOK OF THE SACRED MAGIC OF ABREMELIN THE MAGE, (14th century), The *GRIMOIRE* OF ARMADEL, (17th century), and ASTRAL PROJECTION, RITUAL MAGIC AND ALCHEMY. Mathers was a former friend, turned enemy, of dark occultist Aleister Crowley. The Book of SACRED MAGIC OF ABRAMELIN THE MAGE, is a story about a magician named Abramelin who taught a system of magic to Eleazar of Worms. The manuscript is dated 1458, [619] the year the rabbi died, although there is no authentication, except the date on the manuscript.

Contesa Calomira de Cimara published a 1913 French translation of *SEPHER YEZIRAH* in Paris, and in a translation by E. Bischof. [620]

In Philadelphia, Phineas Mordell published another version of *SEPHER YETZIRAH* in THE ORIGIN OF LETTERS AND NUMERALS ACCORDING TO THE *SEPHER YETZIRAH*, as a separate publication from his earlier article in 1914. It was similar to his 1894, 1912 and 1913 versions, but contains additional historical data and quotes. [621]

---

[619] Translation by S.L. Mac Gregor Mathers 1900, London. "Translated from the Original Hebrew into the French, and now rendered from the latter language into English. From a unique and valuable MS. in the "Bibliothèque de l'Arsenal" at Paris."

[620] Kaplan, Aryeh, *SEPHER YETZIRAH:* THEORY page 336.

[621] JEWISH QUARTERLY REVIEW, New Series 2:557-583 (1912), 3:517-544 (1913). Published separately in Philadelphia in 1914. Reprinted by Samuel Weiser, York Beach, ME in 1975. See reference in *SEPHER YETZIRAH*: THEORY by Kaplan, Aryeh, page 335.

Cover of Gustav Meyrink's *"DER GOLEM."*

Author Johannes Hess produced a four act play in 1914 called *DER RABBINER VON PRAG* (Drama)– The Rabbi of Prague. [622]

Austrian novelist and banker Gustav Meyrink (1868-1932) wrote his most successful novel DER GOLEM· (The *Golem*) in 1915 Leipzig. It is first published in serial form in 1913-1914 in *"DIE WEISSEN BLATTER,"* and in book form in 1915. It was adapted for film and theatre by director Paul Wegener, [623] translated into English as THE GOLEM in 1964, and made into a Yiddish play as DER GOLEM by H. Leivick (1914-1959). [624] A fragment of this film is available in the public domain. [625]

The first film on the *golem* was released in 1915 as a silent horror flick called DER *GOLEM*. It was written and directed by German actor Paul Wegener (1874-1948) and Henrik Galeen (1881-1949) and starred Wegener as the *golem*. It told the 16th century story of Rabbi Loew who saved the Jews from persecution by creating a *golem* to protect the community. A second film was released two years later and was shown in the United States as "THE MONSTER OF FATE." Wegener released three films on the *golem* through 1921. [626]

In 1916, Auguste Hauschner (1850-c.1924) published a German edition of *DER TOD DES LOWEN* (Novellle), repeating the story of Rabbi Loew and his *golem*. [627]

---

[622] Gustch, Johannes Hess, *DER RABBINER VON PRAG (REB LOB): KABBALISTISCHES DRAMA IN 4 AKTEN*; NACHE E. *PRAGER LEGENDE*, 1914, 79 pages.

[623] Gustav Meyrink, THE *GOLEM*."

[624] H. Leivick, *DER GOLEM VON H. LEIVICK*, Hamburger Kammerspiel, 1995, 32 pages.

[625] THE GOLEM, 1915 lost film fragments," at https://archive.org/details/TheGolem1915LostFilmFragments

[626] "The *Golem* (1915 Film)," Wikipedia.com.

[627] Agusta Hauchner, Fleischel, *DER TOD DES LOWEN*, 1916. Volume 2 of *DIE FELDBUCHER*, 159 pages.

Czech writer and director Antonin Fencl (1881-1952) produced a play and book in 1916 about Rabbi Loew and his *golem* creation called "*GOLEM*. FANTASTICKA HRA" ("*Golem*. A Fantastic Play"). Artist Milos Klicman drew the book cover. [628] [629]

Paul Wegener's released his second film on the *golem*, "*DER GOLEM* UND DIE TANZERIN" ("THE *GOLEM* AND THE DANCER") on January 15, 1917. It was a satirical depiction of an actor who impersonated the *golem* he made famous. Wegener again starred as the *golem* in the film. [630] The first *golem* movie was released in 1915, second in 1917 and the third three years later.

Irma Singer wrote a children's story in 1918 titled "*Wohin der Golem die kranken Manner bringen lieb*," ("the *golem* bringing healing to the sick men") that presented the *golem* as a miracle-worker. [631]

Noted author and Rabbi Chayim Yitzchak Bloch (1865-1948) published a novel in 1920 titled *Der Prager Golem* (The *Golem*, legends of the Ghetto of Prague), about R. Loew and the *golem* in Berlin. By this time, the *golem* is well known in arts, writings and film. Four years later, he published a controversial, unknown letter from the *Maharal*. The English edition is published in 1925.

In 1921, Czech writer Karel Capek's (1890-1938) science fiction play R.U.R. (ROSSUM'S UNIVERSAL ROBOTS) coined the term "robot." [632] In the play, a scientist discovers a way to create precision human-like machines. They eventually dominate the human race, but the humans are saved at the last moment. Capek denied that his robot character is modeled after the *golem* even though there are similarities in the plot.

A translation of *SEPHER YETZIRAH* was published in Czech by Otakar Griese (1881-1932) in 1921. [633] H. Leivick (1888-1962) produced a Yiddish-language "dramatic poem in eight sections in 1921 called THE *GOLEM*. [634] As the world's foremost Yiddish poet, this is his best-known work.

The U.S. premiere of Paul Wegener's third silent horror film, *DER GOLEM*: WIE ER IN DIE

---

[628] A. Fencl, *GOLEM. FANTASTICKA HRA*, 1916.

[629] For a summary of the play, see "HISTORY OF THE LITERARY CULTURES OF EAST-CENTRAL EUROPE: JUNCTURES," edited by Marcel Cornis-Pope, John Neubauer, page 311-312.

[630] THE *GOLEM* AND THE DANCING GIRL (1917) at IMDB.com.

[631] Pierre Brunel, COMPANION TO LITERARY MYTHS, HEROES AND ARCHETYPES, page 473.

[632] "*Golem*," Wikipedia.com.

[633] Idel, Moshe, *GOLEM*: JEWISH MAGICAL, page 334.

[634] "*Golem*," Wikipedia.com.

WELT" [635] ("THE *GOLEM*: HOW HE CAME INTO THE WORLD") was released on June 19, 1921. It was co-written and co-directed by Paul Wegener, who also starred as the *golem*. The film continued the theme of R. Loew's *golem* in the 16th century. Wegener wanted to produce the film in 1914, but did not get the investment money he needed from the producer. It premiered in Germany on October 29, 1920. [636]

Wegener also had a disagreement in 1928 with Arthur Holitscher (wrote three-act play *"DER GOLEM"*) who accused him of plagiarizing his 1908 drama, "DER *GOLEM*." But Holitscher was unable to convince the court that the work was stolen. [637] The movie was remade in 1936.

During the summer of 1921, "THE *GOLEM*, WIE ER IN DIE WELT KAM, ERDACHT UND INS WERK GESETZT" ("THE *GOLEM*, HOW HE CAME INTO THE WORLD, devised and put into effect") (Fimmanuskript) played for almost a year at the Criterion Film Theatre in New York. "The *Golem*" is shown for three days at the Lyceum. [638]

Between 1921 and 1922 Albert Kovessy's musical play "The *Golem*" [639] is presented in three-acts at Gabel's Yiddish Theatre on 116th St. in New York. The English version is by James L.A. Burrell and music by Eugene Viranyi.

1922– Auguste Hauschner (1850-c.1924) republished a German edition of *"DER TOD DES LOWEN"* (Novellle) in Leipzig telling the story of about R. Loew. [640]

1923– Knut Stenring published THE BOOK OF FORMATION, OR *SEPHER YETZIRAH* in London. Stenring attributed the information to Rabbi Akiba Ben Joseph, and translated it from the Hebrew with annotations. Stenring uses Goldschmidt's versions. [641] It is similar to Phineas Mordell's study of ORIGIN OF LETTERS. Stenring makes some mistakes in Hebrew, according to Phineas Mordel. [642] His MASTER KEY TO THE THEORETICAL AND PRACTICAL *KABALA* produced

---

[635] Directed by Carl Boese and Paul Wegener. Written by Henrik Galeen and Paul Wegener. From IMDB.com.

[636] "The *Golem*" (1920) at IMDB.com.

[637] John Neubauer, HISTORY OF THE LITERARY CULTURES OF EAST-CENTRAL EUROPE: JUNCTURES, edited by Marcel Cornis-Pope, page 311-312.

[638] "*Golem*," Wikipedia.com.

[639] CATALOG OF COPYRIGHT ENTRIES. Part 1. [B] Group 2. Pamphlets, Etc. New Series," 1921. Page 1792.

[640] Agusta Hauchner Fleischel, *DER TOD DES LOWEN*, 1916. Volume 2 of DIE FELDBUCHER, 159 pages.

[641] Knut Stenring, THE BOOK OF FORMATION OR *SEPHER YETZIRA* in Helsingborg, Sweden through London, Rider & Sons.

[642] "Jewish Quarterly Review, 1928, p 79.

the correspondences between the English and Hebrew alphabets. Waite surveyed the historical background of the *SEPHER YETZIRAH* translations and the text. It was reprinted in 1970.

1923– Romanian opera composer Nicolae Bretan (1887-1968) produced a one-act opera called "THE *GOLEM.*" It was first performed the following year in Cluj and revived in 1990 in Denver, Colorado. [643]

1923– Chayim Bloch published an unknown letter dated 1582 from the *Maharal* (d. 1609) to R. Jacob Gunzberg (d. 1615). In the letter, the *Maharal* explained why it was necessary to create a *golem*, along with what he was going to do it. R. Yizchok Eizik Weiss (d. 1944) published the same letter in 1931, but did not mention Bloch as the source. [644]

1923– Savino Savini published an Italian translation of *SEPHER YETZRIAH* called Il *SEPHER JETSIRAH* (Libro Della Formazione). [645]

1920– The English version of Chayim Yitzchak Bloch's novel, *"DER PRAGER GOLEM"* ("THE GOLEM, LEGENDS OF THE GHETTO OF PRAGUE") is published. [646]

1926, November 14– Pianist and composer Eugen Francois Charles d'Albert (1864-1932) composed a three-act opera with libretto by Ferdinand d'Albert Lion, entitled *"DER GOLEM,"* a music-drama which premiered at the Alte Opera in Frankfurt and performed in other cities. [647]

1927– The opera, *"DER GOLEM,"* was performed in Leipzig.

1928– Canadian born author and mystic Manly Palmer Hall (1901-1990) published a compilation of the *SEPHER YETZIRAH*, his most famous work at age 27, in THE SECRET TEACHINGS OF ALL AGES, a Rosicrucian and Masonic study of occultism. [648] In 1934, he founded the Philosophical Research Society (PRS) in Los Angeles, California. In 1973, he was recognized as a Mason. Over his career he wrote about 150 books and essays, countless magazine articles and delivered about 8,000 lectures in the United States. [649]

1928– Arthur Holitscher again accused Paul Wegener of plagiarizing his drama *"DER GOLEM.*

---

[643] *"Golem,"* Wikipedia.com.

[644] Leiman Shnayer , THE LETTER OF THE MAHARAL ON THE CREATION OF THE GOLEM: A MODERN FORGERY, 2010, the *Seforim* blog.

[645] Kaplan, Aryeh, *SEPHER YETZIRAH*: THEORY, page 330.

[646] *"Golem,"* Wikipedia.com

[647] *"DER GOLEM* (Opera)," Wikipedia.com.

[648] Manley P. Hall, THE SECRET TEACHINGS OF ALL AGES.

[649] From the Manley P. Hall archive and memorial.

GHETTELEGENDE IN DREI AUFZUGEN" (Berlin 1908). [650]

1931– B. Tennen published a Hungarian translation of SEPHER YETZIRAH in "A TEREMTES KONY" in Budapest. [651]

1931– Occultist and writer Francis Israel Regardie (1907-1985) published the popular introduction guide for the general populous, A GARDEN OF POMEGRANATES. It was republished in 1932, 1970 and 1999. Regardie became a contemporary of occultist Aleister Crowley in 1928, [652] and a member of the Hermetic Order of the Golden Dawn, an organization dedicated to the study and practice of the occult, metaphysics and paranormal activities. Westcott and Samuel Mathers were two of three founders of the Golden Dawn. [653] Regardie broke with the Order's secrecies and published many of their practices.

1932– Israel Regardie published THE TREE OF LIFE, A STUDY IN MAGIC about the tradition of the *Kabbalists*. It was considered as Regardie's magnum opus and is a contemporary source of knowledge for the aspiring 20th century American *Kabbalist*.

1932– German born Israeli philosopher Gershom Scholem (born as Gerhard Scholem, 1897-1982) published "*Jezirah*" in the ENCYCLOPEDIA JUDAICA. [654] He continued to produce numerous books on SEPHER YETZIRAH and the *Kabbalah* that became the standard source in the field. Scholem is regarded as the founder of Modern *Kabbalah* and was the first professor of Jewish Mysticism at the Hebrew University of Jerusalem. [655] The author of this book has relied on Scholem's work for decades.

1934– Beate Rosenfeld published DIE GOLEMSAGE UND IHRE VERWERTUNG IN DER DEUTSCHEN LITERATUR (The *Golem* Legend and Its Use in German Literature). [656] She linked the *golem* legends to German literature.

1936– Paul Wegener's "*Der Golem*," is remade and retitled "*Le Golem*" and directed by Julien

---

[650] Marcel Cornis-Pope, John Neubauer, HISTORY OF THE LITERARY CULTURES OF EAST-CENTRAL EUROPE: JUNCTURES, pages 311-312.

[651] Kaplan, Aryeh, SEPHER YETZIRAH: THEORY page 336.

[652] "A GARDEN OF POMEGRANATES," Wikipedia.com

[653] "Hermetic Order of the Golden Dawn," Wikipedia.com

[654] ENCYCLOPEDIA JUDAICA, (Berlin), vol. 9, col. 104ff.

[655] Gershom Scholem, Wikipedia.com.

[656] Marcel Cornis-Pope, John Neubauer, HISTORY OF THE LITERARY CULTURES OF EAST-CENTRAL EUROPE: JUNCTURES, page 397.

Duvivier in Prague. [657]

1939– Reform Rabbi and author Joshua Trachtenberg (1904-1959) published the popular JEWISH MAGIC AND SUPERSTITION, A STUDY IN FOLK RELIGION with a forward by Idel, Moshe (b. 1947). It was published again in 1961. The author of this book has also relied on Trachtenberg and Idel, Moshe's work for decades.

The 1940 Disney film "FANTASIA" brought Johann Goethe's poem, "The Sorcerer's Apprentice" to the celluloid screen. Cartoon character Mickey Mouse played the apprentice who lets the wayward enchanted broom get out of control. The segment was repeated in the sequel "FANTASIA 2000."

Gershom Scholem published MAJOR TRENDS IN JEWISH MYSTICISM in 1941, a major study on *Kabbalah* and related subjects.

1952– Saul Raskin provided the Hebrew text with English and Yiddish translation of *SEPHER YETZIRAH* in an 80-page edition of *KABBALAH* IN WORD AND IMAGE. [658]

1958– Argentinian author Jorge Luis Borges published a poem about Rabbi Loew's *golem* called *"JUDA LEON."* [659]

1960– Gershom Scholem published Jewish Gnosticism, *Merkabah* Mysticism and the Talmudic Tradition. The translation was based on the 1960 edition.

1960– A German publication of Gershom Scholem's *ZUR KABBALA UND IHRER SYMBOLIK* (ON THE KABBALAH AND ITS SYMBOLISM) was published in Germany.

1962– A reprint of the 1884 Warsaw edition of the *SEPHER YETZIRAH* was published in Jerusalem. [660]

1965– An English translation of Gershom Scholem's ON THE *KABBALAH* AND ITS SYMBOLISM was published by Schocken Books in New York City. A paperback edition is issued in 1969.

1965– Kabbalist Rabbi Bentzion Moshe Yair Weinstock (1899-1982) published *YOTZER OR* IN Jerusalem. It included the long version and a commentary to *SEPHER YETZIRAH*. It was originally written by a 13th century unknown author, possibly in France, and attributed to R. Saadia Gaon

---

[657] "The *Golem*: How He Came to Be," Wikipedia.com.

[658] Kaplan, Aryeh, *SEPHER YETZIRAH:* THEORY, page 335.

[659] Nicolas Kraushaar, THE ESOTERIC CODEX: CZECH LEGEND AND FOLKLORE, page 18.

[660] Kaplan, Aryeh, *SEPHER YETZIRAH:* THEORY, page 320.

("Pseudo-Saadia"). [661] Weinstock composed numerous books on *Kabbalah* and *Chasidism*.

1967– An article titled THE *SEPHER YETSIRAH* AND THE ORIGINAL *TETRAGRAMMATON* (Ernst E. Ettish) by Eliyahu Rosh-Pinnah is published in the "Jewish Quarterly Review." [662]

1966– Georges Vajda (1908-1981) edited a version of Elhanan ben Yaqaar's (R. Yaqaar, c.1240) commentary on *SEPHER YETZIRAH*. [663] [664]

1968– French writer, painter and *Kabbalah* author Carlo Giuseppe Suares (1892-1976) published his popular, and widely referenced, translation of *SEPHER YETZIRA*: INCLUDING THE ORIGINAL ASTROLOGY ACCORDING TO THE *QABALAH* AND ITS ZODIAC. [665] It was reprinted by Shambhala Publishing in 1976.

1965– Gershom Scholem published Jewish Gnosticism, Merkabah Mysticism and the Talmudic Tradition. The translation is based on the 1960 edition.

1965– British esotericist and occult author Gareth Knight (b. 1930) published A PRACTICAL GUIDE TO QABALISTIC SYMBOLISM One Volume Edition: Volume 1 - On The Spheres of the Tree of Life; Volume II - On The paths and the Tarot by Samuel Weiser, Inc. It was republished in 1978. Knight is a member of the Fraternity of the Inner Light, founded by occultist Dion Fortune. He composed dozens of books on the occult over the following decades. [666]

1966– *SEPHER HA-RAZIM* (BOOK OF THE MYSTERIES OR SECRETS) is reconstructed in Hebrew from fragments of the Cairo Genizah and other sources by Mordecai Margalioth in Jerusalem. He believed the original materials were copied between the fourth and the fifth centuries. It was reprinted in 1983.

1970– In Israel, the 1902 edition of *SEPHER YETZIRAH* is reprinted. [667]

1970– THE BOOK OF FORMATION (*SEPHER YETZIRAH*) including the 32 Paths of Wisdom, their Correspondences with the Hebrew Alphabet and the Tarot Symbols by Rabbi Akiba ben Joseph,

---

[661] Kaplan, Aryeh, SEPHER YETZIRAH: THEORY, page 320.

[662] "*Jewish Quarterly Review*," January 1967 Volume 57, No. 3, pages 212-226

[663] *KOBETZ AL YAD*, 16: 145-197, pages 145-97.

[664] Kaplan, Aryeh, SEPHER YETZIRAH: THEORY, page 327 and by Joseph Dan, Ronald C. Kiener. "The Early Kabbalah," page 40.

[665] Carlo Suares, SEPHER YETZIRA: INCLUDING THE ORIGINAL ASTROLOGY ACCORDING TO THE QABALAH AND ITS ZODIAC.

[666] "Gareth Knight," Wikipedia.com

[667] Kaplan, Aryeh, SEPHER YETZIRAH: THEORY, page 320.

is published from 1923 edition from the Hebrew with annotations by Knut Stenring and an introduction by Arthur Edward Waite. Waite cites the 1552 Latin translation by the Christian mystic Gulielmus Postellus (Postel) and the 1877 English edition. [668]

1971– Rabbi Gershom Scholem published The Messianic Idea in Judaism and other Essays on Jewish Spirituality.

1971– Ithamar Gruenwald (born in 1937) published A Preliminary Critical Edition of Sepher Yezira, from Israel Oriental Studies. This was a critical examination of the history and Hebrew words used in various editions. As of 2015, he was a faculty Humanities member of Tel Aviv University. This author has relied on Gruenwald's work for decades. Gershom Scholem's book *Kabbalah* is reissued as Origins of the *Kabbalah* (JPS).

1972– A critical edition of the first chapter is published by Yisrael Weinstock called *LeBirur HaNusach shel Sepher Yetzirah, Temirin* 1:9-61. This edition was based on all printed editions, commentaries and manuscripts available. [669]

1971– Gershom Scholem published the book *Kabbalah*. It provides a comprehensive survey and in-depth study of Jewish Mysticism. It was reissued in 1987.

1973– Gershom Scholem published Sabbatai Sevi: The Mystical *Messiah*.

1973– 777 And Other Qabalistic Writings of Aleister Crowley: Including *Gamatria* & *Sepher Sephiroth*, is republished. It is a collection of paper based on Hermetic Qabalah by English occultist, poet and painter Aleister Crowley (1875-1947) with an introduction by Israel Regardie.

1974– Z'ev ben Shimon Halevi (his English name is Warren Kenton, b. 1933), published Adam and the *Kabbalistic* Tree in London. He published about a dozen more books on the *Kabbalah*. [670] A *golem* character appears in three of Marvel Comics "Strange Tales" series during the same year. [671]

1974– Charles Ponce published Kabbalah: An Introduction and Illumination for the World Today in London by Gemstone Press. [672] It contained over 100 illustrations and

---

[668] Rabbi Akiba ben Joseph, The Book of Formation (*Sepher Yetzirah*), KTAV Publishing House, Inc., New York. Reprinted in 2015 by Reink Books.

[669] Kaplan, Aryeh, *Sepher Yetzirah:* Theory, page 320.

[670] "Z'ev ben Shimon Halevi," Wikipedia.com.

[671] Nicolas Kraushaar, The Esoteric Codex: Czech Legend and Folklore, page 18.

[672] Published by National Book Network. Library of Australia Online Catalog. http://catalogue.nla.gov.au/Record/133199

reproductions of historical plates, diagrams and charts.

1975-1977– While in college, Robert E. Zucker (born in 1954) conducted two years of research on Hermetics, parapsychology and *Kabbalah* for independent study credit in five disciplinary departments at the University of Arizona (Anthropology, Judaic Studies, Journalism, Psychology and Sociology). Two manuscripts were produced and submitted to professors. That study became the basis for continued study over the next four decades and the foundation of this volume.

1976– Carlo Suares republished his popular, and widely referenced, translation of SEPHER YETZIRA: INCLUDING THE ORIGINAL ASTROLOGY ACCORDING TO THE QABALAH AND ITS ZODIAC, by Shambhala Publishing. [673]

1976– Professor and author Andrew Sharf's (d.1990) 1976 book on THE UNIVERSE OF SHABBETHAI DONNOLO contained critical discussions from the 1880 book by David Castelli, Firenze, II COMMENTO DI SABBATAI DONNOLO LIBRO DELLA CREAZIONE. [674]

1977– Irving Friedman published his translation and commentary, BOOK OF CREATION, from Samuel Weiser, Inc. [675] The second printing of Isidor Kalisch's 1877 edition on SEPHER YETZIRAH. It was reprinted in 2006. [676] Z'ev ben Shimon Halevi published A KABBALISTIC UNIVERSE, from Samuel Weiser, Inc. It was republished in 1988. [677]

1978– Emory University Professor of Judaic Studies David R. Blumenthal published a two-volume textbook on medieval Jewish intellectual history, UNDERSTANDING JEWISH MYSTICISM (KTAV Publishing House). [678]

1979– Z'ev ben Shimon Halevi published KABBALAH: A TRADITION OF HIDDEN KNOWLEDGE, from Thames and Hudson. [679]

1982– Composer Eugen d'Albert's 1927 opera "DER GOLEM," was revived in Saarbrucken,

---

[673] Carlo Suares, SEPHER YETZIRA: INCLUDING THE ORIGINAL ASTROLOGY ACCORDING TO THE QABALAH AND ITS ZODIAC

[674] Gruenwald, Ithamar, A PRELIMINARY CRITICAL EDITION OF SEPHER YEZIRA, page 224.

[675] Friedman, Irving THE BOOK OF CREATION, from Samuel Weiser, York Beach, ME. ISBN 0-87728-289-7, Library of Congress Catalog Number 76-15537. Citation in SEPHER YETZIRAH, by Kaplan, Aryeh, page 335.

[676] Kalisch, Isidor, SEPHER YETZIRAH Book Tree, 2006, 124 pages.

[677] by Gateway Books.

[678] OCLO World Catalog

[679] "Z'ev ben Shimon Halevi," Wikipedia.com.

Germany.

1982– Samuel Weiser, Inc. published American Orthodox rabbi and author Aryeh Moshe Eilyahu Kaplan's (1934-1983) MEDIATION AND *KABBALAH*. It was published again in 1995. Kaplan is well known for his translations of the *TORAH* and various *Kabbalah* works. I have relied on Kaplan's work for decades.

1979– Z'ev ben Shimon Halevi published THE WORK OF THE *KABBALIST*, by Gateway Books. It was republished in 1993 by Samuel Weiser, Inc. [680]

1983– *SEPHER HA-RAZIM* ("BOOK OF THE MYSTERIES") is reprinted by Michael A. Morgan with an annotated translation of the Hebrew edition published in 1966 by Mordecai Margalioth. This is the first English translation of this work considered to be the text of one of the original 4th century copies of *SEPHER RAZIM*. [681]

1987– Scott J. Thompson translated Gershom Scholem's *TSELEM*: THE REPRESENTATION OF THE ASTRAL BODY.

1987– Robert Zucker began to re-translate the *SEPHER YETZIRAH* using a database program called HyperCard. The stack was called *SEPHER YETZIRAH*: THE MAGIC OF FORMATION. Robert used the program for personal study until HyperCard was discontinued. Then, the entire project had to be recreated using a FileMaker Pro solution. With the expanded capabilities of FileMaker, additional "Solutions" were created to develop a "*Kabbalah* Wheel" to spin the 231 Gates and other techniques possible through a database program. The content was extracted from the two programs to provide the text for this volume.

1988– Historian and philosopher Moshe Idel published several books, *KABBALAH*: NEW PERSPECTIVES (Yale University Press, New Haven and London), THE MYSTICAL EXPERIENCE IN ABRAHAM ABULAFIA (translated from the Hebrew by Jonathan Chipman. Albany, State University of New York Press), and STUDIES IN ECSTATIC *KABBALAH* (Albany, N.Y., State University of New York Press). He continues to publish books on *Kabbalah* for decades. His book, *KABBALAH* is a major resource on Judaic mystical studies.

1989– Moshe Idel published LANGUAGE, *TORAH,* AND HERMENEUTICS IN ABRAHAM ABULAFIA, translated by Menahem Kallus. (Albany, State University of New York Press).

1990– Moshe Idel published *Golem*, Jewish Magical and Mystical Traditions on the Artificial Anthropoid (Albany, State University of New York Press). It is the most comprehensive survey of

---

[680] Ibid.

[681] Published by Society of Biblical Literature, 1st edition, January 1, 1983. Sssa Special Publication, Book 25, 108 pages.

the *Sepher Yetzirah* and *golem* legends.

1991– Z'ev ben Shimon Halevi published THE WAY OF *KABBALAH*, from Gateway Books, and republishes his 1981 edition of PSYCHOLOGY AND *KABBALAH*, from Gateway and the 1972 edition of AN INTRODUCTION TO THE CABALA: TREE OF LIFE from Samuel Weiser, Inc. [682]

1994– Idel, Moshe published HASIDISM: BETWEEN ECSTASY AND MAGIC (SUNY Press, Albany).

1997– Gershom Scholem published ON THE MYSTICAL SHAPE OF THE GODHEAD: BASIC CONCEPTS IN THE *KABBALAH* from Schocken Books. A critical edition of the medieval *grimoire*, The Sword of Moses, [683] published by Moses Gaster in 1896. [684]

---

[682] "Z'ev ben Shimon Halevi," Wikipedia.com.

[683] This manuscript was formerly called Ms. Faster 78, now London. British Library Ms. Or. 10678.

[684] "The Sword of Moses," Wikipedia.com. Published by Israel scholar Yuval Harari.

21st Century (2000-on)

In the early part of the 21st century, a comprehensive Hebrew edition called *SEPHER YETZIRAH HASHALEM* was published in by Harav Moshe Tzuriel. It contained both the short and long versions and included all of the commentaries found in the 1562 Mantua version by Saadia Gaon, Eleazar of Worms, *RASHI, RAAVAD, RAMAK, RAMBAM,* Moses Botriel, and others with a commentary by Rabbi *Gra* on Genesis and a commentary by Ari on the BOOK OF CREATION. The volume also contained a reprint of Sabbathai Donnolo's *SEPHER CHOKMONI,* a discussion on the 231 Gates, *MA'ASEH BERESHIT* and a half dozen other collections.

2002– Moshe Idel published ABRAHAM ABULAFIA , AN ECSTATIC *KABBALIST,* TWO STUDIES (edited by Moshe Lazar, Labyrinthos, CA.) and ABSORBING PERFECTIONS: *KABBALAH* AND INTERPRETATION (Yale University Press, New Haven). It was based on Abraham Abulafia's ecstatic *Kabbalah.*

2008– Z'ev ben Shimon Halevi published INTRODUCTION TO THE WORLD OF *KABBALAH,* from the *Kabbalah* Society: Tree of Life Publishing (UK). [685]

2005– Moshe Idel published *KABBALAH* AND EROS (Yale University Press, New Haven) where he explored erotic love in Judaic mysticism.

2006– Byron L. Sherwin composed his novel The Cubs and the *Kabbalist* - How a *Kabbalah*-Master Helped the Chicago Cubs Win Their First World Series Since 1908. Rabbi Jay Loeb creates a *golem* named Sandy Greenberg to win the World Series for the Chicago Cubs baseball team. He performs a secret ritual in Wrigley field to remove the legendary Billy Goat curse against the Cubs. While they win at home, they are defeated on the road. So, the good rabbi takes his ritual along with the team where he performs his magic to ensure a Cubs win. [686]

2007– An English edition of *PARDES RIMONIM* (ORCHARD OF POMEGRANATES) from Rabbi Moshe ben Cordovero (1522-1570) is translated by Elyakim Getz and published by Providence University. [687]

2009– Z'ev ben Shimon Halevi publishes THE PATH OF A *KABBALIST*: AN AUTOBIOGRAPHY,

---

[685] "Z'ev ben Shimon Halevi," Wikipedia.com.

[686] The Chicago Cubs broke the curse when they won the 2016 World Series Championship.

[687] ISBN: 1-897352-17-4

Kabbalah Society: Tree of Life Publishing (UK). [688]

2011– Moshe Idel published *KABBALAH* IN ITALY 1280-1510 (Yale University Press, New Haven) and SATURN'S JEWS, ON THE WITCHES' SABBAT AND SABBATEANISM (Continuum), London, New York, 2011).

2013– Helene Walker published her novel, THE *GOLEM* AND THE JINNI, about a female *golem* named Chava who is brought to life. [689]

2014– Jonathan and Jesse Kellerman writes the novel THE *GOLEM* OF HOLLYWOOD, bringing the *golem* of Prague to the 21st century where the *golem* exacts his revenge on a serial killer. [690] Moshe Idel publishes MIRCEA ELIADE: FROM MYTH TO MAGIC (Peter Lang, New York) and REPRESENTING GOD, edited by H. Samuelson-Tirosh and A. Hughes (Leiden, Brill). Idel serves as Emeritus Max Cooper Professor in Jewish Thought at the Hebrew University in Jerusalem.

2015– THE BOOK OF FORMATION (*SEPHER YETZIRAH*) by Rabbi Akiba ben Joseph is republished from 1970 edition. [691]

2017– Robert Zucker publishes *KABBALAH'S* SECRET CIRCLES, a historical survey of the *Kabbalah,* and the *SEPHER YETZIRAH* with meditative techniques, and an instructive guide to create a device called a *Kabbalah* Wheel to interpret the second chapter of the *SEPHER YETZIRAH.* The steps to make the Wheel follow in the Appendix.

End of Volume 1.

---

[688] "Z'ev ben Shimon Halevi," Wikipedia.com.

[689] Nicolas Kraushaar, THE ESOTERIC CODEX: CZECH LEGEND AND FOLKLORE, page 18.

[690] Aryeh, Kaplan, *SEPHER YETZIRAH:* THEORY, page 325. Pages 50c-56c.

[690] Nicolas Kraushaar, THE ESOTERIC CODEX: CZECH LEGEND AND FOLKLORE, page 18.

[691] THE BOOK OF FORMATION (*SEPHER YETZIRAH*), by Rabbi Akiba ben Joseph, from Reink Books.

Appendix

Hebrew & English Letters

his is a chart of the 22 letters of the Hebrew alphabet, the English pronunciation and equivalent letter, the traditional numerical value, along with the traditional meaning assigned to the letter.

Hebrew (Name)		English Equivalent	Value	Meaning
א	*Aleph*	A	1	Ox
ב	*Bayt*	B	2	House
ג	*Gimel*	G	3	Camel
ד	*Daleth*	D	4	Door
ה	*Heh*	H	5	Window (air)
ו	*Vav*	V	6	Nail
ז	*Zayin*	Z	7	Sword
ח	*Chet*	Ch	8	Fence

ט	Tet	T	9	Serpent
י	Yod	Y	10	Hand
כ	Kaf	K	20	Palm
ל	Lamed	L	30	Ox goad
מ	Mem	M	40	Water
נ	Nun	N	50	Fish
ס	Samech	S	60	Prop
ע	Ayin	Ay	70	Eye
פ	Peh	P	80	Mouth
צ	Tzadek	Tz	90	Fish hook
ק	Qof	Q	100	Back of hand
ר	Resh	R	200	Head
ש	Shin	Sh	300	Tooth
ת	Tav	T	400	Mark, or sign

Letter Correspondences

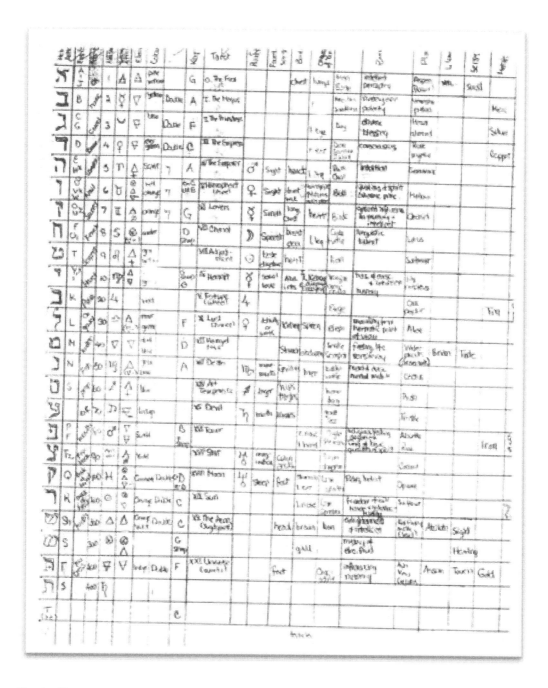

Chart of letter correspondences compiled in the late 1970s by author Robert Zucker.

SEPHER YETZIRAH Chapters

While there are hundreds of variations of the SEPHER YETZIRAH, the basic concepts remains constant.

These first two chapters are an abbreviated English version with a verse-by-verse commentary. The text is gleaned from both the long and short recensions and comments are based on interpretations from *Kabbalists* through history.

The footnotes contain my own commentaries for the first few chapters and how they can be interpreted for today's culture and used in conjunction with the construction of a *Kabbalah* Wheel.

The first chapter explores the Universe and its structure, while the second chapter provides the steps to permutate the 22 letters of the Hebrew alphabet. Based on the passages in Chapter 2, the instructions to create a personal *Kabbalah* Wheel follow this section. The concepts in these two chapters were discussed for centuries by Judaism's leading rabbinical authorities, as described previously in this volume.

This section is planned to be part of a more complete volume that explores each chapter, verse and word in detail based on my forty-year study of unpublished personal notes and charts.

Chapter One: The 10 *Sephiroth*

1:1 • The 32 Paths

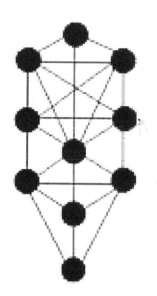

By means of 32 Mystical Paths, [692] There is a hidden Wisdom carved (engraved) by the Holy Name, and

Engraved with three "books" (*Sepharim*):

Letters *(sephar ‏ספר‎)*,

Numbers *(sephar ‏ספר‎)*, and

Speech *(sippur ‏ספר‎)*. [693]

---

[692] The 32 paths are the sum of the 10 *Sephiroth* (the "spheres," represented as dots in the above diagram of the Tree of Life) and the 22 pathways (the intersecting lines) between each *Sephiroth*, as described by earlier rabbis. Wisdom is carved ("engraved," or spoken) with the voice.

[693] The 3 *Sepharim* (themes or "books"):

1. **Letters:** their meanings (the archetypal symbol, **Universal**).
2. **Numbers:** numerical values of each letter (its order, placement and **Time**).
3. **Sounds** of each letter through speech (communication from the **Soul**).

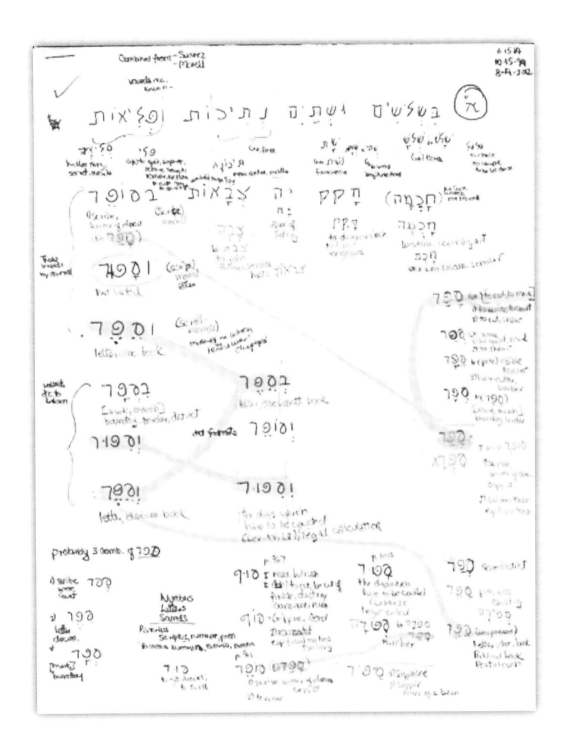

These are part of my personal notes from the 1980s with the first verse and a breakdown of the Hebrew word *Sepher*.

1:2 • **The 10 Sephiroth & 22 Letters**

The 10 *Sephiroth* of Nothingness (*Beli-Mah* בלימה). [694]

And, the 22 Foundation Letters. [695]

They are divided as the:

Three Mothers	ש מ א (ו ה י) [696]
Seven Doubles	ב ג ד כ פ ר ת [697]
And Twelve Simple (elemental) Letters	ה ו ז ח ט י ל נ ס ע צ ק [698]

---

[694] *Beli-Mah* means abstract or nothingness. The 10 *sephiroth* (spheres) do not have any boundaries. At this point, the *sephiroth* are like ten gaseous "spheres" in dark space.

This lists the different sets of numbers to be covered in this book- 10, 22, 3, 7 and 12. The 10 *Sephiroth* are the 10 spheres of the Tree of Life. They were referred to as 10 Names of God in the previous verse. The list of 10 Names of God may refer to each one of the 10 *Sephiroth* discussed throughout this chapter, The Names describe a feature or nature of God's personality. These are the 10 in the Universe.

[695] The 22 letters are the letters of the Hebrew alphabet (and the 22 paths of the Tree of Life).

[696] The 3 "Mother Letters" are the three *A, Sh, M*. They are related to the three-letter Name of God (*Y, H, V*) often referred to as the Father letters.

[697] The 7 double letters s are the 7 letters of the Hebrew alphabet that have a double (hard and soft) sound.

[698] The 12 simple letters, the elemental letters, are the remaining letters that are not doubles or mother letters.

1:3 • Five Opposite Five

The 10 *Sephiroth* of Nothingness (*Beli-Mah* בלימה).

In Number, like Ten Fingers, five are opposite five.

With a single covenant between them:

The circumcision *(MLT* מלט*)* of the tongue, [699]

And the circumcision *(MLT* מלט*)* [700] of the membrane. [701]

---

[699] Besides the description of the 10 *sephiroth* in a Tree of Life diagram, here, the 10 *Sephiroth* layout is displayed in human forms as five fingers facing five fingers. In between the two hands is a single entity (called a "covenant"). When it is between the ten fingers, it is the tongue. When referring to the ten toes, the covenant is the penis.

Add the sum of the 10 fingers and the tongue (total =11); and the ten toes and the penis (total =11). Those two sums equal 22– the 22 Hebrew letters. Each finger and toe and their respective covenants are assigned a specific letter of the Hebrew alphabet.

[700] *MLT* is translated in most texts as "circumcision." The tongue is dividing between the 2 sets of fingers; and the same with the 5 toes and its "covenant."

[701] The word "membrane" or skin (*MAyVR*) is often referred to as the penis in most texts.

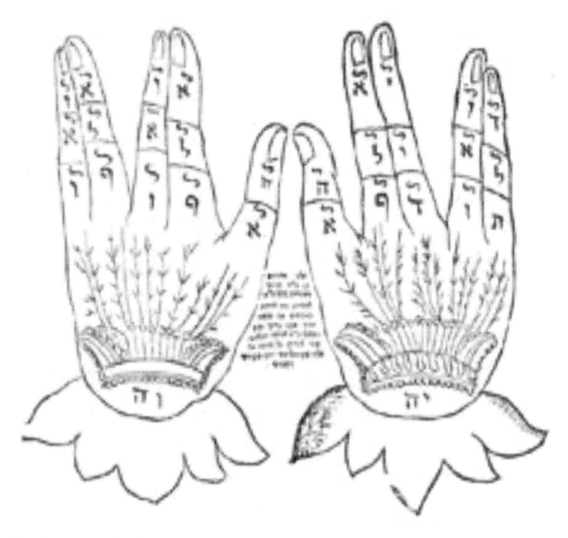

Five fingers opposite five, as represented in a Medieval graphic. Zedcor Graphics.

1:4 • Examine and Probe Them

The 10 *Sephiroth* of Nothingness (*Beli-Mah* בלימה).
10 and not 9. 10 and not 11.

Understand this with Wisdom.

Be wise with Understanding.

Examine them. And probe them.

Make each thing stand on its essence,

And make the Creator (Master) sit on His base [702]

---

[702] This verse emphasizes that there are only 10 *sephiroth*. The one that governs them all does not count as part of the 10. Neither does the single "covenant" that is in between the 10 fingers and the 10 toes. Knowledge and Wisdom are an allegorical representation of the 2 "covenants" between them. The balance between Wisdom and Understanding gains insight to both levels of consciousness at the same time. *Chockmah* ("Wisdom") = non-verbal part of the mind. *Binah* ("Understanding") = verbal consciousness. Just pondering this concept makes one the Master over

1:5 • Depths of the 10 *Sephiroth*

The 10 *Sephiroth* of Nothingness (*Beli-Mah* בלימה) have no end. Their measure is 10:

A depth of beginning.　　A depth of end.
A depth of good.　　　　A depth of evil.
A depth of above.　　　　A depth of below.
A depth of east.　　　　　A depth of west.
A depth of north.　　　　A depth of south.

The Master (ruler) dominates them all from His Holy dwelling. Forever and ever and ever. [703]

---

the entities that are being examined. *Chokmah* and *Binah* are the 3rd and 4th *sephiroth* of the Tree of Life.

[703] The 'spheres of nothingness' may be endless, but they can be restrained within five dimensions to give them form– a vessel. The Creator who governs over all of the *sephiroth* is one point that is defined within this space. From this point, the 10 *sephiroth* emanate (or descend into a depth) of 4 areas and 6 directions from beginning to end, above to below, east to west, and north to south. The graphic on the next page of the directions in space is from the book *KABALAH* by Charles Ponce, page 43.

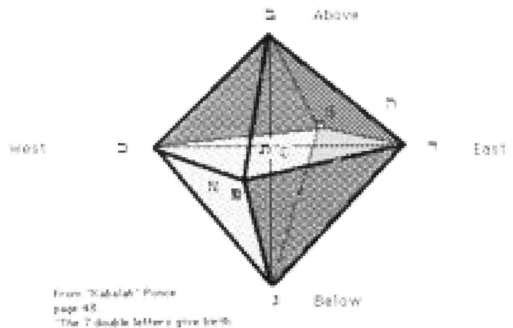

From "Kabalah" Power
page 46
"The 7 double letters give birth
to the directions of space , causing order to the midst of the original chaos "

1:6 • The Appearance of Lightning

Awakening to the sun (Zedcor Graphics).

The 10 *Sephiroth* of Nothingness.
Their vision is like the "appearance of lightning."
Their limit has no end.
And the 'Word' within them is "running and returning.
They rush to Him like a whirlwind.
And before His throne, they prostrate themselves. [704]

---

[704] If your mind keeps going and going, still it with silence. Balance between awareness and unconsciousness (as it is written in Ezekiel 1:14 "And the *Chayyot* (living creatures) were running and returning, like the appearance of lightning." This concept further explained in SEPHER YETZIRAH 1:8. When the Tree of Life is viewed correctly, from top to bottom, it is visualized like a "lightning flash."

1:7 • Like a Flame to Coal

Like a flame to a burning coal (Zedcor Graphics).

The 10 *Sephiroth* of Nothingness.
Their end is embedded in their beginning.
Their beginning is embedded in their end.
Like a flame to a burning coal.
For the Master is singular.
There is no second.
What can you count before One? [705]

---

[705] The interconnection between the 10 *sephiroth* are like burning coals– fire *Shin* (ש) connects

the coal to the air *Aleph* (א) where its emanates as heat *Mem* (מ). There is no defined place where the *sephiroth* actually begin or end. The Master, again, is the one who is at the center of these ten *sephiroth*– 5 side by side. But the Master (the one acting as the Creator) is not counted

1:8 • *Chayyot* "Running & Returning"

"Spirits" artwork
by Robert
Zucker. 1970s.

T he 10 *Sephiroth* of Nothingness.

Stop your mouth from speaking.
And, your heart from thinking.

If your mouth speaks or your heart runs,
Return it back to the place.

As it is written (in Ezekiel 1:24):
"The *Chayyot* (living creatures חיות) are running and returning."
On this, a covenant was made. [706]

---

as one of the *sephiroth* ("10 and not 11"). The Master is one and single.

[706] Now that the 10 *sephiroth* and the "Master" in the center are defined meditate on each of them (number), their directions (letter and names (sounds). Meditate by not speaking or thinking. If your mind runs with loose images and thoughts, refocus on the main point of meditation. The covenant (see 1.3) is between the Creator (God) and the "Master (the invoker)."

1:9 • The Holy Breath

O ne: Breath
of the
Living God.

The voice of breath
and speech.

This is the Holy
Breath. [707]

Art work by Robert Zucker in 1975 of William Blake's "Ancient of Days." The original art was published in 1794 as a front piece to EUROPE A PROPHESY, a prophetic book by Blake.

---

[707] The Holy Breath of God is the source ("crown" or spark) of life and from this comes the breath to give life to each soul. Breath enables both sound and voice. Psalms 33:6: "With the Word of God, the heavens were made, and with breath (*Ruach*) of His mouth, and all their hosts."

1:10 • The 22, 3, 7 and 12

wo: Breath from Breath. Engrave and carve [708] the 22 Foundation Letters—

Three Mothers ש מ א (י ה ו) [709]

Seven Doubles ב ג ד כ פ ר ת [710]

Twelve Simples ה ו ז ח

ט י ל נ ס ע צ ק [711]

And one Breath is from them. [712]

---

[708] Engrave each of the letter in the imagination and carve each letter using the breath to sound out it the letter, as instructed in the next chapter.

[709] The 3 "Mother Letters" are the three *A, Sh, M*. They are related to the three-letter Name of God (*Y, H, V*) often referred to as the Father letters.

[710] The 7 double letters s are the 7 letters of the Hebrew alphabet that have a double (hard and soft) sound.

[711] The 12 simple letters, the elemental letters, are the remaining letters that are not doubles or mother letters.

[712] The 2nd *Sephiroth*, is from breath also, but not the Holy Breath of Life. This is the breath that sustains each life or soul. From the 22 letters divide them into sets of 3, 7 and 12 and, the one Master, which is the "breath of breath."

1:11 • **Water from Breath**

Three: Water from Breath:

With it engrave and carve the 22 letters
From chaos and void, mud and mire.
Engrave them like a garden.
Carve them out on a wall.
Cover them across a ceiling. [713]
And pour snow over them, and it becomes dust.
As it is written: "To the snow, He said, become Earth." [714]

---

[713] Imagine the 22 letters laid out like a row in a garden, one next to each other. Those letters can also be imagined as if they are stacked up, one on top of each other, like they were written on a wall in a column.

[714] The 3rd path is compared to water deriving from breath. Steam produces water when it

715

condenses. From breath, comes voice or sound. From sound, the letters are formed. They are engraved (with breath, sound) and carved out (visualized or imagined) in the mind. If the 22 letters were written (carved) like plants in a garden, they would be in rows. One long row would be one set of 22 letters. Stand them up, like they were against a wall. The first letter, *Aleph*, would be at the top. The quote, from Job 37:6 omitted in some versions, emphasizes the fluid state of the letters which eventually become solidified.

[715] This is an example of the first 8 of 22 foundation letters that are engraved "like a garden" and carved "like a wall," and standing like a column, as described in SEPHER YETZIRAH 1:11

1:12 • Fire from Water

Four:
Fire
from Water.

Engrave and carve the Throne of Glory: *Seraphim, Ophanim* and the Holy *Chayyot*– the ministering angels. [716]

From these three, He founded His dwelling.

As it is written: "He makes His angels of breath. His ministers of flaming fire (Psalms 104:4) [717]

---

[716] The *Chayyot* are the Holy Living Creatures. The roles of the three are further discussed in an upcoming volume.

[717] A clue is that "Fire kindles water," Isaiah 64:1.

1:13 • The 6 Directions in Space

66 "**C**hoose three letters from among the elementals. Set them in His Great Name and with them, seal 6 extremities"

5: Seal above and face upwards. Seal in *YHV.*
6: Seal below and face down. seal it in *YVH.*
7: Seal east and face forward. Seal it in *HYV.*
8: Seal west and face backward, Seal with *HVY.*
9: Seal south and face to right. Seal with *VYH.*
10: Seal north and face left. Seal it with *VHY.* [718]

Y= י   H= ה   V= ו

---

[718] There are numerous interpretations to the correct order of the 3 Mother Letters (*Y H V*). My choices agree with Rabbi Abulafia.

	My choice:	Kaplan, Suares:	Gra:	Abulafia
5:	*YHV*	*YHV*	*YHV*	*YHV*
6:	*YVH*	*HYV*	*YVH*	*YVH*
7:	*HVY*	*YVH*	*HYV*	*HVY*
8:	*HYV*	*VHY*	*HYV*	*HYV*
9:	*VYH*	*YVH*	*VYH*	*VYH*
10:	*VHY*	*HVY*	*VHY*	*VHY*

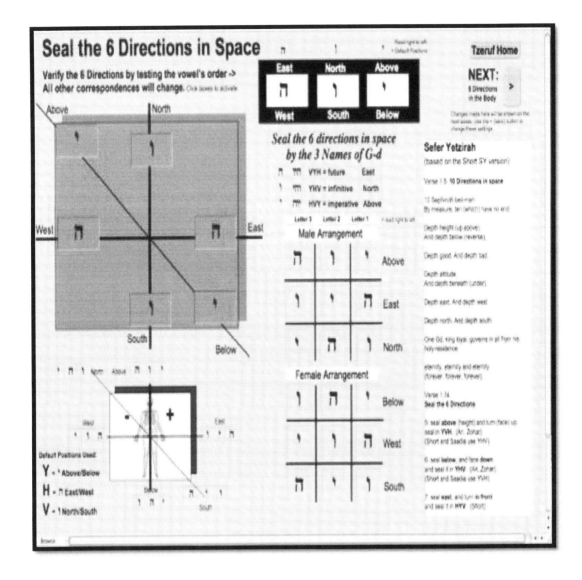

This chart, from my personal notes and a page from a FileMaker software program developed on *Kabbalah* during the 1990s, depicts the six directions in space and their relationship to the Holy Letters *Y H V*.

1:14 • Summary

These are the 10 *Sephiroth* of Nothingness.

Breath of the Living God.
Breath from Breath.
Water from Breath.
Fire from Water.

Up, Down, East, West, North, South. [719]   End of chapter 1

---

[719] This is a summary of the 10 *Sephiroth*– the one breath (air from air), breath from breath, water from (air) breath, fire from water, and from the 6 directions: above and below, east and west, north and south.

Chapter Two: Construct the *Kabbalah* Wheel

The second chapter of *SEPHER YETZIRAH* describes, in code, how to construct the 231 Gates, based on the explanation of the letters' roles in Chapter one. The second chapter also describes the steps to create a device like a *Kabbalah* Wheel to spin the 231 Gates in sequence.

While the *SEPHER YETZIRAH* does not provide specific instructions to create such a device, the second chapter does suggest how to combine the letters into the 231 Gates either by a chart or a wheel. The above image is a homemade *Kabbalah* Wheel.

2:1 • The 22 Letters- 3, 7 & 12

The 22 Foundation Letters, 3 Mothers, 7 Doubles and 12 Elementals (Simples)

The 3 Mothers are *Aleph* (א), *Mem* (מ) and *Shin* (ש).

Their foundation is
A scale of merit and
A scale of liability.

And the tongue tips the balance between them. [720]

---

[720] The 3 Letters, *Aleph, Mem* and *Shin* are equally weighed. This principle is repeated in Chapter 3, verse 1. Weighing implies balancing – the concept of balancing the two opposing forces (positive and negative, etc.) of each of the three Mother letters. These three letters have special significance. They are equated with the three Father Letters, *Y, H, V,* respectively. The tongue controls the proper sound of each letter.

2:2 • Engrave the 22 Letters

The 22 Foundation Letters.
    Engrave them. [721]   הקק
    Carve them. [722]   חצב

Permutate them. [723]   צרף

Weigh them. [724]   סקל

Transform them. [725]   צור

And with them, depict all that was formed,
And all that will be formed. [726]

---

[721] These are the instructions how to form the Gates. Each of the 22 letters are "engraved" with the voice (speak the sound of letters).

[722] Carve the letters out with breath (when speaking them) by shaping their form in your imagination.

[723] Permutate (join them together) them by combining them together (in pairs) to change their sequence, as in "*Aleph* with all of them and…"

[724] Weigh them like a balance– one against each other- as a pair.

[725] Transform them into new concepts. Each new 2 letter combination creates a new word. There are 231 combinations made.

[726] When all of the 22 letters are permutated with each other, then everything one needs to know has been created into the 231 Gates.

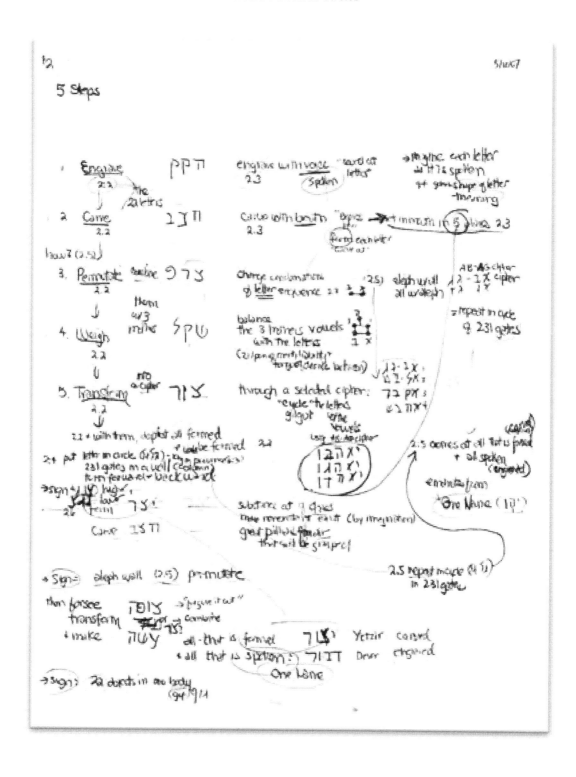

From Robert Zucker's personal notes, the 5 Steps of Letter Permutation, according to the instructions provided by the *Sepher Yetzirah* 2.

2:3 • Set Them in 5 Places

The 22 Foundation Letters (includes 12 simple letters, 7 double letters and the 3 Mother Letters).

Engrave them with the Voice.
Carve them with the Breath.

Set them in the mouth in 5 places. [727]

---

[727] The 22 letters are pronounced from five select parts of the mouth.

Gutterals	throat	*Aleph, Chet, Hey,* and *Ayin*
Palatals	palate	*Gimel, Yod, Kaf,* and *Qof* (middle of tongue)
Linguals	tip of tongue	*Daleth, Tet, Lamed, Nun,* and *Tav*
Dentals	teeth	*Zayin, Samech, Shin, Resh,* and *Tazik*
Labial	lips	*Bayt, Vav, Mem,*and *Pe*

When each letter is spoken (engraved) it becomes formed (carved or "hewed") through the exhalation of breath. The imagination creates the form (the letter) that the sound embodies.

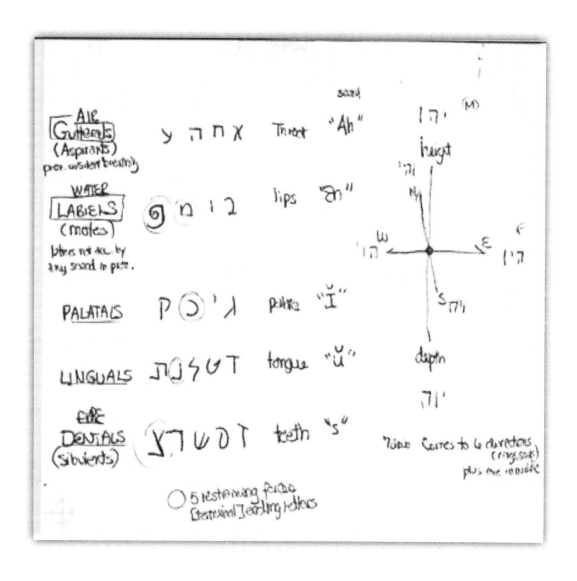

Diagram of the 5 sounds made through the mouth, their Hebrew letter correspondences and design of the 6 directions, from Robert Zucker personal notes.

2:4 • The Wheel Rotates

The 22 Foundation Letters.
Place them in a circle (ring),
Like a wall with 231 Gates.

The Wheel rotates back and forth.

A sign for this is:
There is nothing in good higher than Delight.
There is nothing evil lower than Plague. [728]

---

[728] This is the how to use the *Kabbalah* Wheel, as described later. The 22 letters of the alphabet are visualized in a long column and wrapped around like a circle. Rotating this Circle or Wheel back and forth changes the arrangement of the letters.

Using the three letters *Ay N* and *G*, as an example: when a letter added at the beginning, the Wheel "turns" in front of each letter as if turning front of "*Ay*" becomes "*Ay N G*." When letter added at end of word the Wheel "turns" from behind and "*Ay* becomes "*N G Ay*."

If one can combine the letters in the proper order, the creative process used by God in the formation of the world can be re-enacted. R. Azriel of Gerona, in his Commentary on SEPHER YETZIRAH suggests that the forward combinations of the letters create and the backward combinations undo the creation. He follows this assumption further in his COMMENTARY ON GENESIS RABBA (pages 254-255) and includes copies of the tables of vocalizations as they occur in R. Eleazar of Worms' SEPHER HA-SHEM. These tables also occur in Rabbi David ben Yehudah he-Chasid's writings, under influence of R. Joseph who wrote that there is a certain order for creation and one for destruction. He uses the term *golem*, but not in connections with an artificial creation.

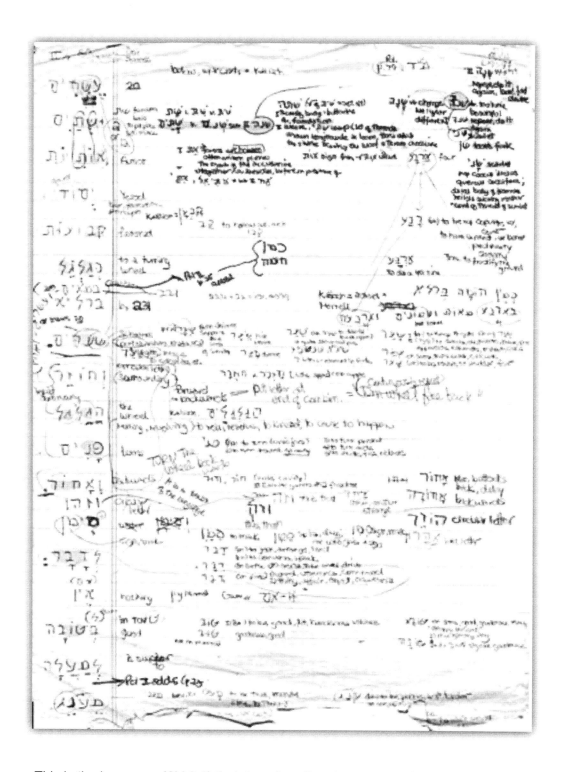

This is the key verse (SY 2:4) that describes the steps to complete the *Kabbalah* Wheel and how to spin it.

2:5 • *Aleph* with all of Them

How?
Permutate them, weigh them and transform them

Aleph (א) with them all
And all of them with *Aleph*(א).
Bayt (ב) with them all
And all of them with *Bayt* (ב).

They repeat in a cycle (circular movement)
And exist in 231 Gates.

And, all that is formed
And all that is spoken
Emanates from One Name. [729]

---

[729] This is the key verse to construct the letter combination technique. In order to permutate each of the letters, they need to be matched with a secondary letter. This creates the "Gate." As described in the instructions to devise a *Kabbalah* Wheel later in this book, when these two Gates are rotated up and down, separately, they make 231 combinations. All that is formed (carved, shaped, or created) is spoken (engraved with voice) from the combination of the 22 letters and the vowels of the Divine Name (*YHVH*).

Aleph with all of them... אב, אג, אד , אה,, או,אז...

And all of the with *Aleph*... בא , גא, דא, הא , וא , זא...

This pairing of letters, forward and reverse, generates the "combinations" also called "Gates." By pairing the "combinations," one can make non-existence exist and, theoretically, create something out of nothing.

X

This chart of the 231 Gates, produced by Rabbi Eleazar of Worms in the 12th century, has been used for centuries to create the list of 231 permutations of the Hebrew alphabet. This exercise can also be demonstrated using the *Kabbalah* Wheel. To read this chart, start in the upper right column on the second line (at the X). As instructed earlier, read the row of letters, like a column (or a wall). Read each column downwards:

אב

אג

אד...

בג

בד

בה...

2:6 • *Creatio ex-nihilo*

Form substance out of chaos
And make non-existence into existence. [730]

Carve great pillars from the air [731]
That cannot be grasped.

This is a sign:
[*Aleph* with all of them and all of them with *Aleph*...]

Foresee, transform and make
All that is formed and all that is spoken in One Name. [732]

End of Chapter 2. [733]

---

[730] This verse reiterates the 2nd chapter's main points. To make the non-existent exist, one must first visualize the correct arrangement of the 231 Gates (using the concept of "columns" of letters"), and then intertwine each Gate (permutate the letters, according to Rabbi Eleazar's chart) with the One Name (the 3 "Fathers").

[731] The great pillars of air represent the 2-letter gates stacked up on top of each other—like a column. Since it is to be visualized in the imagination, the "pillars of air" are not yet material entities.

[732] The proper execution of this act (speaking the letter combinations out loud in the correct order), produces something out of nothing— imagination turns into reality.

[733] There are four more chapters, but the first two are most pertinent to this study. The entire six chapters will be explored in an upcoming edition.

Chart of the 231 Gates where each letter of the Hebrew alphabet is paired with the next, in succession, until there are 231 pairs. This is the chart described by Rabbi Eleazar of Worms and reproduced in many commentaries since the Middle Ages.

Create a *Kabbalah* Wheel

In an attempt to better visualize the instructions to combine, weigh and permutate the letters, a more imaginative method has to be devised. The familiar 231 Gate chart constructed by Rabbi Eleazar of Worms in the 12th century was concise, but it's cumbersome to remember. And, his chart only reveals a portion of the complete method.

There is another way to visualize Eleazar's chart– as a Wheel or a cylinder.

The concept of a *Kabbalah* Wheel was revealed in the 12th century by Rabbi Judah Halevi in *Sepher Ha-Kuzari* [734] where he elaborated on the combinations of the Hebrew letters by means of a "wheel" to produce the 231 Gates.

To better conceptualize those rotating and spinning Gates, as described in the ancient *Sepher Yetzirah*, a more material model is needed. The ancient code can be recreated with a *Kabbalah* Wheel, a simple, hand-held mechanism, similar to an abacus, that provides letter permutations – that anyone can create.

There are two clues to how to construct such a device. According to *Sepher Yetzirah* 1:11, "Engrave them like a **garden**. Carve them like a **wall**. Cover them like a **ceiling**." Build the letters in a garden (rows) and lay them out vertically (like columns) instead of horizontally (like plots). The verses in *Sepher Yetzirah* 2:4 and 2:5 can also be interpreted to create the Wheel in the form of a circle, or rather a tube (an elongated wheel).

The *Kabbalah* Wheel conforms to the description in *Sepher Yetzirah* to "make them like a wall" with "231 Gates." Spin the columns forward and backward, rotate the vowels, and see the arrangements in your own hands. This Wheel can be used to enhance your understanding of the formations.

This *Kabbalah* Wheel is easy to make and easy to use. I was inspired to create the *Kabbalah* Wheel one evening in the early 2000's while trying to develop a prototype *Tzeruf* Key for a *Kabbalah* software program I was working on. Perhaps someone else in time came across this idea. I have yet to see this technique published or mentioned elsewhere in any manuscript or teaching at any time in history besides Rabbi Halevi's clues. But, it works!

---

[734] Halevi, Judah, THE *Kuzari*, introduction by H. Slonimsky. Schocken Books. 1964. First published in 1905. Translated from the Arabic by Harwig Hirschfeld.

How to construct a *Kabbalah* Wheel

This is a finished *Kabbalah* Wheel with five columns (rows), as on a casino slot machine. The 1st, 3rd and 5th columns (From right to left) are displayed by the three vowels (*YHV*). The 2nd and 4th column are the two Gates using the 22 letters of the Hebrew alphabet.

To construct a *Kabbalah* Wheel, these basic household items are needed:

- Paper towel cardboard tube or any tube about 3" wide and 5" or more long
- Scissors
- Tape (either scotch tape or masking tape)
- One sheet of paper
- Marking pen (or thick pen)

1. Take the cardboard paper towel tube (see illustration above).

2. Cut in it half down the middle (see below).

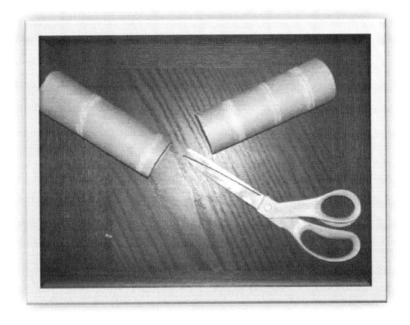

3. Cut each half of the tube down the length (see below).

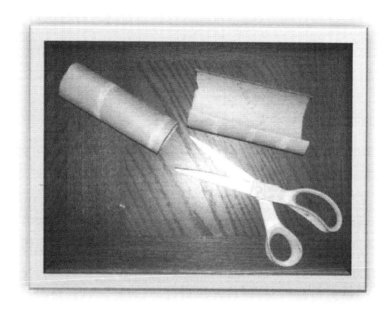

3. Connect the two cut tubes to form a single, wider tube. The hole of the tube should be at least twice as large as normal. Use tape to hold the two pieces together (see example below of the two cut half tubes taped into one).

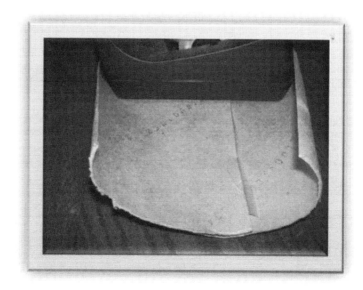

The next steps require the sheet of paper (and a pen, if needed) to form the columns.

5. On the sheet of paper, write or type the Hebrew letters in a long, vertical column (start with the letter *Aleph* (א) at the top, then *Bayt* (ב) below that, then *Gimel* (ג) below that, etc. to the end of the alphabet). The list should be long enough to wrap around the outside of the tube. (see illustration below). Print 2 columns of letters.

If you do not know Hebrew, you can substitute the English equivalent (see Chart of Hebrew and English Letters earlier in this edition), but its effectiveness will be limited. While writing down the letters yourself in Hebrew is preferable, you can take the easy way and duplicate a copy of the column of Hebrew or English letters provided in a chart earlier in this volume.

Columns of Hebrew Letters. These are the two columns of Hebrew letters (from *Aleph* to *Tav*). Two letters side by side form one Gate. The following letters can be copied to make each of the two columns needed to form the *Kabbalah* Wheel.

א
ב
ג
ד
ה
ו
ז
ח
ט
י
כ
ל
מ
נ
ס
ע
פ
צ
ק
ר
ש
ת

א
ב
ג
ד
ה
ו
ז
ח
ט
י
כ
ל
מ
נ
ס
ע
פ
צ
ק
ר
ש
ת

This is how one column of letters should look after it is cut into a long strip and taped to form a circle.

Read from the *Aleph* (**א**) down. Note that the letter *Tav* (**ת**) is above the *Aleph* (**א**). Two columns of letters are needed to form one Gate. These columns are the pillars of air that "cannot be grasped." By writing them down in a column, they become a visible entity out of one's imagination.

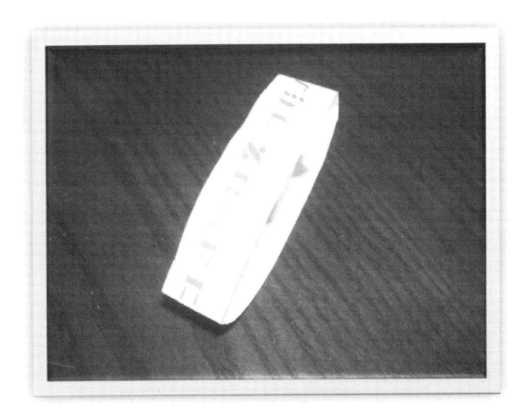

4. Duplicate the column of letters into 2 thin strips. (Hint: print a copy of the page instead of rewriting the second column).

7. Write out third column for the vowels– *Yod* (ʼ), *Vav* (ו), and *Heh* (ה). Space these vowels farther apart (see example below of the three separate columns. The column of the vowels is in the middle, balanced by a column of letters on each side).

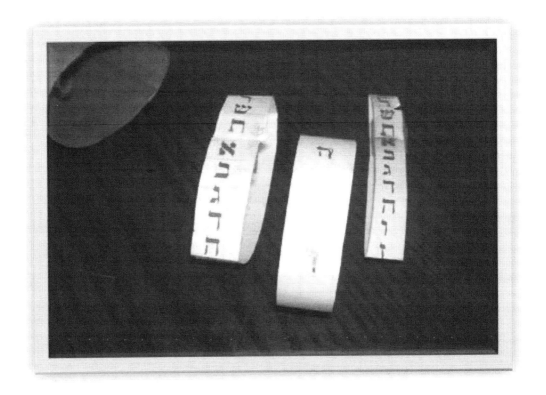

8. Roll each column, like a ring, [735] and connect the two end together with tape. The first letter of the alphabet, *Aleph* (**א**) should be below the last letter *Tav* (**ת**). Do the same with the second strip of letters and for a third strip for the vowels (see illustration above.

The *Kabbalah* Wheel with 3 "rings" of letters: the consonant letters are on the outside and the Vowels ring is in the middle.

9. Wrap each strip around the paper tube, side by side like columns, and tape together the ends of each strip so that each forms a "ring." Put the Vowels ring between the two letter rings (see above).

There are now 2 sets of Gates (the two 22 letters on the outside columns) and the Vowels (column in the middle). Adjust the strips so they line up *Aleph* to *Aleph*. The Wheel can be spun back and forth. Rotate the column strips upwards and downwards to form letter combinations

---

[735] According to SEPHER YETZIRAH, chapter 2:4: "The 22 Foundation Letters.

Place them in a circle (ring), Like a wall with 231 Gates. The wheel rotates back and forth."
Adapted from SEPHER YETZIRAH: THEORY, by Aryeh Kaplan, page 108.

(i.e. *Hey, Tav, Mem, Vav*).

Hebrew is read from right to left.

Column 1 (Far right): **Vowel** - i.e. ה *Hay* H

Column 2 (2nd from right): **Letter** of the Gate - i.e. ת *Tav* T

Column 3 (Middle): 2nd **vowel** - i.e. י *Yod* Y

Column 4 (3rd from right): 2nd **Letter** of the Gate - i.e. מ *Mem* M

Column 5: (far right): 3rd **vowel** - i.e. ו *Vav* V

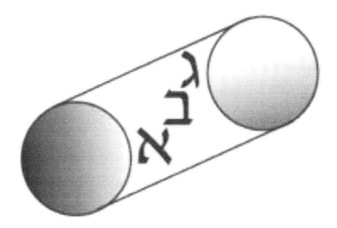

A Wheel like a Wall...

"*Assemble the Wheel, like a wall, with 231 Gates.* [736]

Accounting to *SEPHER YETZIRAH* 2:4: The sign for "this" is when you rotate, or oscillate, one column up or down (back and forth), you change the pair of Gates.

Each combination of two letters, which correspond to the limbs of the body, are combined with all the other letters to form a two-letter "Gate." It seems the magical activity begins with the combination of the letters.

Then, continue with verse 2:5: **Permutate** them. **Weigh** them and **transform** them. *Aleph* (A) with them all. *Bayt* (B) with all of them, and all of them with *Bayt*. They **repeat in a cycle** and exist in **231 Gates**. It comes forth that all that is **created (formed)** and all that is **spoken** emanates (is created) from One Name.

All 231 Gates can be generated by rotating the strips up and down. Rabbi Abulafia instructs to "Turn the wheel in the middle, and begin to combine until the two hundred and thirty-one gates [are computed], and [then] he will receive the influx of Wisdom. When he receives the influx, let him [then] recite speedily the circle of velocity, which is the divine spirit." [737]

---

[736] *SEPHER YETZIRAH* 2:4.

[737] Abraham Abulafia, quoted in "THE *GOLEM*: JEWISH MAGICAL by Idel, Moshe, pages 97-98.

Spinning the *Kabbalah* Wheel

The most popular method to permutate the letters is the "*Aleph* (א) with all of them...all of them with *Aleph*" technique, described by R. Eleazar of Worms in the 12th -13th century.

The permutations (combinations) are formed by pairing each letter with all the other letters of the alphabet. This pairing of letters, forward and reverse, generates the Holy Gates. By pairing those "combinations" and rotating the wheel, one can make non-existence exist– create something out of nothing, according the *SEPHER YETZIRAH*.

R. Eleazar mentions one method is permutation of the first eleven letters from *Aleph* to *Lamed* with each of the 22 letters, often associated with the creation of the *golem*. Eleazar lists the combinations of 21 letters with each of 22 letters and their various positions. This gives 462 combinations or 231 (when halved). He says to obtain the proper combination, only eleven letters are doubled. The other 22 letters are left as they are.

This is the key to the *Aleph to Lamed* (א—ל) technique - avoid repeating the same letters twice. The *A-L* (א—ל) method is often mentioned when constructing the 231 gates. [738]

Forward Rotation (the circle closes before...):

A B   א ב

A G   א ג

A D   א ד

Reverse Rotation (the circle closes behind...):

D A   ד א

G A   ג א

B A   ב א

Through these "gates" (the combination of two letters) the creative power goes out into the

---

[738] These charts are reprinted in Rabbi Aryeh Kaplan's *SEPHER YETZIRAH*: THEORY, page 303 (Appendix III), "The 221 Gates of Rabbi Eliezer Rokeach of Wormes (Rabbi Eleazar of Worms)." It is reprinted from the Przemysl edition (1889).

universe. The 231 Holy Gates are created by pairing each of the 22 letters of the Hebrew alphabet with one another until all 231 letters combination are formed. These mathematical calculations were often inscribed in this chart or devised by memory– letter by letter.

With the *Kabbalah* Wheel, each Gate can go in either direction– the combination could be forward or backwards. The instructions on how to use the *Kabbalah* Wheel is precisely described in the second chapter of the *SEPHER YETZIRAH* 2:4:

"The 22 Foundation Letters. Place them in a circle (ring), Like a wall with 231 Gates. The wheel rotates back and forth. The sign for "this" is when you rotate one column up or down (back and forth), you change the pair of Gates." [739]

Each two-letter combination is called a "Gate." The combination of the 22 Hebrew letters is permutated with each other to produce 484 sets.

Eliminate the 22 double sets ("mirrored" letters, i.e. גג בב ,אא). Divide the remainder in half. The result is 231 sets. The grid chart provided by R. Eleazar of Wormes (Worms) (above) is the cipher of those Gates.

The "Gates" are formed by pairing the forward and reverse combinations of the letters. Each "Gate" in the circle stands as a combination of two consonants of the Hebrew alphabet. When the letters are pronounced, the creative power emanates through these two outer "Gates."

Through the combination of all the letters– forwards and backward– all of the Gates are completed. The combination of the letters is used to both create words and to reveal the Secrets of the Universe. Through these Gates the creative power emanates out into the Universe, which is sealed on all "six sides," according to the *SEPHER YETZIRAH*.

The two-letter Gates can be imagined as a tall column with each Gate stacked up on top of each other and then "bent" into a circular wall– like a wheel. Each two-letter combination can rotate independently as two separate wheels. This is the description of the *Kabbalah* Wheel.

---

[739] *SEPHER YETZIRAH* 2:4.

So, how was this Wheel operated? According to the *SEPHER YETZIRAH*:

Permutate them, weigh them and transform them

Aleph (א) with them all. And all of them with Aleph (א).

Bayt (ב) with them all. And all of them with Bayt (ב).

They repeat in a cycle (circular movement)
And exist in 231 Gates.

And, all that is formed,
And all that is spoken,
Emanates from One Name. [740]

The combination of the letters is used to both create words and to create the universe. The *Kabbalist* has to be acquainted with the technique to permutate the letters, forwards and backward, until the recitation each 231 of the Gates are completed.

All of the words from this combination of the letters are permutated with the four-letter name of God– called the *Tetragrammaton*. Combining the letter *Aleph* with all the other letters, and all the other letters with *Aleph*, and so forth, through the entire alphabet, creates a spiritual experience.

---

[740] *SEPHER YETZIRAH* 2:5.

The "Wheel" rotates back and forth and emanates the power of the Heavens. Zedcor Graphics. Graphic from Gustave Doré's White Rose, "The Saintly throng in the form of a rose." Plate 34. Illustration to Canto 31 of Dante's "Paradiso," from the "Divine Comedy," translated by Laurence Grant White. New York, Pantheon Books. Zedcor Graphics.

Rotating the Wheel

Turn the Circle Forward & Behind...

"so the circle | גלגל galgal|
closes before and behind." [741]

The 2nd chapter of the *SEPHER YETZIRAH* provides the instructions to use the *Kabbalah* Wheel in order to perform the various letter combination techniques described by the Rabbis and in the *SEPHER YETZIRAH*. They can rotate in either direction– up and down, forward or backward, as described in *SEPHER YETZIRAH*. The Middle Pillar– the Hebrew vowels which represent the Holy Name– are also rotated in a specific order.

Using the *Kabbalah* Wheel, set the *Aleph* (א) and *Lamed* (ל) at eye-level- with the *Aleph* in the right column. The next line below should read *Bayt* (ב) and *Mem* (מ)– and the *Bayt* is in the right column. The two lines spell out *AL* and *BM*. It also follows with the next verse that explains "*Aleph* is placed in combination with all the others, all the others with *Aleph*..." These are the gates to creative activity. The assumption is that if one combines the letters properly, the creative process used by God in the formation of the world can be re-enacted– creating something from nothing.

According to the *TANYA,* [742] the letters of speech descend, degree by degree, by the substitutions and transpositions until they reach their completion through the 231 Gates. This is how the "life-force" is infused into an object. R. Eleazar suggested to combine the letters that corresponds to each of the limbs of the body with the letters of the Divine Name, *Y-H-V-H*. The role of the letters is to animate the organs and limbs of the object. To accomplish this, *Kabbalists* insist, one has to be familiar with the Hebrew alphabet, the combination techniques of the Hebrew letters, and how to construct the 231 Gates. Rabbi Abulafia instructs one to "turn the wheel in the middle, and begin to combine until the two hundred and thirty-one gates [are computed], and [then] he will receive the influx of wisdom. When he receives the influx, let him [then] recite speedily the circle of velocity, which is the divine spirit." [743]

---

[741] *SEPHER YETZIRAH* 2:4.

[742] *TANYA*, Chapter 1.

[743] Abraham Abulafia, quoted in "THE *GOLEM*: JEWISH MAGICAL by Idel, Moshe, pages 97-98.

"Magical evocation is the ritualistic experiment of stimulating and externalizing neuroses, complexes and any subconscious process (force) into a selected Archetypal Image (form).

And, through the act of projection, one unites the unconscious processes into a state of consciousness.

By identifying and integrating unconscious or subconscious forces into conscious 'forms' or symbols, one has the capacity of becoming aware of, and dealing with, the latent potential within the 'self.'

This is accomplished by the use of the Will and Imagination.

Evocation has for its aim, the same objective as psychotherapy." [744]

---

[744] Robert E. Zucker quote from HERMETICS: CONSCIOUSNESS & HYPER-PERCEPTIVITY (1976), page 108.

Major Editions of SEPHER YEZIRAH

There are the three main sources of the *SEPHER YETZIRAH* that are still used today. The first two were originally written down in the 10th century. The third, *Gra* Version, became popular in the 18th Century. All subsequent versions are based on either of these and have been reproduced for centuries.

1. the Saadia Gaon version– the most popular;
2. the short recension first used by Dunash ben Tamin;
3. the *Gra* version (from 18th century Gaon of Vilna)

Other editions of the *SEPHER YETZIRAH* mentioned in this volume. See the index for referring pages.

- 10th century. Commentary on the *SEPHER YETZIRAH*, BARZILLAI by Judah ben Barzillai [745] of Barcelona (Bargeloni), a Catalan *TALMUDIST*. It was later published in 1885 by Z.H. Halberstam as *PERUSH SEPHAR JEZIRA* in Hebrew, then in 1971 and again in 2007.
- 10th century, a commentary on the long version of *SEPHER YETZIRAH* written by Shabbathai Donnolo.
- 10th century a Commentary on the *SEPHER YETZIRAH*, by R. Eleazar of Germiza (Worms). Fragments published in Mantua in 1562. Complete edition published at Prezmysl, 1889 and in 2004, Hebrew, in Israel.
- Commentary on *SEPHER YETZIRAH*, by Azriel of Gerona.
- Commentary on *SEPHER YETZIRAH* by R. Joseph ben Shalom *Ashkenezi*.
- Commentary on *SEPHER YETZIRAH* by ibn Malka.
- 1877 *SEPHER YEZIRAH*, A BOOK ON CREATION; OR THE JEWISH METAPHYSICS OF REMOTE ANTIQUITY, with English translation. Preface, Explanatory Notes and Glossary by Rev. Dr. Isidor Kalisch.
- 1881 *SEPHER YETZIRAH* [BOOK OF CREATION] & SAADIA'S COMMENTARY (excerpts) [From Saadia ben Joseph (al-Fayyumi), *Commentaire sur le Séfer Yesira ou Livre de la Création par Le Gaon Saadya de Fayyoum*, trans. & ed., Meyer Lambert, Paris, Emile Bouillon, Editeur, 1891]; translated into English from the French and Hebrew by Scott Thompson and Dominique Marson, San Francisco, 1985.] Walter Benjamin Research Syndicate.
- 1887 *SEPHER YETZIRAH*, THE BOOK OF FORMATION WITH THE FIFTY GATES OF INTELLIGENCE end The Thirty-Two Paths of Wisdom, translated from the Hebrew by W. Wynn Westcott, M.B., J.P., supreme Magus of the Rosicrucian Society of England. Samuel Weiser, 1 BB7, 1 B93, 19BO. Follows Golden Dawn.

---

[745] Born in 1070 AD, few details of his life are known.

- 1889 *SEPHER RAZYA HASHALEM* (BOOK OF SECRETS) by R. Eleazar of Germiza (Worms), extracts from Shabbathai Donnolo's commentary, a study on creation processes through the Hebrew alphabet (*SEPHER ALEPH-BAYT*), the Gates, the names of Metatron, the soul, and the *golem*. Reprinted in 2004, Hebrew, in Israel.
- 1891 *COMMENTAIRE SUR LE SEPHER YEZIRAH PAR LE GAON SAADYA*, Meyer Lambert, Paris. Arabic edition, French translation.
- 1912 THE ORIGIN OF LETTERS AND NUMERALS ACCORDING TO THE *SEPHER YETZIRAH*, by Phineas Mordell, from the "Jewish Quarterly Review," April 1912.
- 1914 THE ORIGIN OF LETTERS AND NUMERALS ACCORDING TO THE *SEPHER YETZIRAH*, by Phineas Mordell.
- 1923 BOOK OF FORMATION OR *SEPHER YETZIRAH*: ATTRIBUTED TO RABBI AKIBA BEN JOSEPH, by Arthur Edward Waite (Editor, Introduction), Knut Stenring (Translator) and R. A. Gilbert (Foreword). Stenring has made a word-for-word translation from several texts, choosing only those parts which he believed to be authentic. He reveals the text's secrets in his diagrams, tables, and extensive notes. His "Master Key to the Theoretical and Practical *Kabala*" is a diagram of the correspondences between the English and Hebrew alphabets and is not found in other translations of the *Sepher Yetzirah*. The introduction by Waite surveys the historical background of the *Sepher Yetzirah* translations and the import of this foundational *Kabbalistic* text. Knut Stenring was a Swedish Hebrew scholar.
- 1930 *DES BUCH JEZIRE* by Johann Friedrich von Moyer, Leip.
- 1941 *SEPHER YETZIRAH*, THE BOOK OF CREATION verse by verse analysis by Dr. M. Doreal, Brother of White Triangle, Inc.
- 1970 THE BOOK OF FORMATION *(SEPHER YETZIRAH)*, by Rabbi Akiba ben Joseph, translated from the Hebrew with Annotations by Knut Stenring, including the 32 Paths of Wisdom, their Correspondences with the Hebrew Alphabet end the Tarot Symbols, with on introduction by Arthur Edward Waite. KTAV Publishing House, Inc..
- 1970 BOOK OF FORMATION (*SEPHER YETZIRAH*: LETTERS OF OUR FATHER ABRAHAM. JEWISH MYSTICISM, English, edited, 1971.
- 1971 *A PRELIMINARY CRITICAL EDITION OF SEPHER YEZIRA* by Ithamar Gruenwald, Israel. Oriental Series, 1 (1971), p. 13-77.
- 1977 *SEPHER YETZIRAH*: THE BOOK OF CREATION: IN THEORY AND PRACTICE, By Aryeh Kaplan. This is the most authoritative text on the study of the *Sepher Yetzirah*. Kaplan's explanations are easy to understand and make common sense. Hebrew with English translations in great detail and insight. A must-have manual for anyone ready to decipher this ancient manuscript. Paperback: 398 pages. Publisher: Weiser Books; Rev. Sub edition (May 1997). Language: English.
- 1977 *BOOK OF CREATION* by Irving Friedman, Samuel Weiser.
- 1975. *SEPHER YETZIRAH* Broy, Guilded Press. 2nd edition, 1976.
- 1975 *SEPHER YETZIRAH*, THE MAGIC OF FORMATION, by Robert E. Zucker. Independent study produced for five departments at the University of Arizona, in Tucson. Non-published, still in manuscript form in personal library.
- 1981 THE *SEPHER YETSIRA*, INCLUDING THE ORIGINAL ASTROLOGY ACCORDING TO QABALAH AND ITS ZODIAC by Carlo Suares, Translated from the French by

Michelinee and Vincent Stuart. Shamabhala Publishing (BM525 A419 S9 13).

- *SEPHER YETZIRAH* (THE BOOK OF FORMATION) COMMENTARY ON *SEPHER YETZIRAH* by Dr. David Blumenthal from UNDERSTANDING JEWISH MYSTICISM.
- *SEPHER YETZIRAH* Bibliography by William Benjamin. Compiled by Scott J. Thompson [The following bibliography combines original scholarship and translation. It combines the substance of the annotated bibliography in Lazarus Goldschmidt's *SEPHER JESIRAH: DAS BUCH DER SCHÖPFUNG* (1894), but has been chronologically arranged in the manner of Adolf Jellinek's *BEITRÄGE ZUR GESCHICHTE DER KABBALAH* (1852) and updated
- Don Karr: NOTES OF EDITIONS OF THE *SEPHER YETZIRAH* (pdf) http://www.digital-brilliance.com/kab/karr/syie.pdf 1991, 1994; updated 2001-2007.

Editions of the Book of Raziel

The *SODEI RAZAYA*, SECRETS OF *RAZIEL*, and *SEPHER RAZIEL HAMALACH* have been published in various editions. Some of these books have been republished recently in Hebrew.

- Amsterdam edition (1701)
- *SEPHER RAZIEL*, BOOK OF THE ANGEL RAZIEL (Regular Size). The size of this edition is 7 inches X 9.75 inches. Clear print. Hardbound
- Steve Savedow (trans.), *Sepher Reziel Hemelach*: The Book of the Angel Reziel, Red Wheel/Weiser (2000), ISBN 978-1578631933.
- Giovanni Grippo (trans.), *SEPHER RAZIEL: DAS BUCH DES ERZENGELS RAZIEL* (German/Hebrew), G. G. Verlag (2009), ISBN 978-398106224.
- *SEPHER RATZIEL HAMALACH*, Publisher: Yarid HaSfarim, Hebrew. Pages: 220.
- *SODEI RAZAYA HASHALEM*- Rabbi Elazar of Germiza
- Rabbi Elazar (Eleazar) of Germiza. Publisher: Berazani. Hebrew. Pages: 443.
- *SODEI RAZAYA*, Language: Hebrew. Pages: 439. R. Eleazar cites and quotes *Merkavah* and *Hechalot* literature. He then describes the realm and characteristics of angels, the Divine Throne, the Chariot, and the Divine Voice. The rest of the work focuses on God's names, the fate of the soul after death, the meaning of dreams, and a large practical guide for the creation of a *golem*. [746]

---

[746] Comment from Nehora.com, book seller.

Recommended Reading

The following books are among the many excellent ones that I have relied on for decades in my library. Some of their references are incorporated into this volume. The best known Western *Kabbalistic* authors of today are Gershom Scholem, Moshe Idel, and Aryeh Kaplan. Some of the titles listed on the previous pages, and referenced in the footnotes, are also excellent sources. This is not a complete list, but highlights some of the most accessible texts, if they are available.

David R. Blumenthal

- UNDERSTANDING JEWISH MYSTICISM, A Source Reader. The *Merkabah* Tradition and the *Zoharic* Tradition. KTAV Publishing House, New York, 1978. The Library of Judaic Learning, Volume II, Edited by Jacob Neusner. ISBN: 0-87068-334-9.

Leonard R. Glotzer

- THE FUNDAMENTALS OF JEWISH MYSTICISM, THE BOOK OF CREATION AND ITS COMMENTARIES. An in-depth study into the *Sephiroth,* alphabet of creation, 231 Gates, the Divine Names, Letters and Vowels. Jason Aronson, Inc., 1992. Moshe Idel

- GOLEM, JEWISH MAGICAL AND MYSTICAL TRADITIONS ON THE ARTIFICIAL ANTHROPOID, State University of New York Press, 1990. ISBN: 0-7914-0160-x.
- STUDIES IN ECSTATIC *KABBALAH*, State University of New York Press, SUNY Series in Judaica: Hermeneutics, Mysticism and Religion. 1988. ISBN: 0-88706-604-6.

Aryeh Kaplan

- MEDITATION AND *KABBALAH*, Published by Jason Aronson, Inc. 1982, Kaplan; 1995, Aronson. ISBN: 1-56821-381-6. Titles from the GREATER HEKHALOT, Textbook of the *Merkabah* School; The Works of Abraham Abulafia; Joseph Gikatalia's GATES OF LIGHT; THE GATES OF HOLINESS; GATE OF THE HOLY SPIRIT, Textbook of the Lurianic School of Hasidic Classics.
- *SEFER YETZIRAH* THE BOOK OF CREATION IN THEORY AND PRACTICE. Samuel Weiser, Inc. 1990. ISBN: 0-87728-726-0. English and Hebrew commentary in English, includes bibliographical references.
- THE LIVING TORAH, 1981. Kaplan's widely used English translation of the *TORAH*.

R. Isaac Luria (1537-1572)

- *SHA'AR HA-GILGULIM* (GATES OF REINCARNATION), recorded by his disciple R. Chayim Vital. English translation published in 2003 by Yitzach Bar Chaim. 37 Books publishing, Malibu, CA. ISBN: 0-9727924-0-6

Rebbe Nachman of Breslov

- ANATOMY OF THE SOUL, Breslov Research Institute, 1998. A description of the soul in connection with parts of the body, including digestive system, circulatory system, central nervous system, and more. ISBN: 0-930213-51-3

Israel Regardie

- A GARDEN OF POMEGRANATES, 1932.
- THE TREE OF LIFE, 1932.
- MY ROSICRUCIAN ADVENTURE, 1936.
- THE ART OF TRUE HEALING, Helios Books, 1937.
- THE GOLDEN DAWN, 4 volumes (1937-1940)
- THE MIDDLE PILLAR, 1938.
- THE PHILOSOPHER'S STONE, Llewellyn Publications. First edition 1938. ISBN: 0-87542-691-3 (1938).
- THE ROMANCE OF METAPHYSICS, 1945.
- THE ART AND MEANING OF MAGIC, 1964.
- BE YOURSELF, THE ART OF RELAXATION, 1965.
- TWELVE STEPS TO SPIRITUAL ENLIGHTENMENT, 1969.
- THE EYE OF THE TRIANGLE, 1970.

Gershom G. Scholem

- JEWISH GNOSTICISM, MERKABAH MYSTICISM AND TALMUDIC TRADITION, based on the Israel, Goldstein Lectures delivered at the Jewish Theological Seminary of America, New York, 1960. LCC: 60-10743
- *KABBALAH*, Dorsett Press/Keter Publishing House, Jerusalem, 1974. Historical development of *Kabbalah,* Basic Ideas of *Kabbalah*, Influences and dozens of topics and personalities. ISBN: 0-88029-205-9.
- MAJOR TRENDS IN JEWISH MYSTICISM (1940)
- ON THE *KABBALAH* AND ITS SYMBOLISM, *ZUR KABBALA UND IBRER* SYMBOLIK (1960), translated by Ralph Manheim, 1969. Schocken Books.
- THE MESSIANIC IDEA IN JUDAISM, And other Essays on Jewish Spirituality, Schocken Books, 1971. Translated by Michael A. Meyer from German essays.

Joshua Trachtenberg

- JEWISH MAGIC AND SUPERSTITION, A STUDY IN FOLK RELIGION, Meridian Books and the Jewish Publication Society, 1939. Meridian Books.

Author Biography

Author Robert E. Zucker, 2009.

Digging into the mystical past

For over forty years my interest in mysticism has matured into a lifelong study of the ancient Judaic mystical studies and practices. During this time, I have collected a multitude of information and built a tremendous library of some of the best books on *Kabbalah*.

This published work actually began while I was attending the University of Arizona from 1975-1977. Part of my University undergraduate time was spent producing several manuscripts about mysticism for university course credit.

To complete my course requirements, two manuscripts were produced (titled HERMETICS,

CONSCIOUSNESS & HYPER-PERCEPTIVITY, [747] (1976) and MAGIC OF THE MIND, [748] (1977). They were credited by faculty sponsors in five different departments at the University of Arizona: Judaic Studies, Psychology, Sociology, Anthropology and Journalism. [749]

Those years enabled me to study *Kabbalah* at home, build my personal library, fill cabinets with thousands of pages of notes, *and* receive college credit. TWILIGHT OF CONSCIOUSNESS [750] (1981) was a third unpublished work prepared partially from the earlier two pieces during college. This volume was the result of my researching into the waking-dream state.

In between my researching and writing, I conducted mysticism and *Kabbalah* courses through the Tucson Free University, a non-profit education organization managed by a longtime friend who passed away a year ago. After college, I began to publish a series of community tabloid newspapers starting with YOUTH ALTERNATIVES (1978), YOUTH AWARENESS PRESS (1978-1980), TUCSON TEEN (1981-1990), MAGAZINE (1982-1985) and the ENTERTAINMENT MAGAZINE (1985-1992).

With the introduction of personal computers, I saw the opportunity to consolidate my notes into a digital format. I purchased my first Macintosh SE computer in 1987. It was a tiny box with a screen as big as an iPad with a small floppy drive. I began to enter the thousands of pages I collected since I started my studies in the early 1970s into word processing software, like SimpleText, and then, Microsoft Word.

Eventually, with an Apple Macintosh graphic database program called HyperCard, I was able to organize the many different topics and disconnected associations into a multi-dimensional program that incorporated text, images and sounds. I developed several unique programs that read like virtual books. The chapters of *SEPHER YETZIRAH* came alive with music that played while the Macintosh speech program read the chapters.

Unfortunately, HyperCard support was discontinued in 1998 and the Macintosh operating system kept updating until HyperCard became inoperable. I still maintain a few of the older computers and floppy disks.

Another graphic database program compatible with the Macintosh was called FileMaker. I recreated the *SEPHER YETZIRAH* book format and was able to add more features, build a Hebrew

---

[747] ISBN-10: 1939050154 and ISBN-13: 978-1-939050-15-1 (Bowker, 2012).

[748] ISBN-10: 1939050103 and ISBN-13 978-1-939050-10-6 (Bowker, 2012).

[749] University of Arizona department faculty sponsors included Albert T. Bilgray (Judaic Studies), James T. Borhek, Ph.D. (Sociology), Richard W. Cohen, Ph.D. (Psychology), Thomas C. Duddleston, MA (Journalism), and Richard W. Henderson, PhD (Anthropology).

[750] ISBN-10: 1939050200 and ISBN-13: 978-1-939050-20-5 (Bowker, 2012).

alphabet database with correspondences, and a "solution" [751] that "spins" the 231 Gates with word definitions formed by each of the 2-letter Gates.

Unfortunately, attempts to publicly distribute these dozens of "solutions" became problematic– incompatible operating systems (developed on a Mac, but not compatible with PC's using Windows, etc.) and upgrade issues (features, fonts and formats wouldn't update with the OS upgrades). It became too cumbersome to keep redesigning and relinking the databases.

While returning to my university alma-mater to teach from 1992-2005, I pioneered the Internet and launched websites for my print newspaper, ENTERTAINMENT MAGAZINE (EMOL.org) and both journalism departments at the University of Arizona and Pima Community College in Tucson. About the same time in 1995, some of the pages from manuscripts I wrote in college were posted online. Some of those pages and my personal notes can be read at http://emol.org/kabbalah and http://robert-zucker.com/qabalah.

Over the past few years, I began to extract the content from these FileMaker projects and transform them into this print book format. That also presented technology issues. As I am at this point in writing the book, I am already stretching the limits of the software's capability to compose and index these pages. Also, the technology used to print the digital files (a PDF is uploaded to CreateSpace, a printing company owned by Amazon.com) has its limits in file size. In fact, the computer and program crashed within the last hours of finishing!

My study continued during my newspaper publishing and teaching career, and now, into retirement. There was always that quest to understand this lost wisdom and share it with others. This print volume is a culmination of that effort. Yet, there is so much more to include, but I have to stop at some point.

---

[751] A "solution" is a FileMaker term for a database. The first FileMaker version was released in 1985.

This is the main library room where most of my reading has been done over the past years. The room (1 of 3) contains over 1,000 books on *Kabbalah*, Jewish Mysticism, Jewish literature and religious text, parapsychology, Egyptian history and texts, parapsychology, occult and Hermetic subjects. A *Kabbalah* Wheel sits on the table next to my chair.

Personal notes from January 22, 1974 during my college years when I conducted classes in occultism and parapsychology, from 1974-1976, through the Tucson Free University, a non-profit community program operated by a friend of mine, Phil Miles, who passed away in January 2016.

THE UNIVERSITY OF ARIZONA
TUCSON, ARIZONA 85721

COLLEGE OF LIBERAL ARTS
ORIENTAL STUDIES

May 11, 1976

To my colleagues on the Committee on Petitions:

Last semester, Robert E. Zucker, Senior in the College of Liberal Arts, counseled with me concerning an ambitious research project covering five disciplines. The nature of the study required a coordinated approach involving 15 units of independent study. After he received the approval of four other departments - Anthropology, Journalism, Psychology and Sociology, I agreed to sponsor the project.

The final manuscript of more than 200 pages of text and bibliography involves considerable research and is a fine summary of the currently available literature in the field of Hermetics. Mr. Zucker has received the mark of S from all five departmental readers.

Now he has discovered that the grade of S cannot be averaged in his general grade record unless it is converted into the equivalent grade of A.

This creates a special hardship for Mr. Zucker because he would like to qualify for a Board of Regents grant next semester. He has worked assiduously and set his plans for a scholarship. When he planned his research project he was not aware that the grade of S (given for independent study) cannot be incorporated into his semester average.

Because of the unique circumstances, it is my hope that the petition of Mr. Zucker to have his grades of S changed to A will be honored.

Sincerely,

Albert T. Bilgray
Area of Judaic Studies
Department of Oriental Studies

A letter from Rabbi Albert T. Bilgray, from the Judaic Studies at the University of Arizona in a petition the University to convert my letter grade of "S" (awarded for general studies and equivalent to an "A") to count towards 15 numerical credits, rather than just graduating credits. The petition was denied since Independent Studies "cannot be given regular grades" (5/20/76).

THE UNIVERSITY OF ARIZONA
TUCSON, ARIZONA 85721

COLLEGE OF LIBERAL ARTS
DEPARTMENT OF SOCIOLOGY

To Whom it May Concern: 4/18/77

 Mr. Robert Zucker has asked me to write a letter of reference in his behalf.

 I have known Bob for a little over a year now. He approached me with a plan to take an entire semester for individual study and writing. The time was to be provided by four departments. I was very sceptical at first as anyone would be after ten years of U/A students. However, the semester produced a 225 page, well researched, competently written book . Not a term paper but a genuine book length manuscript which I believe has some real possibilties for publication.

 Since that time, Mr. Zucker has continued his research into hermetics and has elaborated and polished the original manuscript.

 Mr. Zucker is a polished researcher who can organize himself and his work and get the results down in good prose without supervision. What else is there to say? If this is what you want, then he is what you want.

Sincerely

James T. Borhek
Department of Sociology
University of Arizona
Tucson, 85721

Letter from James T. Borhek, Department of Sociology, another one of the five sponsoring faculty members to petition for letter grade conversion to the University of Arizona.

"Magic is a (psychological and physiological) mnemonic process so arranged as to result in the deliberate exhilaration of the Will and exaltation of the Imagination, the end result being the purification of the personality and attainment of a spiritual state of consciousness in which the conscious enters into union with the unconscious."

Israel Regardie, TREE OF LIFE, page 150

Books by Robert Zucker

ENTERTAINING TUCSON ACROSS THE DECADES 1950s-1985– Volume 1
ISBN: 978-1-939050069   2014

ENTERTAINING TUCSON ACROSS THE DECADES 1986-1989– Volume 2
ISBN: 978-1-939050076   2015

ENTERTAINING TUCSON ACROSS THE DECADES 1990s – Volume 3
ISBN: 978-1-939050090   2015

ENTERTAINING TUCSON HIGHLIGHTS – Volume 4
ISBN: 978-1-939050137   2015

TREASURES OF THE SANTA CATALINA MOUNTAINS
ISBN: 978-1-939050052   2014

TRAVELING SHOW
ISBN: 978-1-939050030   2013

Other books published through BZB Publishing, Inc.:

SEARCHING FOR ARIZONA'S BURIED TREASURES
By Ron Quinn   ISBN: 978-1939050403   2013

MYSTERIOUS DISAPPEARANCES & OTHER STRANGE TALES
By Ron Quinn   ISBN: 978-1939050045   2013

CANYON OF GOLD
By William "Flint" Carter   ISBN: 978-1939050120   2016

To purchase copies or for more information:
BZB Publishing, P.O. Box 91317, Tucson, Arizona 85752

Phone: 520-623-3733 (accept orders by credit card)
Email: publisher@emol.org
Web Site: http://emol.org/books

Index

This Index can be used as learning tool to look up key words, important phrases, people and sources to better understand the *SEPHER YETZIRAH* and its related teachings. Book titles are in CAPITAL LETTERS. Foreign words are in *italics*.

A

Made in the USA
Charleston, SC
17 January 2017